D0394881

POLITICAL MERCENARIES

Lewis, Lindsay Mark.
Political mercenaries :
the inside story of how
[2014].
33305232969489
gi   03/27/15   WITHDRAWN

POLITICAL MERCENARIES

THE INSIDE STORY OF HOW FUNDRAISERS ALLOWED BILLIONAIRES TO TAKE OVER POLITICS

LINDSAY MARK LEWIS

WITH JIM ARKEDIS

palgrave
macmillan

POLITICAL MERCENARIES
Copyright © Lindsay Mark Lewis and Jim Arkedis, 2014.
All rights reserved.

First published in 2014 by PALGRAVE MACMILLAN® in the United States—a division of St. Martin's Press LLC, 175 Fifth Avenue, New York, NY 10010.

Where this book is distributed in the UK, Europe and the rest of the world, this is by Palgrave Macmillan, a division of Macmillan Publishers Limited, registered in England, company number 785998, of Houndmills, Basingstoke, Hampshire RG21 6XS.

Palgrave Macmillan is the global academic imprint of the above companies and has companies and representatives throughout the world.

Palgrave® and Macmillan® are registered trademarks in the United States, the United Kingdom, Europe and other countries.

ISBN: 978-1-137-27958-3

Library of Congress Cataloging-in-Publication Data

Lewis, Lindsay Mark.
    Political mercenaries : the inside story of how fundraisers allowed billionaires to take over politics / Lindsay Mark Lewis ; with Jim Arkedis.
    pages   cm
    ISBN 978-1-137-27958-3 (hardback)
    1. Lewis, Lindsay Mark. 2. Fund raisers (Persons)–United States–Biography.
3. Political consultants–United States–Biography. 4. Campaign funds–United States. 5. Pressure groups–United States. 6. United States–Politics and government-1989– I. Arkedis, Jim. II. Title.
JK1991.L53   2014
324.7'8092–dc23

                                                                    2014018989

A catalogue record of the book is available from the British Library.

Design by Letra Libre, Inc.

First edition: October 2014

10 9 8 7 6 5 4 3 2 1

Printed in the United States of America.

CONTENTS

*To the previous generation that instilled the need to
fight for the oppressed and the next generation
that will continue the battle:
Jake, Anne, Jo C, Peggie, Lauren, Matt, Amy.*

*And a special thanks to the wealthy
liberals that instilled the fear in me:
we can't ever let you control our democracy.*

ACKNOWLEDGMENTS

LINDSAY LEWIS: I would like to thank my family for all their support. I'd also like to thank my friend and colleague Jim Arkedis, an amazing writer and editor. Without Jim, this project simply doesn't exist. Finally, I'd like to thank the strip club owners, casino moguls, and rich folks who made these stories possible and showed me exactly what I don't want to be. And the hockey goalies, who showed me what I do want to be.

JIM ARKEDIS: I would like to thank all who supported and encouraged me through this challenge—The Arkedii: Mom & Dad, Jean, Kevin & Aidan, and Bob & Beth. And to my good friends: Kevin McTigue, Brad Elkins, Jason Weiss, Vlad Dorjets, Lukas Kohler, Mike Derham, Jed Howbert, Eric Sundström, Lauren Goldbeck, Paul Goldbeck, Joanna Angelides, Joe Mitchell, Dan Blair, Melissa Hersch, Jennie Wellman & the Deuce, Martin Mayerchak, Brian Wingfield, Jeff Jordan, Snuffy, Dan Ingber, Melissa Feld, Allen & Melodee McCrodden, Andy & Katie Cwalinski, Kevin Walsh, PhD, Patrick McCorry, Mike Satlak, Adam Haubenreich, Raj Basu, Ben Berkowick, Jed Donahue, JoeyV, Kevin Dunne . . . and Ort.

LINDSAY & JIM would like to thank: The staff at the F.E.C., who were extremely helpful as we poured over hours of microfilm. Huge thanks to our agent, Sam Fleischman at LAR, a true sage, and Karen Wolny, Alan Bradshaw, Lauren LoPinto, and Lauren Janiec at Palgrave. You all were the few who believed in this project from the get-go—thank you for giving us a chance.

PROLOGUE

I MADE MY FIRST POLITICAL FUNDRAISING CALL IN JUNE OF 1992.
Over the next fifteen years, I would be responsible for raising over $200
million for the Democratic Party's candidates, committees, and causes. I
would raise money to support Democrats at every level of elected office: a
mayor, congressional representatives, senators, governors, and a presidential
candidate.

When I started in 1992, the professional fundraising industry didn't
exist. Fewer than twenty people had full-time jobs raising money for Democrats in the House and Senate; today that number well exceeds four hundred,
and for a reason. As we raised more and more money, I watched the fundraiser go from being an outsider to being the most influential person on a
politician's staff, with control over schedule (the politicians' time) and those
who could influence policy, all because of the chase for political money. It
has evolved from a part-time effort into a 365-day-a-year obsession.

During my fifteen years as a fundraiser, I learned how to work over
donors, how to gamble, how to skirt campaign finance disclosure rules, how
to buy drugs, and how to cover up contributions from a murder victim. I
learned how to use a member of Congress's wife as my drug mule. Most
fundraisers haven't done everything I've done or seen everything I've seen.
But they all know how the political money system pays them well and they
want it to keep growing.

I witnessed the amount of time a member of Congress spent raising money increase dramatically. Time members spend raising money is the biggest problem in American politics today. In 1992, members raised money for about fifteen hours a year. Today, it's at least fifteen hours a *week*. In 1992, the threshold to be considered a viable candidate was to raise $200,000 during the entire election. That was enough to make the race competitive and get out the campaign's message. Today, viability begins at $1 million and is much more if a candidate is running in an expensive media market. In Philadelphia, for example, a candidate needs $2 million or doesn't have a fighting chance.

Being a member of Congress in 1992 is nothing like being a member of Congress in 2014. In the 1980s and early '90s, Members of Congress spent most afternoons and evenings playing poker, drinking, going to dinner with each other—bipartisanship at its best. In 2014, members can't afford to spend time like that; all available time must be spent appealing to individually wealthy donors, lobbyists, and grassroots true believers. The new focus on the never-ending money chase self-selects those who run for Congress.

I have hobnobbed with the likes of Bill and Hillary Clinton, Kevin Spacey, Dick and Jane Gephardt, Howard Dean, Ted Kennedy, Billy Crystal, Patrick Kennedy, David Stern, Ed Markey, Bianca Jagger, George Soros, Steve Wynn, Ed Asner, Terry McAuliffe, Norman Lear, and countless extremely wealthy and important individuals you've never heard of . . . but only because I could raise political money.

Some of the folks I've dealt with, like former senator Bob Torricelli of New Jersey, ended their careers in disgrace after taking illegal contributions. Others, like former Louisiana congressman Bill Jefferson, donor-raisers like John Huang, or strip club owners like Rick Rizzolo, ended up in trouble with the law.

But most important, I helped a few hundred rich, liberal elites take over the Democratic Party, not only by the money they raised and the time they spent with politicians, but by allowing them to control the levers of the Democratic agenda. Bill Clinton was elected president in 1992 and raised

$62 million for that campaign, a record at the time.[1] The new money in the Democratic Party ended up yielding $1.07 billion for President Obama's re-election in 2012: money given directly to his campaign, to the Democratic National Committee, and to outside, unaccountable super political action committees (super-PACs): a mere 2000 percent increase in twenty years.

Many books and articles have been written about the influence of money, the lobbying industry, or the obnoxious political greed of a few wealthy Republicans in recent years. They have all missed the real story: To compete with Republicans' ability to raise money, Democrats sold out not to corporate or lobbying interests but to a very few liberal wealthy elites. The new defensive explanation from Democratic leadership, fundraisers, and super-PACs is simply that they're playing within the system, or "our billionaires are cleaner than Republican billionaires." They aren't, and they have driven the party's priorities to reflect their personal beliefs.

I saw this coming in the late '90s and spent my last few years inside the party's apparatus trying to defeat the onslaught of self-selected monied elites. I failed.

The Howard Dean insurgency seemed to offer hope. Under his tenure as chair of the Democratic National Committee, I became the Democratic Party's top fundraiser, a job many would relish. I didn't. I wanted to use the position to take my shot at changing a system I'd helped build. I oversaw the creation of sustainable, online low-dollar donations, which I thought would dilute the influence of mega-donors and provide a real seat at the table for all Democrats.

It proved to be fool's gold. The race to the bottom to attract small do-nors has done more damage to both parties in the last ten years and is the biggest contributor to partisan bickering today.

In June of 2007, fifteen years after making that first fundraising call, I finally quit party fundraising forever.

THIS WASN'T HOW I THOUGHT it would all turn out. I grew up in a lib-eral 1980s family. At various times, my family worked for Ralph Nader,

ACORN, Greenpeace, and US PiRG. We spent Saturdays protesting, whether at the South African embassy over apartheid, or somewhere else over another tree-hugging flavor of the month.

My father marched on Selma, Alabama, the entire family marched on Washington. I got beat up on my first day in high school for wearing a Mondale/Ferraro button. My first hand-me-down records were the Grateful Dead, Pete Seeger, and Arlo Guthrie. When I was a freshman at the University of Maryland–Baltimore County, I moved into subsidized housing, just to prove a point: I wanted to bridge the racial divide in America. Being a good liberal was in my blood.

My mother is an education writer and took me on a trip as a seven-year-old to meet Harry Briggs in South Carolina. It was a long drive through cotton fields that seemed like it was taking all afternoon. Mr. Briggs handed me a nice tall glass of iced tea, then I went outside to play basketball with the neighborhood kids. I was the only white person there, but that didn't mean anything to me. Years later, I found out Mr. Briggs was a plaintiff in the Supreme Court's first major case on school desegregation. (His case was later lumped into four others to form *Brown v. Board of Education*.)

WINNING AT SPORTS was the most important thing as a kid. It's a personality streak that translates quite well to raising political money: You either close the deal or you don't. But rather than searching for the next check, I should have applied that drive to help the middle class.

I played hockey and played it well growing up. I was always a goalie on a mission to win and was a member of the first American youth hockey team to go to the Soviet Union after the Americans boycotted the 1980 summer Olympics. I was never an elite player but at six feet five, international hockey scouts thought I had the makings of an NHL regular. Al Arbour, the coach and architect of the New York Islanders' four Stanley Cups in the early 1980s, saw me play a game one day at the Capital Centre before the Islanders took the ice that night. As I left the ice he said, "Kid, you could be the next Ken Dryden," something that I will never forget.

Hockey was not a sanctioned sport at Walt Whitman High School, but wrestling was. The wrestling coach, Jim Douglass, pulled me aside one afternoon in the hallway and had an offer. He'd suspended his only heavyweight. If I'd dress for the next match against Whooten, Mr. Douglass would give me an A in his biology class.

It was my first political quid pro quo. The team hadn't lost a match in four years, and that night's would be a done deal by the time they got to my weight class. I wouldn't even have to wrestle; we were supposed to be so far ahead that we could forfeit my match. I just had to be on the team bus by 4 pm. The Wooten High gym was packed with over five thousand people. What an atmosphere.

When the lower weights didn't go as planned, Coach Douglass took me back into the locker room and showed me some moves. Wrestling for dummies, fast-forwarded. I headed out to the mat, the issue in doubt in front of five thousand people cheering for a massive upset. I wanted to win, that's what I was put on this earth to do. I just had to last six minutes without getting pinned, the match would end in a tie, and our streak would be preserved.

The ref blew his whistle. I snapped and did the only thing that came to mind: I jabbed my opponent's jaw with my left hand and cocked a full-blown roundhouse punch to his nose with my right. He went down, out cold. I put my hands in the air and trotted a victory lap around the ring. I saved the day!

I was fined ten points and Whooten got to replace my opponent. The new guy took about thirty seconds to pin me. The local paper's next day headline?

LEWIS BOXES, WHOOTEN WINS

Why am I telling you all this?

I spent my twenties raising money for House Democrats. I started as this idealistic kid working on Capitol Hill when Democrats had the majority in 1992. We lost in 1994, and wanted desperately to win it all back. Money was the answer. I left in 1998 when Newt Gingrich was still the Speaker after four years. I was competitive, and successful when I wanted to be. But for what? I left because I was unhappy raising money from a very small, select group of donors who commanded our elected representatives' most precious quantities: their time and attention.

So I went out in search of a better way to change the world, through local elections for governor and mayor, offices I thought were closer to the people they served. Then I worked for some outsider candidates for Congress, who to my dismay were immediately engulfed by the campaign finance system I'd helped build. Finally, I thought I'd found my messiah, the one who would lead the people to the promised land of political change: Howard Dean. I was wrong again. That same small group of ultra-liberal wealthy elites gobbled up Howard Dean too. I lost all hope. There isn't a happy ending to this story . . . yet.

Along the way, I've had some amazing times. But the story of the explosion of money in American politics over the last twenty years can't be told through charts and graphs and laws and figures. It's best explained by someone who had a front-row seat to it all.

Who are these donors? What drives them? What can fundraisers get away with? And how did we—politicians, donors, and fundraisers—screw up American politics so badly?

That's what this book is about.

PART 1

THE GEPHARDT YEARS

1

THE SENSE OF HISTORY, POWER, AND EVEN THE SIGHT OF THE building itself sent chills through my body. It was June of 1992, and I was twenty-two and had arrived at the U.S. Capitol. Well, I wasn't some policy wonk or power broker; I sat out front as one of the official greeters for Majority Leader Richard A. Gephardt (D-MO), my working-class hero. My incredibly important duties included answering the phones, greeting visitors, and snipping newspaper stories about politics. Even from the lowest spot on the totem pole, it sure beat my friends' jobs: selling cars, working in hotels, delivering pizzas. I was in a very different place, at an institution I revered—the U.S. Congress, the people's House.

I had no idea what went on in Leader Gephardt's closed-door meetings. Not many of his seventy-plus staffers did, either, for that matter, or even had much interaction with him. But I provided customer service to his visitors with a smile. I felt like a butler, but was honored to play my role.

MONEY HAS ALWAYS BEEN IN POLITICS, that's not a secret. But things started to change in the 1970s. First, Watergate happened. Few remember it was actually a campaign finance scandal that unraveled when $25,000 was discovered in the burglars' bank account from Nixon's Committee to Re-Elect the President (CREEP). Reforms followed, which set up donation limits and political action committees (PACs). PACs were a new, legal way for unions and companies to funnel their employees' or members' money to politicians. They favor big organizations. The larger the company or union, the more employees or members there are to donate to the PAC. The Federal Election Committee was created to oversee these new rules. It was and continues to be a weak regulatory body that is driven by partisan politics more than a desire to regulate money.

In 1976, the Supreme Court ruled in *Buckley v. Valeo* that political giving was a form of free speech, a precedent enhanced by *Citizens United* in 2010. *Buckley* opened the possibility for "soft money" to come into play—essentially unlimited cash that could be used for vague "party building activities" and "advocacy" but not directly for campaigning. Soon PACs had "hard" and "soft" money accounts. Hard money paid for the campaigns (rallies, ads, get out the vote), soft money paid for everything else, including staff salaries, benefits, travel, and overhead. It took a long time for politicians to really begin to recognize the power of soft money. When soft money got out of control, Senators John McCain (R-AZ) and Russ Feingold (D-WA) tried to limit it in 2002 through the law unofficially known as McCain-Feingold. It capped donations to parties and essentially killed soft money as we knew it. But the law really just forced soft money away from the parties, as billionaires set up their own outside organizations. A lot more on this later.

In the summer of 1992, Congress was nervous about the role of money in politics. DC had spent the previous summer enthralled by the Keating Five Hearings, a major campaign finance scandal that snared five U.S. Senators for swapping favors for money and time spent with Charles Keating. He looked for help for his business from what would become known as the Keating Five: U.S. Senators Alan Cranston (D-CA), Dennis DeConcini (D-AZ), John Glenn (D-OH), John McCain, and Donald W. Riegle (D-MI). Keating had made legal political contributions of about $1.3 million to the senators, and he called on them to help him resist regulators who were trying to close his savings and loan operation, Lincoln Savings and American Continental. Keating became a personal friend of McCain following their initial contacts in 1981; McCain and his family made several trips at Keating's expense, sometimes aboard American Continental's private jet, for vacations at Keating's opulent Bahamas retreat at Cat Cay. Senator McCain would spend years after this scandal finding ways to look clean when it comes to political money. He has been so effective that few if any still remember that McCain had such a close relationship with one wealthy donor.

In the end, the senators were found technically innocent of breaking ethics rules. But it was clear from the hearings—and I watched them all— that money had influenced them. It wasn't corruption as most understand it—*I give you money, you vote for my issue*—but rather Charles Keating had influenced them by demanding so much of their time. With meetings in DC and Arizona and vacations with Senator McCain, Charles Keating was getting more bang for his money than the average donor, never mind the average constituent.

I didn't understand why a group of bipartisan senators would be so focused on one person, one donor. Democrats and Republicans alike got caught up in Charles Keating's drive to make close friends on Capitol Hill. In hindsight, the net result was that big donors split along partisan lines. Since Senator McCain managed to drag a few Democrats down with him, McCain had accidentally protected himself from the Left's attacks. Politicians noticed. Democrats did not want to be dragged into scandals created by Republicans, and Republicans didn't want to be dragged into scandals created by Democrats. Politicians shied away from wealthy donors who played both sides. The Keating scandal forced donors to become more partisan. Today, the only groups that give money to both sides are corporations and industry associations.

Accused of doing something illegal or unethical, donors and politicians started defending themselves by turning the accusation into a partisan attack. Members of Congress and staffers worried that they might be implicated in a similar scandal with one false move, so they shied away from even the appearance of campaign finance impropriety. Money had been a minor annoyance to senior Hill staff up to this point, but they used the Keating Five as a last stand against the increasing influence of money: It would be the Hill policy staffs' Alamo.

RUNNING FOR ELECTION TO CONGRESS in the late 1980s or early 1990s required raising campaign money, but not like today. In 1992, the candidates running for the U.S. House couldn't compete with the big boys running for

Senate or governor, so House candidates saved the money and spent it more wisely. The average incumbent Democratic member of the U.S. House in 1990 spent about $425,000 on a campaign.[1] Incumbents always have an easier time raising money because they hold power. Throw out a few of the biggest Democratic money raisers (like Dick Gephardt), and the real average was closer to $250,000. Viable challengers could raise half that. Over a two-year election cycle back then, raising money was a part-time undertaking. Your average House of Representatives incumbents would have one event in DC every year and a few smaller ones back home in their districts. Members of Congress didn't make a ton of calls to big donors outside their district or state and celebrated the $5,000 PAC checks they rarely saw.

With fundraising budgets under $425,000 for House members, power rested with groups that could cobble together contributions of $50,000 to $100,000. For Democrats in 1992, that was the labor movement. This was the high point of their influence. Over seventy-five different international unions, each with a federal PAC, collected smaller donations from their membership that they bundled in one lump donation of $5,000 or $10,000. A Democratic candidate could easily raise $200,000 of a $500,000 campaign just from labor. As campaign spending has increased, labor's same $200,000 has meant less and less and labor has lost influence to the big donors around the country.

The labor movement never fully adjusted for the changing landscape of political money. With PAC donations limited to $10,000 to each member of Congress, labor today has become the equivalent of the "nice aunt" of Democratic politics: She sends you that little check on your birthday and you will say thank you, but in the end it doesn't make much difference. Ten $10,000 checks from different unions made labor important in 1992; it could add up to almost 50 percent of the budget for a Democratic candidate for the House. That same $100,000 from Auntie Union in 2014 will be under 10 percent of the million-dollar (or more) budget. The change has been significant, and the failure of the labor movement—the home to middle-class America—to adapt to the modern realities of political money has meant that members of Congress don't reflect its values. In 1992, you had real champions of the working class: Dick Gephardt and David Bonior (D-MI) both had leadership positions. Today, House Democrats have no labor champion in the House leadership, they have only "friends."

DC IN 1992 had only a few fundraising consultants, and the firm Fraioli-Jost was their king. The rest of the Democratic fundraising class in the early '90s could fit into a Volkswagen Bug. Besides Mr. Gephardt and Joe Kennedy (D-MA), Fraioli-Jost worked for nearly every House Democrat. Mike Fraioli and Steve Jost developed the first large sweatshop fundraising firm business model. Each of their clients would get one big cattle-call event every year. That was it. Congress was in session for about two weeks a month. Then take out April, August, November, and December, when Congress was basically not in DC, and that left eight months with two available weeks each, or sixteen weeks, to hold one event for each of their clients. During those two-week windows, Fraioli-Jost would host about twenty separate fundraising events for twenty different members. They'd make sure not to schedule fundraising events at the same time or have events for members of the same committee in the House on the same night. At best, a DC donor or lobbyist might have one or two events in a week to attend. Today it's hard to find a Tuesday, Wednesday, or Thursday (days of the week Congress is in session) that doesn't offer twenty to twenty-five fundraising events, breakfast through dessert.

To rally money from labor unions, rich people, and companies, the firm hired recent college grads for about seven bucks an hour to mail invites and cold-call donors. Because the firm was hosting so many events, tracking the RSVPs could be confusing. So the phone bank boiler rooms got creative. They'd invent names on the "RSVP to" line of each invite; "RSVP to Steve," for example. So if a donor called the boiler room and asked for "Steve," the kid would say, "I'm sorry, Steve's not in, but can I help you with the congressman's event next week?" And no matter what the donor said next, the kid would know anyone calling for "Steve" was RSVPing for

Representative X's event. Calls for "Anna" were RSVPs for Congressman Y's event, and so on.

Fraioli-Jost worked part time for each client, at $2,500 a month. The firm would usually be hired for three months to plan an event, host it, and follow up to collect late checks. The total fundraising bill for a member of Congress was about $7,500 every year, although some members paid for their services throughout the year. Most members now pay at least $7,500 *a month* for fundraising salaries, with travel and event costs on top of that.

Much of the DC donor community would not contribute or attend fundraising events in the "off year," the year with no elections. And since election season didn't begin until late spring of the election year, candidates would raise most of their money in the final two months of the campaign. Of that $425,000 average incumbent member's budget, a candidate could expect to raise $200,000 in the late summer and fall, in the last few weeks leading up to election day.

This system—one big cattle call of an event per year—created a pretty innocent relationship between the donor and the member of Congress: Donors would get one opportunity to be in a room with a member, and they'd be surrounded by hundreds of others just like them. This arrangement limited the influence of any one donor. If a donor or lobbyist wanted to see a member of Congress or their staff, they'd go directly to the member's office on the Hill and ask for a meeting. Although lobbyists donated, turning one down for a meeting wasn't a big deal. If you pissed off one donor, there were so many giving relatively small amounts that it wasn't going to destroy your chances for reelection. Chiefs of staff and legislative assistants were powerful, and they didn't associate much with the lobbyist donor world; that was just beneath them.

It was more important to know the key leaders of groups that could endorse members. Labor unions, senior citizens' groups, women's groups, and some environmental leaders made the cut for the influence of senior Hill staff. Endorsements mattered much more than money, because these groups could turn out the voters.

TODAY, THE MOST IMPORTANT PERSON on members' staff is the fund-raiser. Almost all members of Congress employ full-time consultants or direct staff to raise money 365 days a year. Most top donors are on a first-name basis with the fundraiser but would struggle to name a member's chief of staff.

In 2012, the average price of winning a seat in the U.S. Congress was $1.6 million, a 380 percent increase in just twenty years.[2] Since 1990, the number of individual donors who have given more than $10,000 to poli-tics has quadrupled, from 6,500 to nearly 27,000 by 2010. All those rich people didn't appear out of thin air. They didn't spontaneously decide that they were going to start forking over massive amounts of money, changing politics, and increasing the influence of donors on the democratic process. The self-fulfilling industry of political fundraisers created the need for the billionaires to donate and the need for politicians to appease the donors.

This is how it happened.

2

MIDMORNING ON A SWELTERING DC DAY IN JULY OF 1992, STEVE Elmendorf, Mr. Gephardt's deputy chief of staff, asked me to take an en-velope from Gephardt's office on Capitol Hill over to something called the Effective Government Committee at 80 F Street, NW, on the eighth floor of the American Federation of Teachers building. I jumped at the chance— as a twenty-two-year-old do-gooder, the Effective Government Committee (EGC) sounded like a perfect organization for me.

Turns out I'd be disappointed. EGC was Mr. Gephardt's fundraising shop, his own political action committee. I walked in to my own little Ho-tel California. I would spend the next fifteen years trying to check out but could never leave.

THE EGC OFFICE WAS SET UP with four desks out front and one large private office in back. Three men in their early twenties were all on phones and looked up in unison as I walked in, but they kept talking and pitching prospects. The man in the big office, John O'Hanlon, a burly guy in his late thirties, peered over his sports section of the *Washington Post* and invited me in to see him.

"I'm from Mr. Gephardt's office," I said, beaming, as I handed him my envelope.

He pried it open and pulled out ten checks for Mr. Gephardt's campaign totaling $15,000. My heart sank; had I just broken the law? Taking contributions in the Capitol? That, as the Keating hearings had made clear to me, was illegal: Federal officials can't solicit or receive political money on federal property, which includes congressional offices. What had I done? Was this the beginning of a new Keating Five scandal? Although I was just the courier, I was sure I'd taken part in something dirty.

"Thanks for bringing this over . . . So what's your deal?" John asked in his slight New England accent. He was the first person from any part of Gephardt's operation to show any interest in me, the reception desk jockey.

"What do you mean?"

"You know . . . Where are you from? How'd you get into this business? What do you do for Gephardt? What do you do when you're not here?"

"Oh," I replied. "Not much . . . I'm from Maryland . . . decided that I really liked Tom Harkin so I volunteered on his campaign, then I got an internship over here after it ended . . . and I play a lot of ice hockey. I'm a goalie."

"Awesome. You're a goalie, that's great. I'm a big Bruins fan . . . Now let me tell you about this operation . . ."

I couldn't help but like him. This was my kind of guy, engaging, relaxed, Irish, and he clearly loved sports. He explained he was in charge of raising money for Mr. Gephardt. John made me feel wanted, which is the brilliance of any good fundraiser. He had a knack for becoming your best friend in mere seconds. Then he pitched me.

"Look, Lindsay, you can go back, answer the phones, and clip newspapers in that big, boring office where nobody knows who you are. But I'm sensing that it sounds like you want to be in the action. The action is here, at the Effective Government Committee."

No one in the Capitol office had ever given me a we-want-you speech. I was a cheap date, and John smelled it all over me. In just five minutes I went from despising "dirty money" in politics to desperately wanting to join the guys who raised it. John called the Capitol office and explained to my boss that I was now going to be working at the EGC.

JOHN INTRODUCED ME to the three other staffers: David Jones, Peter Maroney, and David Poger. All in their early twenties, Peter and Poger wore decked-out suits, David Jones wore jeans and a wrinkled sport coat. Instantly I picked out the real star: David Jones—Jonesy—beamed an aggressive confidence that underlined an honest, All-American quality. If David wanted to sell me a used car, I would have bought it on the spot. He was the most creative young fundraiser the party would have over the next few years, and he would lead the charge to revolutionize fundraising for Democrats.

They all gave me a quick once-over. Who was I? What was my deal? Was I some major donor's kid in need of a job? Why was I there? I answered just as I had with O'Hanlon, and I seemed to pass muster with all of them.

O'Hanlon reemerged from his office and announced we were having a "staff meeting." Yes! I was excited to get the feel for my new career. But when I went to grab a seat, everyone else headed toward the elevator. The elevator led us to the Dubliner, an Irish pub across from Union Station and one block from our office. This is where the EGC conducted most of its staff meetings.

Peter seemed to know every waiter and bartender. Turns out O'Hanlon had offered him a job while Peter was slinging drinks there a few months ago. Selling Guinness and selling Dick Gephardt apparently had something in common. Peter was a hustler, projecting the aura of a tough Irish intimidator, which somehow didn't fit his twenty-one-year-old demeanor. David Poger was the village idiot. He went on and on about his latest conquest, some freshman at George Washington University he nailed the night before. Poger's pride in his sexual prowess outweighed any talk about fundraising or politics.

Jonesy was all about the job at hand. He pestered O'Hanlon relentlessly about other folks he could call, new ways to squeeze a few bucks out from a donor here or there. "Patricof in New York, Buddy Chiles in Florida" and many more names I had never heard of. He wanted to win. So did I. But I didn't know how, so I sat there and repeated, "How can I help?" I'd been scared of the "dirty" aspects of money in politics, but if it was helping Dick Gephardt win elections, it was becoming all right by me.

Our staff meeting ran into happy hour. Five hours and about nine beers after arriving for the 1 pm staff meeting, we parted ways. Everyone went home, except for Jonesy, who headed back to the office. They told me to show up the next morning for "normal business hours."

3

I ARRIVED ON MY FIRST FULL DAY OF WORK AT 8 AM, THE "NORMAL" time I'd arrived at the Capitol. The ECG's door was locked. I waited, and waited. At 10:30, O'Hanlon finally emerged from the elevator.

"Wow, how long have you been waiting?"

"Oh, just a bit," I replied, trying not to guilt him.

Jonesy, Poger, and Peter arrived a few minutes later. They put me on my first fundraising project. Peter was in charge of an event in Orlando, two weeks away. He needed to find new donors to invite in the Orlando area. To raise more money, we had to find new donors. Peter handed me a list of three hundred names, people he'd found by digging through old invite lists and campaign disclosure forms down at the Federal Election Commission, or had gotten through word of mouth. Unfortunately, there was rarely a phone number attached—on a disclosure form, donors only have to give their address and profession. My job was to call the information line and find their numbers.

I jumped right in. It was a manageable and even fulfilling task. As soon as I got a number out of the Orlando operator, I'd hand it to Peter, who'd say "Thanks, need more," and he would call the number immediately.

"Hi, this is Peter Maroney calling from Leader Dick Gephardt's office. Mr. Gephardt is coming to town and wants to see you at lunch. How much are you giving, and how many people can you bring?"

Meanwhile, to me Poger didn't seem to be doing much work. He sat at his desk and read the paper, clipped his fingernails, hand-pressed any wrinkles out of his suit, and stared at the clock on the wall: Lunch would be soon, closing time not too long after that. And GW freshmen would be waiting for him after that.

I finished five hours of calls with the 407–555–1212 line in Orlando and found nearly two hundred phone numbers. Jonesy gave me another list for a New York event, and I went to work. Instead of being king of Dick Gephardt's office foyer, I was getting tangible results for my work. Of all the jobs in politics, fundraising is the most black and white: Either you raised the money or you didn't, either I got the phone numbers or I didn't. I was contributing. I was helping Democrats win. If money was the means to that end, I convinced myself that raising it was okay.

FOR ALL THE OUTGOING CALLS, the phone didn't ring that much in the office. If donors called back, they knew they'd be asked for money. But one guy did call every morning for the update: Terry McAuliffe, the Macker. He was the de facto king of Democratic political money and the overlord of Gephardt's money machine, the man Al Gore would later call the "greatest fundraiser in the history of the universe." He's now the governor of Virginia. It was his job to make sure O'Hanlon was closing, and often. After talking with O'Hanlon, he would ask to speak with Jonesy and Maroney. His method—love and intimidation—worked.

"Great job, Jonesy!" he'd cheer when David had hooked a new host for an event in New York. But if there were no new hosts coming from Peter, he'd explain, "You know, the first event I ever did in Orlando I raised over $50,000." If you want to be the next Terry McAuliffe, you need to raise. Otherwise, you just aren't that good.

As the event in Orlando approached, I was full of pride. I helped Peter, and together we helped one of my heroes, Dick Gephardt. We hadn't sealed the deal, however. Terry was ruthless, and wanted to make sure Peter could turn commitments into checks. Terry bought Peter a one-way plane ticket to Orlando. If Peter wanted to come home on Gephardt's dime, he'd have to fax in copies of the checks that totaled at least $25,000.

Peter flew down a week before the event to meet a few of the bigger donors, check out the lunch location, and make more calls. Making calls locally worked; folks seemed to be willing to talk with a "local" over somebody from Washington.

Two days before the event, Hurricane Andrew devastated Florida. Gephardt, not wanting to seem disrespectful of a crushed state (and its donors), pulled the plug on the trip. Fundraising right after a natural disaster wasn't appropriate—a position I'd stick to years later with Hurricane Katrina. Hurricanes didn't float as an excuse to Terry McAuliffe.

He called Peter. "A deal is a deal. Fax in the copies of the checks and you can come home."

"Terry," Peter protested, "the whole state is a disaster area. How can I ask donors for checks when they don't even have running water?"

"I don't care. They just better total $25,000."

Tough-love Terry. Peter needed ten days to collect $25,000 with no event. He went door to door and told donors they still had to cut a check. I imagined Peter stepping over downed palm trees and downed power lines. When he faxed a copy of the last $1,000 check to get his total raised to $25,000, Terry was good to his word and Peter got his flight home.

THIS ROUTINE WENT ON for the next few months: Pick a city, search for names, find "hosts," send out invites, follow up with calls, make more calls, then travel to the site a few days before the event. I never saw Dick Gephardt that year after I stopped working in the Capitol. He never made one fundraising call. He didn't have to—he was the only member of the House with a full-time team of fundraisers. He was unique. Gephardt had run for president in 1988 and had kept his money machine ready by continuing to employ staff. No other House member really had presidential timber or ambitions, so it made sense for Gephardt to have his campaign finance staff ready in case he wanted to run again. No one knew it at the time, but Dick Gephardt's personal drive to be president had a big impact on how the role of money would fundamentally change politics over the next twenty years. With his own staff, he was setting a precedent.

As a member of the Democratic leadership, he had to raise money for his reelection, for the Effective Government Committee, and for other House Democrats. While your average incumbent Democrat in the House was raising less than $500,000 during the 1992 cycle, Dick Gephardt hauled in $3.2 million.[1] Not that he needed it—he won his 1992 race by thirty-one points. But he could transfer a lot of that money to the Democratic Congressional Campaign Committee (DCCC, the committee in charge of electing Democrats to the House), which would help other Democrats get elected. Leadership had to show the other members that they did everything they could to help Democrats win. These internal campaign fund transfers—raising money for your own campaign that you didn't need—were limited in 1992 to only the most senior members and top party leadership. Today it is required for all members of the House Caucus. The party committees like the DCCC simply could not keep their doors open today without direct transfers from all members. No back-benching member from the 1980s would understand this. Even other high ranking members of the Democratic Caucus didn't fund-raise aggressively. Speaker of the House Tom Foley used his wife as his fundraiser; another member of leadership, David Bonior, used Fraioli-Jost, the fundraising firm.

The Gephardt team wanted to build a national network of donors who would not only give the maximum donation of $1,000 but also would be able to raise $20,000 or $50,000 from others for the next Gephardt presidential campaign. In 1992, the thinking was that a candidate in the Democratic primary for president would need to raise $10 million to be a real player, $20 million would win the nomination. Gephardt didn't run in '92, but kept his team around in case he ever wanted to again. So his team built the list of three or four big donors in every major fundraising market: New York, Boston, Florida, Chicago, Los Angeles, Texas, and Philadelphia. Each city had a top donor: Ben Barnes in Austin, Boston was Steven Grossman or Arnold Hiatt, Chicago was Don Sussman, and so on. It was rare for a national politician like Gephardt to make "the ask" for a contribution from these individuals, so when Gephardt came to their city once or twice a year, getting them to write a check was an easy lift.

It was clear why these donors wanted to stay on Gephardt's good side: to enjoy the perks of the White House in a Gephardt presidency. Dick was still tops on the list of presidential candidates, and when his fundraiser called, it was important to be supportive if a donor wanted to serve in his administration or become an ambassador. That was the hook. Top donors in each city would raise money for a prospective presidential candidate from smaller donors, who'd give once the top donor asked. For the handful of Democrats who wanted to be president, it was easy: All they had to do was keep three or four people in each city engaged, and they would do the rest of the work for you. In 1992, if you had fifty of these folks around the country, you had a healthy national fundraising strategy.

This all changed in the next three years. Raising money nationally became no longer about presidential ambition but about members of the House and Senate (with no presidential ambition) raising money by pitching congressional legislation and picking political fights. That's a very different sell to donors. With an explosion of the number of members raising money, more and more donors around the country had to be found to fund them. In 1992, you would be hard-pressed to name the top five Democratic donors in Boston; by 2012, there would be over fifty well-known top targets.

Over the next few years, as Gephardt and his House leadership team forced average House back-benchers to raise money from a national donor network, the party was slowly taken over by the need to keep these individual donors happy. One or two phone calls a year from Dick Gephardt or a senator in leadership like Tom Daschle (D-SD) became one or two a *week* from some House or Senate Committee chairman. That call schedule takes up members' most in-demand quantity: time.

4

AS THE 1992 ELECTION APPROACHED, A STRONG FEELING DEVELoped among Democrats that Bill Clinton might actually win. It had been sixteen years since Jimmy Carter had won the presidential election in 1976, and Democrats had forgotten what holding power was like. With victory almost in hand, Gephardt didn't fund-raise much those last few weeks before the election. Work slowed down at the Gephardt money machine, but we did maintain our daily liquid-infused staff meetings.

The Friday before the election, O'Hanlon and Gephardt's Hill staff decided to dump all the cash out of the Effective Government Committee PAC accounts and spread it around to any and all Democrats running. It was why the EGC existed in the first place. Gephardt had started traveling around the country with John O'Hanlon, David Jones, and Peter Maroney to raise money for several different accounts: for "Gephardt in Congress," his official campaign account: for the Democratic Congressional Campaign Committee (DCCC): and for his political action committee, the EGC, which could also be used to pay campaign staff salaries and travel costs. "Leadership" PACs in 1992 matched the title: Members of a party's *leadership* had them, but the average back-bench member did not. Today, 90 percent of members in both parties have at least one leadership PAC, yet the leadership in the House is still the same number: four. I guess money makes everybody a leader.

He gave away the EGC's money to "buy" loyalty from members of the Democratic Caucus. If another member ever challenged him for leadership of House Democrats, Dick could easily remind the Democratic members of Congress, the voters in leadership races, that he had given them money. With campaigns running about $425,000 on average, that $5,000 or $10,000 from Gephardt was not insignificant. And if a candidate lost by a few hundred votes and Gephardt—or anyone else with a PAC—had not helped them and yet had cash available, that would be hard to explain, if not plain embarrassing, to the other members in the Democratic Caucus. This was the ultimate, legal way to instill loyalty from members: Handing them cash would make it hard for them to vote against you for Speaker, leader, or whip. If you ever had a real internal campaign for leadership, no question that the member-candidate that delivers the most money will always win.

In the middle of September of 1992, our office got a call from one of the postal workers' unions with a simple offer: They had $100,000 left to give from their PAC but wanted to give that money to incumbents who really needed it. O'Hanlon and the others gathered the names and sent the list, via fax machine, over to the Rural Letter Carriers of America. About two days later, the stack of fifty checks arrived to the office, some made out for $1,000, some for $5,000, and addressed to individual members. O'Hanlon told me to take that stack up to Steve Elmendorf in the Capitol. I was opposed to the thought of distributing political money in the Capitol, but I would do the job I was handed.

I watched as Steve ran the few feet from Gephardt's office and tried to track down every member he had a check for. Classic. He was currying favor for himself with each and every member he handed a check to, though he had done nothing to raise the money.

The hypocrisy of the moment was not lost on me a few years later when John Boehner (R-OH), today the Speaker of the House, went to give a few checks out to Republican members on the House floor, and Steve Elmendorf went batshit crazy. My money is cleaner than yours, that's the Democratic motto.

A FEW DAYS BEFORE THE ELECTION, another list came in, this one from Gephardt's Capitol office. One hundred seventy-seven candidates for Congress needed to get checks ASAP or they couldn't use the money before election day. Buying loyalty was in overdrive. We too went into overdrive to assemble 177 donation packets in just a couple of hours. We split up assignments. I would print the letters for each candidate, Jonesy would write the checks, O'Hanlon would forge Gephardt's signature, Maroney would call the candidates to tell them the checks were coming, and Poger would fill out the FedEx forms. We had four hours before the 5 pm FedEx cutoff.

I stacked the letters on O'Hanlon's desk as they came off the printer, and O'Hanlon got to signing "Dick" on each note to a candidate that would accompany the check. Jonesy hand-printed the campaign committee names on checks: "Clyburn for South Carolina, People for Waxman in California," and so on. I would grab the note from O'Hanlon, attach the corresponding check, and hand it to Poger to be placed in the matching FedEx envelope.

At 4:55 pm the FedEx guy arrived just as we sealed the last of the 177 envelopes. He gave them a quick once-over, then looked at O'Hanlon with a puzzled expression. "Let me get this straight: You guys want to send these 177 envelopes right back to this office?"

Poger had pulled a Poger. He had spent four hours writing our office address in the "TO" box on all 177 forms. We didn't have time to meet the FedEx deadline that night, so we came back on Monday and redid all the packages for Tuesday delivery, the day of the election.

5

THE CLINTON/GORE TEAM HAD THE CREAM OF THE FUNDRAISING
crop in 1992; presidential campaigns always do. Clinton raised $62 million
in 1992, a 20 percent increase over Mike Dukakis in 1988. That's where the
real action was—if you wanted to be in the big leagues, you raised money
for the presidential campaign. Gephardt had his team, and a few other
small fundraising shops existed around town, but the talent pool—maybe
twenty full-time fundraisers in 1992—was thin.

After the election, members of the Clinton money team started getting important jobs: Rahm Emanuel would go to the White House as an
advisor, Terry McAuliffe somehow got himself an ambassadorship (to the
Taejon Expo in South Korea, whatever that is), and other fundraisers would
jump onto the transition team and broker themselves a gig. That meant the
Inaugural Committee was short fundraisers. And it needed money, for the
parade, for balls, and for food . . . and to entertain all the big-name stars
coming to town.

Since I really had not been a fundraiser, I didn't want to go to the Inaugural Committee and make calls—I had no confidence I could ask someone
for $5,000 or $10,000. So I went off to work for the "talent team," which
meant we would pamper the visiting Hollywood and music stars. I've never
been a star fucker, at least for Hollywood types. My stars were members of
Congress, but I would do my job for President-Elect Clinton.

JONESY STAYED WITH GEPHARDT to handle donor requests for the inauguration. Maroney got a new job as Congressman Joe Kennedy's full-time
fundraiser. Joe wanted to be governor of Massachusetts and wanted a
piece of the only Democratic fundraising pros outside of Clinton's world,

the Gephardt team. Poger went to raise money full time for the Inaugural Committee.

The Inaugural Committee didn't know about Poger's FedEx problem, but he'd screw things up soon enough. I stopped by the fundraising side of the committee one morning and overheard Poger making a grease-ball pitch to a donor on the phone.

"Beth, I just got off the phone with the president-elect, and he asked me—personally—to call you and request $5,000 for the Inauguration Committee. I would love nothing more than to call him back and tell him that you're sending in that check. Can I do that?"

Utter bullshit. To think Bill Clinton had called Poger to discuss specific donors is beyond fantasy. But Poger probably saw himself hanging out in Georgetown bars dropping the same line: "I just got off the phone with President-Elect Bill Clinton . . . and he thinks you should sleep with me."

Unfortunately for Poger, he had just pitched Beth Dozoretz. Beth was very close to the Clinton family, so close that she could pick up the phone and talk to Bill or Hillary, which she did. Terry McAuliffe heard about the call, lit into Poger, and put him in the doghouse for the rest of the inaugural.

Meanwhile, those of us on the talent committee ran around DC blocking off hotel floors for the big stars: Barbra Streisand to the Mayflower, Billy Crystal to the Jefferson, and so on. We had over a hundred performers appearing at different inaugural events. All of them needed hotels, pampering, and more. As it would play out over the next fifteen years, involving Hollywood stars in Democratic politics would prove to be a massive time suck, as staff and elected officials routinely spend too much time coddling large egos when they should be doing better things, like running the country.

Six days before the inaugural, the talent committee assembled in the basement of our headquarters, where we'd be assigned our talent for the week. The big names were already gobbled up by the top staff, but we put the B-list stars in a hat to be assigned lottery style. I was excited. Maybe

I'd get Fleetwood Mac? Chevy Chase? But when I saw my sheet of paper, I should have taken it as a sign to get out of politics.

I would spend the next six days driving around the Manhattan Transfer in a van to events, dinners, museums, and more. Yep. And they would practice singing nonstop in that van. I shudder every time someone mentions that band today.

My dislike for Hollywood types started with Billy Crystal. The day before the inauguration, we were hosting a presidential gala out at the Capital Centre, the sports complex about ten miles from DC, where the Bullets and Capitals played. Crystal was slated to MC the night, and Barbra Streisand, Michael Jackson, Elton John, Robin Williams, and Chevy Chase would all perform. It would be a full-on liberal coronation love-fest.

But there was one major hiccup. Billy Crystal refused to take a limo; he would only take a helicopter. Seriously. Members of Congress, senators, governors, foreign leaders, and every other performer would all happily ride the ten miles in a limo, but not Billy. The inaugural scrambled and worked with the Secret Service—this is DC, after all—and arranged for his solo ride in the helicopter.

6

DC WAS IN THE MIDST OF A DEMOCRATIC HONEYMOON IN JANUARY of 1993. The White House and both houses of Congress had Democrats controlling them. Bill Clinton was President, Tom Foley was Speaker of the House, and George Mitchell was Senate majority leader. Congressional fundraising remained part time, as the anti–Keating Five culture still hung heavy over the Capitol. Almost no members had a full-time fundraising staff yet. Why pay a fundraiser a salary and benefits a full two years before the next election?

The Gephardt money machine nearly closed down after the election of 1992. With Clinton in the White House, Dick's next chance to run for president was at least four, but more likely eight, years away. And Gephardt could easily raise enough by himself to win his next House election. But Gephardt recognized talent and wanted to keep David Jones around just in case. So Dick kept Jonesy on as his only fundraiser. Meanwhile, Poger was still in the woodshed for his call to Beth Dozoretz. Maroney was gearing up Joe Kennedy to run for Massachusetts governor. John O'Hanlon went into making money and became a lobbyist.

I was in limbo for only a few days. Fundraisers with talent and political connections went into the administration. Beyond that, the Democratic National Committee held the only real promise for a fundraiser's next job. McAuliffe called the new finance director (the DNC's top fundraiser and a job I'd hold by 2005), Nancy Jacobson, and told her to hire me. Getting me a job was a win-win for Terry: He built my loyalty to him, and Nancy was happy to have one of Gephardt's renowned money team on board. Nancy had been raising money for national Democrats for a few years, having worked for Senators Gary Hart (D-CO) and Al Gore (D-TN) previously. Today Nancy runs a group called "No Labels," a centrist group that is supposed to be about "fixing" partisan politics. Of course, Nancy was a leader in creating the partisan money game in 1993.

JANUARY 25, JUST FIVE DAYS after the inaugural, and the DNC's new fundraisers arrived at the third floor of the DNC building. It was a dingy, smelly office with disgusting, stained green carpet. The office fell far short of the new standards in campaign cash. Now that Bill Clinton was in the White House, the role of money in politics was changing. All of a sudden, the memory of the Keating Five scandal faded fast, and the era of soft money—unlimited amounts that could be given to party committees in support of loosely defined party-building activities—was dawning. It was morning in America for those who could write six-figure checks, and Nancy Jacobson was determined to make it rain.

The last time Democrats controlled all three branches of elected government—House, Senate, White House—had been 1977. No one understood, or cared, how such absolute control of the legislative process could translate into political money. Democrats' grip on power meant special interest groups would need to shower Democrats with money to move any nonessential bill through Washington. If a Nancy Jacobson or a Terry McAuliffe did not approve of you, or if you had not done enough for them, you got nothing. Nancy or Terry would just deny you access, and they'd never tell you about the potential access you were being denied. It was a new day.

But most of the party—except for a few other big players—didn't understand that Nancy and Terry were opening the floodgates, and it showed. The Clinton team installed David Wilhelm as the DNC chair, a young Chicago hack from the campaign, but he was not ready for a high-pressure role. Few, for that matter, were.

Combine a disgusting office, a weak DNC chair, and Nancy's desire to raise more money—hard and soft—than ever before, and guess what? The fundraisers took control and moved out of the DNC's offices. Nancy didn't tell anybody, not even Chairman Wilhelm. She found office space next to the White House, above the Old Ebbitt Grill on 15th Street. Donors could see the White House front lawn from its windows. It was the ultimate shake-down shuffle: If you want to get into the White House, I am your point of access. Pony up.

However, because this move was done on such short notice and without the "approval" of the rest of the DNC, Nancy had to choose office space that was not ideal. We shared space—down to the receptionist— with a law firm called Tanaka-O'Leary. In those first few months of the new DNC finance operation, when a donor returned a call they would hear "Tanaka-O'Leary, Democratic National Committee, how may I direct your call?"

It might seem like a small, subtle move for the DNC finance team to end up next to the White House, but it was the coronation of the new world. Policy and money are related. The statement wasn't aimed at traditional DC donors, like lobbyists and PAC directors. Rather, it was aimed at wealthier donors around the country, rich individuals who wanted to be involved and would be impressed by the DNC's proximity to the new president.

In the past, these folks would attend that one big Democratic fundraising event in their city every year. Since Democrats had not occupied the White House since 1980, the small donor community of the very wealthy had been connected to DC only through their home state members of the House and Senate to whom they donated in the final few months of the campaign. New York donors gave to Senator Pat Moynihan, Californians to Alan Cranston, and Ohioans to John Glenn. When those donors came to DC, they would come see their senator and maybe big players like Dick Gephardt, Representative Vic Fazio (D-CA), or Speaker Foley over in the House.

Nancy had sent an important signal that that relationship was changing. If you want to get into the White House, you must stop to get credentials next door at the DNC finance office. In just a few short months, a few elite rich people would begin to dictate which concerns Democrats cared about and how much time the party's elected officials spent kissing their asses, all because of the structure and rules that fundraisers like Nancy put in place. This new group of donors would be heavily associated with President Bill Clinton, and they would remain organized through his and Hillary Clinton's efforts for the next few years.

Then there is another level of donor, a level occupied by a very small handful of liberal elite donors. Billionaires. They participated some but never loved the Clinton operation. He was too moderate, too centrist. After losing the White House in 2000 and with the McCain-Feingold caps on soft money in 2002, they would take over the party by going around it. Keep reading.

7

THE DNC'S NEW FUNDRAISING TEAM HAD NO IDEA WHAT IT WAS doing. We would sit in the mahogany-paneled conference room of our sub-leased law firm office every morning at 8 am. Fifteen of us, not one over the age of twenty-five, including Nancy. Some of our staff was not in DC. Our Los Angeles fundraiser was dating actress Dana Delaney, and Dana would join our morning staff meeting over the phone.

Unlike past presidents, Bill Clinton immediately offered his time to the DNC for a few big events. The 1993–1994 cycle saw the first full-time national committee fundraising operation.

During the last presidential campaign, the DNC had raised $8 million. With soft money now in vogue, this team of green, pimply fundraisers had been charged with raising over $50 million. Peter O'Keeffe, Erica Payne, Hannah Simone, Kimball Stroud, and others had to find a way to make it happen.

Mind you, I had yet to make a fundraising call in my life, but I was a full-time paid fundraiser for the Democratic National Committee.

WE ASSIGNED STAFF to each upcoming event. I would go off to New York with three others to plan a big Radio City Music Hall evening with Barry Manilow. I went with the flow. It was thrilling: twenty-three years old and working an "important" job for the DNC or, as we would say, "working for the President of the United States." We got free rooms at the Loews Hotel on Madison Avenue, which became my home until I flamed out a few weeks later.

We went over to Radio City and discussed the seating charts. Five thousand seats in all, and we'd be generous enough to sell the balcony for $100 per seat. This was part of the new fundraising optics: The DNC could defend taking large checks by pointing to the vast number of small checks it also received. We could point at the balcony and say, "We are the party of little people!"

That left three thousand seats for the best (richest) Democrats in New York. The front two hundred seats would go for $25,000 a pair and include backstage passes to hang out with President Clinton. The next slice of seats went for a $15,000 donation (but no presidential hangout), then $10,000, $5,000, $2,500, and $1,000. If we sold out, the evening would raise over $10 million for the DNC, which would be a record. It proved too much to handle. They never could sell the tickets and moved the event to a more manageable location with fewer seats, Lincoln Center.

This was the problem with starting the race for dollars so early in the election cycle. It's about the timing. The next election was so far away, and a pitch focused solely on winning the next election didn't go over well because donors felt tapped out from trying to win the one that just happened. So fundraisers began to divide the class of wealthy donors into two groups—"regular" rich people who might have other priorities for their money and a class of a select few very wealthy individuals who would automatically write checks because they had too much money to know what to do with it. This elite network of donors who could write $100,000 in soft-money checks without blinking started with these types of events in the spring of 1993.

It changed how politicians talked and acted toward donors. Before, a politician asked for a check because it made the difference between winning and losing. Raising so much money so early from the wealthy elite changed what the donor got in return. Making a call to a donor six weeks before the election took only a few minutes on the phone and was accompanied by a simple ask: "Please donate so I can win." Getting the elite donor class to pony up twenty-four months before the election meant coddling them, spending time with them, and giving them access.

Elections and fundraising were seasonal prior to 1993. Since then, they have been year-round.

WE DIVIDED UP the Clinton/Gore and Inaugural Committee donors. All I had to do was raise $3.3 million and some change . . . more money than I could possibly imagine. But I was representing the President of the United States; how could a donor say no to that *and* an evening with Barry Manilow? My list had some heavy hitters: VPs at Goldman Sachs, Lazard Frères, Dime Bank, JP Morgan, and the like . . . a who's who of Wall Street Democrats, folks who made more in one day than I did in a year. I would never have anything in common with them, but my job was to raise and raise.

I started with donors who had written checks of $25,000 or more in a combination of hard and soft money. My very first donor meeting was with an investment banker. We had a superficial conversation, where a guy in his fifties pretends to care about a twenty-three-year-old kid in a cheap suit who was about to beg for a check. Except I never got the chance to beg. He complained about all the money he'd given and said he needed a break. To my own amazement, I agreed. Twenty-five grand is a lot of money, and what right did I have to ask him for so much again just a month after the inauguration? Donors had always had a honeymoon after the election, and I wanted to respect that tradition. That break does not exist anymore.

But I felt that our fake conversation might just have built a bond between us. Confident he would give that $25,000 before the event—I had two months still to work on him—I did what I thought a fundraiser did: I marked him down on the commitment sheet for $25,000. I had never asked him for the money, he had never offered, but I was confident.

I had fifteen meetings that first week. I was traipsing around New York, sitting down with the richest of the rich and talking presidential politics. I was king of the hill . . . for a day or two. But then the script of my first meeting repeated itself all over town. Everyone was tapped out from the campaign and the inauguration. I didn't put in a single ask for money. And that's the critical part: Fundraisers don't raise money unless they ask for it, and for a specific amount. At that point in my career, I just assumed donors would give sooner or later. I marked down each donor for the amount they'd given previously, without a single actual commitment. I sent my list of "commitments" at the end of that first week in New York to Nancy. My total was $375,000.

ONE OF MY LAST MEETINGS that week was with what I would come to know as a "donor fake," a David Poger in reverse: a donor who bullshitted as well as a fundraiser and would never write a check. As fundraising exploded between 1993 and 1995, donor fakes would become more common. They're a double whammy: Not only do they fail to cough up enough money, they demand more and more time from the politician, who usually believes a large check is around the corner with just a little more work. Hollywood types are the worst donor fakes. And fundraisers, like me, would buy into this false hope and allow politicians to continue coddling them.

David Bender was my first donor fake. My list didn't have a dollar amount next to his name, but he was still high up near the top: #44 out of 500. Since the list seemed to go by dollar amounts, with the biggest donor at the top, he had to be big time.

His assistant answered the phone, "Please hold for Mr. Bender."

A minute later, Bender picked up. "Lindsay, how are you doing? I would love to talk about this event! Perhaps you could come to my office and we could go to lunch?"

Something was off. Mr. Bender sure sounded a lot like his assistant. I didn't care, I had a new "whale." I walked over to his office in Midtown Manhattan. It wasn't really an office building, it was an old apartment block. I didn't pay much attention; in New York lots of offices were in apartments. I buzzed up, and Mr. Bender's assistant answered.

"Please come up, Mr. Bender will see you now."

It was the smallest studio apartment I've ever seen, maybe two hundred square feet, with a couch that doubled as a bed, a TV, a coffeemaker, a hot plate, a bookcase, and a toilet. No closet. No bathroom. No shower. It was hard to find a seat.

We talked about President Clinton and all Mr. Bender had done to help, which sounded like not much, frankly. I really wanted to ask where his assistant was. It was killing me. Was he under the toilet? Maybe outside on the window ledge? David had a deal for me, for the president, Nancy Jacobson, and the Democratic Party. He opened a little box on his floor and pulled out a plate, a plate stamped with a picture of Bill Clinton, Al Gore, and the presidential seal.

"Why are you showing me these, David?"

"Lindsay, if you really want to raise a ton of money, and I mean a ton, and if Nancy does too, these plates are the ticket. You should offer them as gifts to your top donors."

"Well, I'm not—" I started to reply.

"Just think about it," he cut me off. "I have a dealer who can score these sweet babies for us for $14.95 a plate and maybe get us a bulk discount!"

My new pitch was obvious: Give the DNC $25,000 and you too can eat a turkey sandwich on Bill Clinton's face! I was desperate to escape. Now, it was 1993, so I didn't have a cell phone, and I didn't carry a pager. I had no way out of Bender's shoebox studio, and we still had to go to lunch.

"That's great, David, I think everybody at Goldman Sachs will want those in their homes!"

We walked to the Russian Tea Room. At least he had some class, and I could only assume his assistant had made the reservation. Actor/comedian Alan King came in a few minutes after us. David yelled at him. Alan gave the what-the-fuck-are-you-doing-here-and-no-I-am-not-your-friend wave back. "Hi, David." He kept moving.

After an excruciating hour, the check came. And it sat on the table, just staring at us. I got the message and hoped I had enough money in my account to cover it. I walked back to the hotel with tears of laughter streaming down my face. I marked him down for $25,000. Why not?

I KEPT SENDING NANCY the list of "commitments." I was rocking out. By the end of the second week, I had over $1.2 million on paper. Nobody else in that office had more than $100,000. Suckers. Then my house of cards crashed down. Nancy picked up the phone to thank the donors. The calls did not go too well. Not one of those nice people I had spent time chitchatting with, bonding with, being friendly with, "working," would confirm they had committed. Not one.

Nancy gave me my last paycheck and had me on the next train back to DC. I had managed to work a total of one month for the DNC.

8

I DIDN'T LIKE FUNDRAISING. ALTHOUGH I HAD A GOOD TIME THOSE few months with John O'Hanlon, David Jones, Peter Maroney, and Poger. If I wanted to make a difference in the world, it was becoming clear that fundraising wasn't the way. How could I help the underserved if I was begging rich folks all day? Maybe I could get a new job on the Hill doing some policy work? Fundraisers had no say in policy. At least that was the case in early 1993.

David Jones called. He had heard about my great Democratic National Committee fundraising success, but he "still believed in me." That meant he could get me cheap, as his assistant for the revamped Gephardt money machine, which he led. I should have said no. But I needed a paycheck, and he could get me $18,000 a year.

Since the downsizing of the Gephardt fundraising office, Jonesy had moved the operation to a little basement on Capitol Court NE near Union Station. It was a dark, dank office, but it would be the home of the Gephardt money machine for the next two years. Gephardt didn't need the full-time fundraiser operation he had had before, since the White House was occupied by a Democrat and Democrats controlled the House and the Senate. Fundraising in 1993 didn't require attention or work. It was like shooting fish in a barrel. Democrats held all the levers of power, so money would begin to flow in naturally, even to fundraisers like me.

David was hard-edged New Jersey all the way. He understood the money game. And he understood how to game the game. One of my first days in the office, I sat in awe as I listened to Jonesy berate some poor Verizon phone representative for over an hour. Jonesy wanted to change our office number, which began with a 636 extension. He wanted one that started with 225, same as the U.S. Capitol exchange. Caller ID was becoming more popular, and he wanted donors to think he was calling from an office in Congress. His message was simple: I'm close to power. Brilliant.

Verizon said no.

THE ROUTINE HADN'T CHANGED: Raising money meant finding new donors. We'd cull through lists of people who'd given to Gephardt before or pick up new names from other fundraisers at the DNC (and the list of names I had stolen on my way out the door at the DNC), or go down to the Federal Election Commission (FEC) and tear through disclosure forms for people who'd given to other Democrats. Then I'd call the information line to track down their numbers. We needed as many leads as possible to make the biggest possible target list. That was key: The more names, the less worry when somebody said no.

The closing rate for political fundraising is around 2 percent. Call one hundred people, two will say yes. Send one thousand letters asking donors to host an event, twenty—with a follow-up call—will say yes. Recruiting hosts is how to raise more money and increase attendance. Hosts agreed to raise or write $1,000, $2,500, or $5,000. We'd set different levels for hosting; maybe a gold host would be $5,000, silver $2,500, and bronze $1,000. Since the individual giving limit in 1993 was $1,000 (in 2014, it's $2,600), the idea was to get people to raise more money for us from their friends and colleagues after they'd given all they could. We'd tell them to ask their spouses, coworkers, neighbors, anyone. When hosts recruited new donors, we'd add them to our database, expanding our universe. We called them hosts to make them feel important: They'd be listed on the invite as a friend and supporter of Dick Gephardt, and we'd send the invite to thousands of people. Woo hoo.

Floyd Stoner was the head lobbyist of the American Bankers Association. He called me back in response to one of the host letters he had received and talked to me for over thirty minutes. He was a nice guy and I enjoyed talking with someone who seemed to be important. He wanted me—and thus Mr. Gephardt—to know that he was happy to contribute the maximum of $5,000 from the American Bankers PAC but that he could not be listed as a host. His excuse? The association didn't want to be seen as helping Democrats publicly. Sure the donation would show up on the FEC report, but he did not want his name floating around DC as being a big supporter of Democrats.

When we had stopped fishing for hosts and printed the invites, we would code each invite and send ten or twenty extras to each host. John Boland, for example, would receive twenty invites to pass out to his friends and colleagues with a little "JB" in the corner. When someone sent in a check on a "JB" RSVP, we knew whom to credit. That was 1993. Today, when so much money is raised online, there's usually a box on the Web page that asks donors to name the host who referred them.

Meanwhile, a political action committee could give $5,000. PACs are funded by many smaller contributions from individual union members or company employees, all in the name of spreading the respective organization's influence. It is average people's money. They give to the PAC run by their company or union, which bundles it together and donates it to make a large impression on behalf of the PAC's parent organization. But the higher limit meant PAC directors of all stripes jumped at being hosts. All they had to do was write a check funded by other peoples' money, and not spend time recruiting others. And, of course, they didn't have to write a personal check themselves.

With a bigger check, PACs had outsize influence but it was easier money for me to raise. All I had to do was reach out to a PAC director once:

one call, one check, done. I didn't have to spend time with them, I didn't have to beg them with weekly calls. Best of all, in 1993, *Gephardt* never had to spend time calling them.

Then there were independent lobbyist firms. They had PACs too. Since access was their stock and trade, they were a little stingier with the automatic "yes." They wanted more coddling, more time with the member so they could brag to clients about their relationships. If a hired K Street lobbyist agreed to be a gold host for $5,000, I had to stay on top of them, work them, make sure they got the attention they needed to send in that $5,000. If they could only write $1,000, they had to find another $4,000, and I had to motivate them to do that. Maybe a little time with the chief of staff would motivate you to produce? Or how about we send you one of those flags that flew over the Capitol? It was a constant battle to entice these people.

IF AFTER ALL THAT SPECIAL ATTENTION you still did not produce all the money you said you would, we'd put you on the deadbeat list. Mr. Gephardt would hear about the deadbeats. And we made sure everybody knew when we would send him the list. In truth, Gephardt never cared, but we fundraisers wanted the donor community to think he did.

At first, donors thought we were joking. But as political money grew in importance, so did the list. It began to inspire fear. To avoid being on this list, lobbyists and donors would create reasons to get us even more money to be sure they'd never get anywhere near it. Soon lobbyists' kids started opening checking accounts to funnel us money. We'd get $1,000 from Lobbyist Smith, but Lobbyist Smith's five-year-old daughter gave too . . . just to stay off the deadbeat list.

Then lobbyists became desperate to claim credit for as many donations as possible. If the Trial Attorneys' PAC gave $5,000 to host an event, within hours I would get calls from every outside lobbyist who ever worked for the trial attorneys taking credit for the check. I'd pass Tommy Boggs on the street, one of the most successful lobbyists in town, and he'd yell out that he had gotten that $5,000 check for us. All you could do was feign a weak "thank you."

We loved the extra money, but I hated the ass-kissing. We decided donors had to actually hand-deliver us the check or we would not credit them. Deadbeats be beaten! David Jones drew a line in the sand, and taking credit for the money had become important. The fundraiser's power was on the rise.

WE'D START PLANNING for the big events about six weeks beforehand. We knew we could only count on five or six days of fundraising time with Mr. Gephardt in 1993, so we had a short window to raise enough money to justify our salaries and employment. That seemed okay to me: With lots of people at a big event, no one would have too much time to lobby him about any one issue. Except for those couple events, we never saw Gephardt that year. He never made fundraising calls. He didn't visit our Capitol Court basement. He was busy working as majority leader in the House.

After President Clinton asked California congressman Leon Panetta to join his cabinet, Gephardt took a trip out west to campaign for Panetta's replacement in a special election. We decided to tack on an LA fundraising event. David was given two months to raise some money. We came up with about 2,500 possible hosts, printed letters, and forged Gephardt's signature. After dropping them in the mail and waiting a few days, David called them all, then he called again. And again. I culled for more names, spending hours at the FEC looking for any donor who had written $500 or more in Los Angeles. It was eye popping. As I read through various FEC filings, I got to understand different donor profiles: lots of "homemakers" (a term all fundraisers used when a donation disclosure form had to be filled out and we didn't know a woman's profession), lots of lawyers, few business executives, but very few Hollywood types. Actor Ed Asner showed up here and there with $250 contributions, but that was about it. In those days, Hollywood liked to show up, but never gave much money.

David was a closer; he relished calling folks for money. By the end of week one, he had over thirty hosts. By week two, he had over fifty. Then he called every Democratic member of Congress in the LA area and asked them to be "honorary hosts" of the event, which just meant we could list them on the invite. Most wouldn't event show, but donors didn't need to know that.

Three weeks out from the event, David flew to LA so he could work donors on the ground. I stayed in DC to design the invitation, get it printed, and mail it to five thousand people, including twenty to each host so they could invite their friends. Not one of them had ever spoken to Dick Gephardt, but that didn't matter; getting thirty seconds with him was enough to fork over $1,000.

David had failed to switch our phone exchange, but he was not done insinuating our relationship with the Capitol. We designed the invitation with a gold dome in the Capitol's shape. If you didn't know any better, it looked like official correspondence from the U.S. Congress. That was the point: If you wanted to be near the action in Congress, money is the way to do it.

I double-checked the names and made sure I had everybody listed and took the invite over to the printer to get five thousand invitations. I sent them out. David called me two days later. "Love you, man, but you fucked up. You misspelled Congressman Xavier Becerra's name." Damn. I was the worst fundraiser ever. In hindsight, I wish I'd been fired.

WE USED ONLY TWO of the five offices in that basement, so we rented one to Peter Maroney, now Congressman Joe Kennedy's full-time moneyman. Outside of Gephardt, the only full-time non-DNC fundraisers worked for Ted and Joe Kennedy. A new breed was popping up, as the handful of fundraisers around town realized that they could strike out on their own and sign House candidates—often gullible long shots who didn't know any donors and needed to hire people who did. With campaign budgets well under $500,000, candidates needed to know the labor leaders and individuals in their districts; that was more than enough to hit their campaign's fundraising targets.

Enter Bruce Keiloch. He was friends with Jonesy though I never knew what they had in common. Bruce was in his late twenties, with smelly, nappy dreadlocks down to his waist. Bruce was a member of the new fund-raising consultant class, and his client list showed it: long shots who didn't know they didn't need him, like a candidate for Congress in Chicago who was living in Cabrini Greens—the infamous housing project—who spent most of her campaign funds on new hats. This is how the industry grew— by preying on clients who could be convinced they needed a fundraiser. Jonesy rented the last office to Bruce.

The four of us set up our shops in that basement. Everybody made calls, set up events, tracked down new donors. Then things got punchy. Bruce and Peter had a love-hate relationship. Peter was most excited about his newfound ease in picking up young women. It was one thing to show up in a bar and flash a "Congressman Richard A. Gephardt" business card; the average college sophomore had no idea who he was. But business cards bearing the Kennedy name put Peter in sexual conquest heaven.

I am pretty sure Bruce was in unrequited love with Peter. Bruce often gave Peter rides home. Peter wanted to live close to Georgetown and its students. Bruce and Peter got into some argument in the car and Bruce very maturely blasted the Dead Kennedys on the stereo in response. Peter demanded Bruce pull over, and he jumped out of the car on Rock Creek Parkway. These were the new stars of Democratic fundraising.

OUR ROUTINE CONTINUED for the next year and half. Events in DC, New York, California, Vegas, Chicago, Florida, all in the same mode: maybe once every month or two, with no committed time from Gephardt to make calls. Assemble donors, find phone numbers, mail host invites, fol-low up, confirm hosts, follow up. Call. Call again. Expand the universe of people who could give us money. Rinse. Repeat. Monotony set in. My office was filled with trash, trash from reams of paper listing names, forgot-ten invitations, and, at times, piles of checks. David and I both got fat over the next eighteen months—we ate McDonald's breakfasts most mornings to put off making calls.

Fundraisers were still viewed as seedy characters. Very few politicians truly understood what we did or how we could be used to their benefit. With most members of Congress sticking to only one or two events a year, they had no use for full-time fundraisers. The path to a rich lobbying gig on K Street was still as a subject area expert in a congressional office, not as a fundraiser like so many today. Those lobbyists knew the legislative process, and that was what your clients paid for. Fundraising was just a sideshow.

Fraioli-Jost's business model was under threat. Campaign budgets were creeping up. Members of Congress needed to lavish more attention on more donors; the one or two big cattle-call events a year wouldn't cut it anymore. The emerging class of fundraising consultants was beginning to have success picking up new clients: a member here, a challenger there, maybe even a senator. Fundraisers were beginning to convince politicians that money would win elections and, of course, pay their own salaries. The new fundraising consultants concentrated on just one or two clients, which meant they could be more attentive, both to them and to the expanding class of high-maintenance donors they were creating.

9

I WANTED OUT, BUT I HAD NO CLUE WHAT I'D DO FOR A LIVING. NO matter how hard I tried to convince myself that I was helping the president, Leader Gephardt, or any other Democrat by raising money, I knew I was corrupting the political process, one check at a time. I had to get out of fundraising and find another way to make the world a better place.

In 1994, I announced I was running for the Maryland House of Delegates in District 39, a new seat carved out after the 1990 census. The district was way out in Germantown, Maryland, a very long way from the Capitol. Since I didn't live anywhere close to Germantown, I had to rent a tiny apartment to comply with the law. I furnished it with a TV, bed, and chair. It was home, sort of. With no money to my name, I had to keep my day job working for Gephardt. The commute was a killer, but elected office was my chance to make a difference.

In an article with the *Frederick News,* I focused on keeping government pure:

> Mr. Lewis was critical of incumbent lawmakers who, in his words, needed tougher public ethics laws. He said he would refuse all lobbyists' gifts, regardless of their value, and would push for new ethics laws . . . [so] that "the public does have full disclosure between representatives of the people and representatives of special interests."

A little ironic that I spent my day raising money from DC lobbyists and yet attacked them at night. Jonesy made calls for me. I held my first fundraising event at the infamous Hawk 'n' Dove on Capitol Hill. Terry McAuliffe came, as did other friends of Gephardt. I raised $10,000 that night, including $4,000 from Sunkist Growers of California. Not that they had much interest in District 39 in Maryland; they cared that David Jones, Dick Gephardt's chief fundraiser, had called them.

I organized weekend get-out-the-votes and invited my new fundraising and lobbyist friends from DC to help. My friends Kate Moss, Kimball Stroud, and David Jones all came out and knocked on doors for me. At the height of the campaign, I had over twenty DC power brokers wearing my T-shirt and knocking on doors. Although my campaign had no real message beyond vague promises of change, they did their best. Unfortunately, the most common response my powerful door knockers got from voters was, "I met her last week, I like her." They didn't even know I was a man.

I came in fourth in the primary, with 8 percent of the vote. But I still was the only person to get $4,000 from the Sunkist Growers!

10

IT WAS 1994, AND THE CAMPAIGN FINANCE WORLD WAS ABOUT TO change dramatically. All the fundraising innovations after the 1992 election would seem like child's play compared to what was about to happen. Newt Gingrich had signed a contract with America, and his band of Republicans was taking over Washington. Democrats had controlled the House of Representatives since the 1950s, but no more.

The summer of 1994 had been tough on Democrats. The first eighteen months of legislative pushes from President Clinton had taken a political toll. Carbon tax, gays in the military, the assault rifle ban, and health care reform had been tough votes, and they essentially forced many moderate Southern House Democrats to retire from Congress: Over fifty announced they would not be running for reelection. This stretched the party's limited resources—incumbents could raise money easily (they control power), but challengers always have a tougher time.

It was clear to anybody really paying attention that it was going to be a bloodbath on election day. Over forty years in charge of the House had made many in the party too comfortable. Sure, maybe we might lose a few seats, the thinking went, but it will still be a Democratic majority.

I got a call from David Jones on the Friday before the election. He was in St. Louis with Gephardt trying to raise some last-minute money. He gave me a task: Track down weekend phone numbers for George Soros and Arnold Hiatt, two mega-donors. Gephardt and Senator Tom Daschle had panicked, and both decided they would come up with $1 million each, $2 million total, to try to save the majority.

It was wrong on so many levels to me. How could you spend that money in the closing days? TV advertising time would be reserved already, and it was too late to design and send direct mail. Maybe we could set up some phone banks, but we couldn't find enough callers in America to make $2 million worth of calls. It was all going to be a waste of money.

But then I understood what they wanted to do: Tell these donors that the money would be spent on the election, but in the end use it elsewhere. They wanted to save it to pay bills after the election, but who would give so much after a massive loss?

I reached Mr. Soros's secretary in New York, and she was not dumb. She asked, "Why does Mr. Gephardt want to call over the weekend? Can't this wait until next week?"

I did my best to bullshit her about the call. "Mr. Gephardt is just calling to wish him a happy weekend and talk about the election." She didn't go for it, and we didn't raise our $1 million.

NEWT GINGRICH'S VICTORY that November was monumental, and total. Republicans took the Senate too. Democrats everywhere, fresh off Bill Clinton's big win in 1992, were beside themselves: distraught, confused, stunned, and reeling. No one knew what to do. How would the party react? Change the message? Blame Clinton? Attack Gingrich?

Democrats' reaction to the loss would forever change the role of money in politics. Their conclusion was definitive but simple: We lost because we didn't have enough money. Safe incumbents could have raised more. Challengers should have raised more. The party committees needed more. And Dick Gephardt wanted more: Win back the House in 1996, and he'd be the next Speaker. If you could fit all the Democratic fundraisers into a VW Bug in 1993, you'd need a cruise ship by mid-1995.

President Clinton would recover and win a landslide victory in 1996; much of that would come from his raw political skill and focus on centrist voters. But the secret piece of the puzzle was the massive amount of money that the Democratic National Committee raised in 1995 and 1996. The

Clinton White House, hurting in the polls before the '96 election, had gone into full panic mode. The DNC went into overdrive. The new M.O. for both was to do anything to suck up money, which they could because Clinton was still the president after all. Nancy Jacobson had started it on a small scale in 1993, but by January 1995, money was the central focus of Democrats.

House and Senate Democrats would try to copy them that election cycle. But House and Senate Democrats had what to offer, exactly? A Capitol tour? They'd been flying high after the 1992 election with complete control over the legislative process at both ends of Pennsylvania Avenue. By losing both houses of Congress, the power vanished. A real panic set in for Hill Democrats, who had little to offer donors compared to White House coffees and sleepovers in the Lincoln Bedroom. A full-time money war was on inside the Democratic Party, and the fundraisers became the frontline soldiers.

HOUSE DEMOCRATS HUDDLED mere days after Dick Gephardt, now their highest-ranking member, had handed the Speaker's gavel to Newt Gingrich. As minority leader, Gephardt could appoint loyalists to key positions, and his first was the strongest signal that money was now the only thing that mattered. Gephardt appointed Texan congressman Martin Frost as the new head of the Democratic Congressional Campaign Committee (DCCC), the party committee in charge of electing Democrats to the House. In fifteen years of fundraising, I have never met a member of Congress who loved raising money as much as Martin Frost. He'd try to pass that love on to anybody who'd listen.

Frost's impact was immediate. Days later, he made a presentation to the House Democratic Caucus: A minimum of twelve hours a week should be scheduled for each member to raise money. There was even a formula: Twelve hours would raise $15,000, and $15,000 over the next ninety-five weeks before the 1996 election would mean close to $1.5 million per member. Raising money in a member's official office on Capitol Hill is illegal, so the DCCC set up a new phone room for members, about forty phones spread out in little cubicles. Walk on over across the street, have some free coffee, some soda, relax, and dial for dollars.

Next were "dues." In the past, members had been asked to contribute $5,000 a year to the DCCC from their campaign accounts, a minimal fee used to pay the organization's operating expenses. Nobody ever really paid, and no member ever was called out for not contributing.

Frost established mandatory payments for everyone, then raised the stakes. If you wanted to be the Number 1 Democrat on a committee, Frost and Gephardt required a $50,000 annual payoff. It was revolutionary. Imagine being a long-serving member of Congress who had worked hard to become the top dog on a committee—an incredibly powerful position and the crown jewel of many members' careers. Most likely the member in question had risen to the committee chair because he had a safe seat and could concentrate on legislating and never really have to raise much money. Now members had to buy their power, with a minimum $100,000 contribution to the DCCC that election cycle: $50,000 in '95, $50,000 in '96.

At every caucus meeting, Frost would hand out a score sheet that listed members' contributions. Frost wasn't celebrating those who had paid. Rather, he had his own deadbeat list; he was embarrassing those at the bottom. Seniority would now be based on money, not legislative skill. For the first time in history, House Democrats had made money the central measuring stick of success. Republicans weren't there yet, though they followed suit quickly.

Members who didn't want to raise money at the new pace would not be considered "good" members of the caucus. The message was clear: If you had trouble in your next election, don't expect any help from Dick Gephardt, Martin Frost, or the DCCC. No money for staff, for independent advertising, or for ground troops. It wasn't a hollow threat, as the fight was on to get back to 218 House Democrats—the majority, and they would help any Democrat on the ballot who paid.

The threat did get members to raise money early. If incumbents could raise enough money in the first few months of 1995, two things would happen. A full campaign account might scare away opponents. Who wants to run against an opponent who has $500,000 in the bank from day one? If Democrats took the House back in 1996, it was made clear that members who had raised the money would be chosen to lead committees. Seniority was tossed out the window and replaced by a financial scorecard.

TO THE OLD GUARD, the new way of doing business was a massive shock. They held one or maybe two fundraisers every election cycle and raised a couple hundred thousand dollars. Without the constant chase for campaign dollars, the old guard focused on representing their districts and spent time getting to know their colleagues on the other side of the aisle and hammering out bipartisan legislation. Their time was fading fast.

The new demands of political money demanded a different type of candidate. By 1996, the average Democratic member was already raising more—$620,000[1]—just enough to be a member in good standing. The new standards applied to challengers too. If candidates couldn't show the DCCC that they could raise real money—$500,000 to $1 million—the DCCC would not support them. The easiest way to hit that level was to be rich and write your campaign a big fat check. Yep, the DCCC under Martin Frost went out to recruit candidates who had money. It was a new type of Democrat.

THE DOMINO EFFECT of these decisions would help change politics forever. Since the party decided it needed more money, that meant it needed to hire more staff to raise it. Fundraisers needed to justify their salaries, so they needed to raise more money. That meant scheduling more events, which meant members of Congress had to spend more time cultivating donors and less time doing their jobs.

These decisions created a new power base, an emerging center of political gravity: the fundraiser. As members needed to spend more and more time raising money, they'd spend more time with their fundraiser. Chiefs of staff, legislative directors, and policy staff started to mean less and less. Fundraisers began having a say in every aspect of the member's day: policy decisions, political decisions, and scheduling decisions. Fundraisers became gatekeepers to Congress in just a matter of weeks.

ALL THAT SEEMS FAIRLY INNOCENT on one level. Republicans had won and had been raising more money. But they also had a simple message that resonated with their rich donors: "Give money to us because we keep taxes and regulations low." Democrats needed to compete, and without that message, had to find and then offer new rich donors influence and access. Easy enough, and they set out to do it.

But it was not innocent in the halls of Congress. Newt and his team responded to Democrats firing the first money shot by increasing pressure to raise on their members, of course.

Even worse, by the summer of 1995, House leadership on both sides of the aisle circulated new cheat sheets. Nobody talked much about them, and they were never widely distributed. I never saw the Republican version of the sheets, but I was told that Democratic House leaders just copied what the GOP did.

Not all senior staff knew about them. Gephardt's chief of staff at the time, Tom O'Donnell, never mentioned them to me, and I doubt he knew about them. Gephardt's deputy chief, Steve Elmendorf, casually laughed about them. He did it in a way that made sure we fundraisers knew what was on them.

The lists were campaign finance goals for new legislation. A tax proposal was worth $200,000 per member on the Ways and Means Committee; a proposal for a trade deal was worth $100,000. The lists went through every committee that could plausibly raise money in connection with legislation. Members played both sides, too—half the time lists were to scare opponents: "We will pass this bill unless you find us money not to."

To this day, reporters and reformers talk about the evils of lobbyists and the Gucci gulch of K Street. They refuse to accept or say that the members of Congress forced this system on them. The lists are still used today, but they started in 1995 because the Democrats had a money panic.

11

AFTER THE 1994 ELECTION, OUR BASEMENT ON C STREET WOULD no longer suffice. We moved the Gephardt operation to the "pink palace" on Pennsylvania Avenue. Keiloch came with us, Maroney did not. We hired more fundraisers, more assistants. The full-blown money machine was ramping up again. Patrick Kennedy had been elected to Congress from Rhode Island in 1994, and we rented space to his new fundraiser, Jamie Whitehead.

And I was "promoted" to raising money for Jonesy. He gave me my first task, Gephardt's big annual DC event. This would be the first real test, not only for me but also for House Democrats. In the minority for the first time since the 1950s, whether donors would give was an open question. With all the power in Newt's hands, would they care? Confusion and fear ran deep.

But I had my chance. I was a fighter, I had bought into the message: We needed to raise money to win back the House. I did what David Jones had taught me: I sent out those host letters, then I called potential hosts. And I called them again, often spending close to twelve hours a day on the phone. I was scared for my party and my job. I wanted to win.

I didn't have David Bender's Clinton/Gore plates, but I had some of my own juice: first, a host committee breakfast meeting. Yep, not only would hosts get the chance to be listed on the invite for the big event, but I invited them to a special, exclusive breakfast meeting with Gephardt. We had begun servicing our big donors.

Next, I got call time with Gephardt, a new tool. I was able to put him on the phone with donors, and often. Dick would call twelve hours a week, just like everyone else. Gephardt was no Martin Frost, who'd pick up the phone and ask anybody for money. He was his good ol' Midwestern self; he couldn't make the ask for a dollar amount. But he would do his job mechanically.

To ingratiate myself to donors, I would dial them and chitchat for a minute about life. I did this not because I really cared about them but to imprint in their minds that I, the fundraiser, was their point of access to power. After my short chat I would announce that I had somebody with me who wanted to say "Hi," though I'd never say who it was. Gephardt would sit and read the paper and wait for me to get somebody on the phone. His standard greeting was "How *are you* doing?" to every person he talked to. He would listen, not care what anyone said on the other end, then go into his big pitch about House Democrats winning in 1996. He closed with "By gosh, I need you to help me and hope that you can join me for my next event. Lindsay can give you all the details." Good-bye, that was it. On to the next call.

Gephardt spoke slowly. And, by speaking slowly, he dominated the conversation, avoided tough questions, and took up the few minutes he had to speak with a prospect. Ninety percent of the time he had no idea to whom he had just spoken. That was his game, creating distant relationships.

Now, the other members of Congress never had the luxury of being the party leader. They had to call and actually have real conversations with donors. Long, time-consuming conversations, schmoozing donors because they didn't have Gephardt's power. Some corporate or union donors would respond right away with an immediate yes, but others made members beg. Making a member beg meant the donor would say, "Call me back next week and I will see if I have it in my budget." It was a strategic ploy by the lobbyist or political action committee director; you never know what bill a client wants to talk about next week, so a lobbyist has done his job by getting a member to call back.

GEPHARDT'S BIG EVENT was just over the horizon. I was relentless: faxing, mailing, and calling nonstop. I had secured over a hundred hosts, three weeks beforehand, which meant at least $150,000 in firm commitments. I took those hundred names, put them on the invitation, and mailed out ten thousand invites. I *did* double check to make sure I had spelled everybody's name right. I might have been the worst fundraiser ever, but I learned from my mistakes!

I called as many of those ten thousand people as I could over the next three weeks. I could fit in 150 calls a day, as most calls wound up in voice-mail boxes. When somebody confirmed their attendance, I immediately sent a note thanking them and telling them where to send the check. With each thank-you note, I enclosed two extra invites and asked that they pass them to a friend. The biggest possible checkwriters would receive a special thank you call from Leader Gephardt.

WE RENTED OUT B. SMITH'S RESTAURANT at Union Station—a mammoth hall the length of the building—for the first fundraising event in over forty years when Democrats were in the minority in the House of Representatives. This was my chance, my moment, my Alamo. Failure was not an option, and I was worried.

I added some touches of flair. American flags everywhere. What says pride in America like a bunch of checkwriters sipping fancy wine with the Democratic leader of the House? I paid $500 to a balloon guy to decorate the entrance. Slight hiccup with that—he showed up with four balloons. What the fuck, $125 a balloon? But my new strategy was a sign of the changing times: I wanted to show donors a good time, and that meant spending more of the money they'd donated. Make it big, make it grandiose, spend their money to make them feel important . . . and they will come back.

Before 1996, members would usually spend about 10 percent of their campaign accounts to raise money. With this new emphasis on money, the cost would go over 20 percent in 1996. We ended up with plenty of $125 balloons and the like, but it was all about the volume of cash: Spend it to get it.

We invited all the remaining House Democrats to join the party as our guests. That may sound like a nice thing to do, but it was about filling the room. Nobody ever knows how much you raise in a night, but if they see an event packed with people, donors assume you raised a lot. Almost every Democratic member of Congress showed up.

And the donors did too, in droves. Lines out the door. Every Democratic lobbyist you could think of showed up and left a check. Gephardt's big event the prior year raised about $200,000, at a time when he was in the majority and had real power. That night, in the minority, we collected over $500,000 in a massive showing of cash, pride, and momentum. I saw it in the eyes of the members of Congress who walked around that event: We can do this. We can raise money. We can win the House back. Money is the answer.

I was now a fundraiser.

12

IN THE DAYS AND WEEKS AFTER MY SMASHING SUCCESS, A FUNNY thing happened. House Democrats—the powerful men and women in elected office? those who I admired?—started calling me, twenty-four-year-old me, just to say hello. I'd see them in the halls of Congress and they'd wave at me and smile. When I showed up at the Democratic Congressional Campaign Committee offices, members put their phones down and sweet-talked me. I had raised so much money for Gephardt; surely I could help them.

I became King of the New DC Bullshit. I'd never been elected, never done any policy, never written legislation, never done much of anything of consequence. But I could raise new DC money, and they all wanted a piece. Two years earlier, no member of Congress knew the top fundraisers by name; they could barely remember the name of their own. They never saw them, talked to them, or dealt with them outside of one or two events a year. But by 1995, fundraisers picked up the golden touch, and members of Congress wanted to run with it.

Donors realized it too, and realized that I had time with and access to Gephardt no one else did. I started getting gifts. Real gifts: tickets to any sporting event I wanted. Bored on a Friday? I'd call up George Tagg, the FedEx lobbyist, and he would have a private plane waiting at National Airport to fly us anywhere. If you wanted to be on my good side, don't take me to some sandwich shop for lunch; the Capital Grille would be fine. As campaign staff, not a single regulation or ethics rule restrained me.

As glorious as this might sound, deep down I was extremely uncomfortable. I hated it. The whole idea that the monied class had something that everybody else didn't—access to power—bothered me. I wanted to take care of the donors and friends who represented the middle class (unions, mostly) and to cut off the insanely rich interests who wanted something in return for their money.

I COULD SQUEEZE only about $300,000 a year from labor. That sounds like a lot, but when you are raising $10 million a year, in hard and soft money, it wasn't that much. Even though they didn't have the kind of money that some of the big donors had, I found myself making sure that the labor folks had access to and time with Gephardt. I went out of my way to do private events with just labor leaders. I didn't care, these were my kind of folks.

Pretty soon, I began to hate Capital Grille lunches with big bank and insurance industry lobbyists. Spending an hour or two with Paul Equale, the chief lobbyist for the Independent Insurance Agents, was becoming a painful thought. I wanted to escape. Don Kaniewski and Tim Scully saved me. Don represented the Laborers' International Union and Scully worked at Philip Morris, although Tim had been with the Teamsters for a long time before. They had little get-togethers on Fridays at Old Glory, the Georgetown barbecue joint. It was far enough removed from Capitol Hill that we would never run into other lobbyists. Brilliant.

My first lunch adventure with Tim and Don didn't work out too well. You know what goes well with ribs and BBQ chicken? Draft beers, about eight of them. To complicate matters, I had call time with Gephardt at 3 pm. I left Old Glory just a little on the tipsy side. Walking into the office at

2:30 pm, I downed some coffee and told my new assistant, Liesl, that I was going to take a short nap, for just fifteen minutes.

"When Gephardt shows up for call time, please wake me up," I murmured to her as I slithered under my desk, George Costanza style.

At 9 pm, with a big headache and no idea where I was, I found a note mysteriously taped to my chest: "Hi Lindsay, I tried to wake you but you wouldn't budge. Mr. Gephardt came and left when he could not find you. Hope you have a good weekend, Liesl."

People get fired for much, much less. But fundraisers were becoming so powerful that we were untouchable. We would throw parties at Chief Ike's in Adams Morgan and could make everyone come, just because we were so powerful. I'd show up not completely sober some mornings. Once I forced my way into a meeting with the Dalai Lama, just because I thought I deserved to be there. And I continued having lunch with Don and Tim on Fridays, but stopped scheduling call time on Friday afternoon.

13

WE MADE A BIG DECISION: GEPHARDT WOULD SPEND ON AVERAGE one weekend a month in St. Louis, the congressional district he represented. He'd spend one weekend at home in Herndon, Virginia, with his family. And he'd spend two weekends a month raising money, for his campaign, for the Effective Government Committee, for the DCCC, for other members. Anywhere Jonesy and I could come up with. Politicians were now spending significantly more of their time raising money.

DC money had showed up for the big event—it was easy; companies, lobbyists, and unions had political giving budgets. But would lots and lots of rich Democratic donors outside DC and outside his network of presidential campaign supporters care about Dick Gephardt, now minority leader? It was a big risk—a new kind of donor in new cities—but time to prove I could do it all.

Gephardt's schedule permitted roughly twenty-five fundraising trips a year around the country in the 1995–1996 cycle. Compare that to the five or six traveling events before the 1994 election, and it worked out to about a 500 percent increase in fundraising time on the road. Add that to the now-regular twelve hours of call time Tuesdays, Wednesdays, and Thursdays while the House was in session, and Dick Gephardt (and others in Congress) spent a majority of their time with us, the fundraisers. Not with his chief of staff, his legislative staff, or any other of his seventy staffers on the Hill. Not even Gephardt's wife, Jane, spent that much time with him. Raising money was becoming his central preoccupation, taking most of his time, dictating his schedule, and occupying his thoughts . . . time that should have been spent on legislation or building relationships with Republicans.

JUST LOOK AT A MAP and you can see potential one-day trips outside of DC. If you hustled, it was possible to hit Baltimore, Philly, and New York in just eighteen hours. Jonesy's first road-trip assignment took me up I-95 to Baltimore. Gephardt was set to grab a 7 am train out of DC, pull into Baltimore for breakfast, ride up to Philadelphia for a lunch, and hit New York for a big-money dinner. He could jump on a 10:30 pm shuttle out of LaGuardia and be in bed in DC by midnight. The kitty for this East Coast whirlwind? At least $100,000. My sole responsibility was the Baltimore breakfast meeting, where I needed to raise $30,000.

I did some quick math. If I could get a hundred people to donate $500 for a breakfast reception with Leader Gephardt, I'd haul in $50,000 and be a star. I booked the Baltimore Center Club for a hundred for breakfast and got to work. After I had just raised over $500,000 in DC, $30,000 would be simple, a piece of cake.

A few names stood out, like Baltimore Orioles owner Peter Angelos and a few trial attorneys. I had learned from Jonesy to go after as many folks as you can, and I did. One donor intrigued me, a guy named Willie Runyon, who owned an ambulance company in Baltimore. He had given $25,000 to the Democratic Senatorial Campaign Committee (DSCC) the year before.

I started calling invitees. And calling. And calling. And calling. It's what fundraisers do.

One hundred unanswered, unreturned phone calls quickly became two hundred. I didn't exactly panic, but I was starting to become frustrated. Do people in Baltimore not care about politics? Next, I mailed out an invite, designed on a fancy card that looked like it came from an important office at the U.S. Capitol. Surely that would impress rich people. The card was embossed with a gold dome on the front and a return address marked "Democratic Leader Richard Gephardt." I sent three thousand.

And I kept calling. And calling. And calling. Raising money outside DC was proving a big challenge.

I made Gephardt call too, trying to shake the trees a little more with his help. He didn't have much luck either. But I stayed positive. If I left enough messages, they'd start talking about this amazing Gephardt fundraiser over rounds of golf, cigars, and poker games. But Willie was still on my mind. He represented at least another $25,000. So I applied myself. When he didn't call back on day one, I called him on day two, then on day three. Every day, 9:30 am. For forty-three straight days.

On day 44 he took my call.

"What the hell?" He was gruff but likable. "What the fuck could you possibly want? Can't you understand I don't want to talk to you?"

Just happy that a big donor was talking to me, I gave my best pitch. "Well, Mr. Runyon, I work for Leader Richard Gephardt, and we're having a breakfast meeting at the Center Club so he can get to know some of the local businesspeople."

"Fuck off. I have no interest in spending my morning at the Baltimore Center Club with a bunch of tight-ass lawyers." Willie was a good ol' boy from West Virginia. I loved this guy. He shared my pain. "Now, if Dick Gephardt wants to come visit me in my office, I'd be happy to chat."

Make Dick come to me, that's how money outside Washington works. So I set it up for right after our breakfast: We would drive over to see Willie.

With thousands of invitations out the door and a barrage of follow-up phone calls, I was positive at least seventy-five guests would show. The night before the event, I had only four confirmed RSVPs, but I knew I'd worked hard. Maybe the new breed of non-DC bigwigs didn't bother to respond. Nervous but confident, I hopped on a 6 am train and arrived at the Baltimore Center Club an hour early. I made sure the tables were preset with fruit plates—I wanted to seat and feed the guests quickly before Gephardt spoke—and reserved the head table for my top targets. The glass bowl that would receive all the checks sat on the edge of the check-in table.

At 7:55 am, the lobby phone rang. It was Gephardt's deputy chief of staff, Steve Elmendorf, calling to say they were downstairs. Steve was a typical Hill staffer of the early '90s, with some skill and political ability. But at that time, he lacked an understanding of and an appreciation for the new role money was beginning to play. At first, he disdained the money and the lobbyist world and wanted to protect Gephardt from it. The Steve Elmendorfs of Capitol Hill tried to hold on to power against the wave of money, but in the end they just seemed lost in the new political process. Since he couldn't beat them, he'd eventually join them.

Steve had joined Gephardt in 1992 after being Congressman Dennis Eckart's (D-OH) chief of staff. The Democratic Party still hadn't fully embraced supporting gay rights, and in one of the first off-the-cuff conversations I had with Terry McAuliffe he told me that, "had we known Steve was gay, we would have never hired him." Terry, as with most Democrats, has updated his views and now supports gay rights, but at the time, Steve didn't fit in with Terry's boys' network.

Terry McAuliffe and Steve Elmendorf both have evolved since 1992. Terry evolved on the gay issue, and Steve soon started to play ball with big money. He realized that raising a lot of money from a few folks had merit to it, no matter what the trade-offs. Today Steve is one of the highest-paid lobbyists in DC and has given over $383,000 of his own money to candidates just in the last ten years.[1]

When Steve called up that morning, I seized. One of the ten most powerful people in the country was about to walk into a room—a room I was responsible for filling—and almost no one had arrived. Gephardt made a grand entrance into a breakfast with four people, two of whom I'd let in for free as a favor. I raised $200 from two donors. To Gephardt's credit, he put on his best face and joked whether his four supporters would be able to find somewhere quiet to have a serious conversation. Gephardt finished his chat in thirty minutes and looked like he was about to grab the other ninety-six plates of fruit and take them with us.

BY THAT TIME, Steve was just beginning to realize the potential of big money and wanted Jonesy and me to start only focusing on large donors around the country. He smelled that Willie was a potential whale, and wanted to impress the point on Dick. Steve would give lip service to the labor guys, but he never understood or appreciated how important they were to Gephardt's political coalition. The mismatch of Dick Gephardt, the champion of labor and the middle class, with a senior staffer who didn't appreciate some of his key supporters would later end Gephardt's political career, and Dick never saw it coming.

Right after that failed Baltimore breakfast, we headed to Runyon's office. The place stunk and seemed like a major fire hazard: Medicare forms, insurance packets, brochures, ambulance service forms lay everywhere. Willie didn't like computers. The nice lady out front walked us back to Willie's private office—a dingy smelly closet no bigger than a hundred square feet. So small that Elmendorf had to stand for the meeting, while Dick and I sat on a little green couch that had to be forty years old.

Willie was happy. He liked having the Democratic leader in his office. He glowed regaling Dick with stories about West Virginia politics and a few heart-tugging tales about his problems with a Medicare reimbursement audit that he seemed to want Dick to look into. Gephardt loved Willie as much as I did, though I don't know if it was enough to help him with those Medicare problems. If Dick represented a middle-class, middle America success story in politics, Willie represented one in business. Steve spent the entire thirty minutes about as uncomfortable as he could be. Steve had nothing in common with Willie.

"Well, all right," Willie concluded with a twinge of West Virginia on his lips. "Leader Gephardt, how do you want me to write this here check?"

I saved Leader Gephardt the trouble of making the ask.

"Willie, you have a couple options. You could write $2,000 to Leader Gephardt's campaign account, 'Gephardt in Congress.' That's $1,000 for the primary and $1,000 for the general election. Then you could write a $5,000 for the Effective Government Committee, Leader Gephardt's political action committee, that will allow him to donate to other Democrats running for office around the country. Or you could do $15,000 for the DCCC, to help Democratic House candidates in general. We're trying to win the House back this year."

The sonuvabitch wrote all three checks on the spot, totaling $22,000, and handed them over to Gephardt. I loved Willie. He surely had saved my ass, and maybe my job. Fundraisers have to produce, and my breakfast hadn't. Gephardt and Steve jumped on the next train to Philadelphia. I went back to the Center Club for some fruit.

14

BY THE SPRING OF 1995, THE PRESSURE TO JUSTIFY OUR SALARIES had become intense. The previous year had been a little more innocent: They didn't pay Jonesy or me much, and, consequently, we didn't do that much with only five or six trips a year. Now with twenty-five trips to schedule, our salaries had gone up, but we had to find enough donors to make it worthwhile.

As I had learned with my Baltimore experience, we just could not parachute into a new city, send a bunch of invites, and expect to raise money. Maybe the president could do that, but the "lowly" Democratic leader of the House sure couldn't.

We innovated. We decided we needed wealthy people who had access to money, people who could find friends and colleagues around the country who could pull together fifteen or twenty people who'd write checks for $1,000 or more. We had to find, cultivate, service, and kiss the asses of the few Democrats in each city who could help us. In return, these individuals would be granted ultimate access. In 1995, they became a crucial constituency of the Democratic Party that still exists today.

We created "donor-raisers." In years prior, having one person pull together $10,000 from friends was a big deal. Only a few of those gems existed for House Democrats, and more important, since we didn't need that much money in those days, our donor-raisers only got "begged" to pull money together every few years. Today, every member of Congress—not just leadership—makes that ask, constantly.

This new reliance on the big donor-raiser ("big" being relative; the $10,000 donor-raiser no longer matters, today it's the $100,000 donor-raiser) created a new problem for the very wealthy: the checks for $25,000 or $50,000 that they wrote themselves started meaning less. Individual checkwriters who didn't also raise money from others started losing control of the party. They are fighting this battle to this day. Today's billionaires began by using a mechanism called the "Democracy Alliance" to gain back power. More on that later.

AS WILLIE SUTTON, the infamous bank robber, said, go where the money is. There aren't many places around this country with donors who can raise that kind of big money. As we scoped out upcoming trips, a trend became clear: New York had enough rich people to handle seven or eight trips a year; Los Angeles, five or six. Florida, Boston, Chicago, Texas, Philadelphia, maybe one or two. Middle America didn't make the cut anymore: Cleveland, Milwaukee, Indianapolis, and Kansas City were out. Our new donors wouldn't drink beer from a can or understand traditional middle-class struggles—buying health insurance, building a nice place in the 'burbs, finding money for the kids to go to college—that the Democratic Party had paid attention to. Our new donors drank champagne from flutes.

In previous years, Gephardt had done a trip to the North Carolina Outer Banks with some labor leaders and other Democratic lobbyists. It was a way to spend some time with donors outside of the typical DC event. Two or three days at the beach with Dick and Jane Gephardt was a great way for them to bond with donors, grant access, and build loyalty.

But this was 1995: We needed donor-raisers, not DC checkwriters. We banned lobbyists from attending—our goal was to find twenty major donors around the country who would eventually host Gephardt and raise him money in their cities, $20,000 kind of money, or more.

We chose the days after the 4th of July. Jonesy and I had gone down to Duck, North Carolina, and rented ten massive, expensive homes on prime beachfront real estate for the week. We decided we would put two couples in each home, our way of bonding donors together and with Gephardt. The week cost over $100,000 for rent, booze, food, and transportation. Sure, it was a lot of money, but it was about investing in the future. We charged each couple $2,500 to recoup some costs, but we were still $50,000 in the hole.

I loved my labor union political directors, so I made a simple suggestion to Gephardt's deputy chief of staff, Steve Elmendorf. "Steve, let's not hide who we are, why not spend a few days at the beach with both labor and the rich folks we're trying to cultivate?"

Steve laughed it off. "No way, no how, not going to happen."

"You know this is the coalition that Dick needs if he wants to run again for president," I shot back.

"No labor," he insisted. "We've got them already, and we can't squeeze any more out of them. This weekend is about building relationships with rich donors who can lead us to even more money. Period."

Steve was the boss, so Jonesy and I set out to find rich Democrats who wanted to go to the beach with Dick and Jane and could raise at least $20,000 a year. To add some spice to the invite, and because we knew members had been inspired to raise more money, we invited a few to join us. This first trip would include Bob Torricelli from New Jersey, who'd later go on to be a senator, Bill Jefferson of Louisiana, and Tim Holden of Pennsylvania.

We sent out about three hundred invite letters: big shots on Wall Street, Hollywood studio heads, investment bankers in Chicago and Boston, insurance salesmen, and corporate attorneys. It took some effort, but fifteen couples joined us. Clive and Ann Cummis from New Jersey, the owner of the Aladdin Casino in Las Vegas, a Puerto Rican insurance mogul from Harlem, a real estate investor from Atlanta, and the members of Congress.

Jonesy and I went down a few days early to set everything up. We needed to be careful about which couples were housed together so they got along. Jonesy and I took the biggest house to host evening cocktails and dinner, and we stacked each house with gifts: liquor, food, magazines, chocolates . . . five-star treatment for our new donor-raisers.

One of my jobs for the week was to make sure the members of Congress got to the beach. Tim Holden drove down from Pennsylvania, so no problem. Bob Torricelli flew in on a private jet with his then girlfriend, Bianca Jagger. Bill Jefferson flew into Richmond with his wife. Fucking Richmond, two hours away. So on day one of this glorious week at the beach, I drove two hours to Richmond and two hours back.

I arrived early at the Richmond airport. With no idea what he looked like, I walked around for an hour trying to find Bill Jefferson. When I finally did, an hour later, he was mad as hell, which led to one long-ass, silent two-hour drive to the beach. In 2009, Bill Jefferson was found guilty on eleven counts of bribery for using his position on the House Ways and Means Committee to funnel business to companies that had paid him off. The FBI found $90,000 cash in his freezer, and he began a thirteen-year sentence in 2012.[1] If that money would have gone to his campaign instead, he never would have had a problem. He came to the beach that year not because of loyalty to Gephardt but because of the money people he might meet.

THE DONORS STARTING ARRIVING. Most drove; a few took private planes. Carlos, the insurance mogul from Harlem whose last name escapes me, arrived in style: His entire family—his wife and five kids—pulled up in a Rolls-Royce he had driven from Harlem, gold rims and all. The daily ritual was pool time, beach time, and a get-together for dinner. The politicians all tried to find private time with each donor to make the pitch. So did Jonesy and I, while Dick and Jane just enjoyed the time at the beach.

Drinks and dinner started at 7 pm at the main house. Kelly's Outer Banks down in Nags Head catered, and our one menu instruction was to bring only Budweiser products and one case of Miller Lite. Gephardt represented St. Louis, Budweiser's hometown, but Jane Gephardt hated it. She was a Miller Lite lady. But since she obviously couldn't be seen drinking a Miller product, we handed her bottles of Bud Light filled with Miller Lite, with a wink and a nod.

One of our daily activities at Duck was playing pickup basketball each afternoon before dinner. Not everybody played, but usually Richard Sullivan, the DNC's finance director, and Dick Gephardt would join me with one other for a little two on two. I was slightly hung over on one day and was just happy to stand under the basket and let Gephardt pass me the ball. I was taller than everyone else, so I could reach over them and drop it in the basket pretty easily. The strategy worked. We won big. And to this day, the nickname that Gephardt gave me stuck: the Chief. He compared me to the Indian chief in *One Flew Over the Cuckoo's Nest*.

The trip was an unquestioned success. By the end of the week, we had arranged a bunch of new events, Harlem, Las Vegas, and others. We had discovered a new way to connect with the biggest of the best of the new breed of Democratic funders. We would repeat this several times: Telluride,

Colorado, a return to Duck, Nantucket, and elsewhere. Over the years, other members of Congress would pick up the idea, and today every weekend is filled with exotic trips with donors. It all started and ramped up with a Rolls-Royce in Duck, NC.

15

WE HAD TWO FUNDRAISING TRIPS A MONTH, AND WHEN WE COULD handle the travel arrangements through commercial planes, we did. But when we couldn't for whatever reason, we had to find a private plane. A fleet of the Democratic Party "friends'" private and corporate jets sits at National Airport to this day. Senators got prime choice, House leadership like Gephardt got second choice, and other members of Congress never got calls returned.

The rule was straightforward: We could use any plane as long as we paid the owner first-class airfare for Gephardt. If the United first-class fare from DC to Dallas was $900, that's what we paid. And not a penny more. With few regulations on campaign staff, fundraisers flew free. It saved time and hassle to have the jets ready to fly. Friday afternoons in the tiny private jet lobby at National was the most powerful room in Washington, full of a quorum of senators, Dick Gephardt, Newt Gingrich, and House Majority Leader Tom DeLay (R-TX) waiting around for booze and food to be loaded onto the private planes before taking off for a weekend of fundraising, work, or pleasure.

We split up the list of the planes from best to worst. It had nothing to do with the quality of the planes but everything to do with how much effort was involved in securing their use.

The gold standard was Archer Daniels Midland, the food processing giant just up the road from Dick's hometown of St. Louis. The company had four or five jets at all times at National Airport. We would call the CEO's office, tell them our needs, and they would respond right away. Nobody from ADM would be on the plane, just the pilots and us. Our other top choices were Philip Morris, FedEx, and Aflac.

The planes of two Democratic donors, Jack Rosen from New Jersey and J.J. Cafaro from Ohio, ended up at the bottom of the list. J.J. was a pain in the ass, but when we got desperate we would call for his plane. What this meant was that J.J. would be flying with us, and we would have to talk to him throughout the flight. J.J. was a consistent presence in my career.

EVEN AS THE DEMOCRATIC LEADER, Gephardt kept raising money not only for himself and his PAC but also for the Democratic Congressional Campaign Committee. One of the hidden chunks of Democratic cash lay on the beach down on this little island called Puerto Rico. I didn't understand why it was such a hotbed, but Jonesy told me to travel down with Dick and Jane for a weekend of DCCC events. We would have two major fundraisers, one at the Hilton in Puerto Rico and one over on St. Thomas at the home of Hess Oil owner, Leon Hess. Combined, we would raise over $200,000 for the DCCC that weekend. Equally important to Dick and Jane was some quality vacation time paid for by the DCCC.

The three of us boarded a private jet at Dulles Airport and took off. Over a hundred police officers met us on the tarmac in San Juan, lined up like for a presidential visit. Three bodyguards watched over me twenty-four hours a day. Dick and Jane had eight. The cops closed off all the streets along the route of our caravan—complete with helicopter overhead—so we could get to the Hilton in under ten minutes.

We got settled in at the Hilton and had a few hours before that evening's dinner fundraiser. Dick and Jane donned their bathing suits and headed out to the beach, I watched from my balcony, smiling from ear to ear, as eight bodyguards dutifully followed. When the Gephardts went swimming, so did two of their minders, still dressed in suit jackets. I wasn't sure what the threat was; maybe Scarface had surfaced in San Juan. The evening event was a spectacle. Blaring music, a rope line for Dick, and a packed room full of white suits. I guess this was high society for the Puerto Rican elite. I loved every minute of it.

We got up the next morning and went off for the brunch fundraiser at the Hess home. Different crowd, mostly white Northern folks who had settled down on the islands. It was much more akin to a DC event. Fine with me. We did our job and raised the money.

We still had a day and a half of downtime to hang out at the beach. Jane called the next morning. "Dick and I would love to hop over to the U.S. Virgin Islands today. Could you call and arrange the plane?"

"No problem, Mrs. Gephardt." I was going too.

This change in plans caused quite a stir with our bodyguards. They couldn't handle the request, so we agreed that they'd take us to the airport and meet us when we got back. Besides my swimming trunks, all I had to wear was my business suit. Off we went. When we landed, Dick and Jane set off on their own. I went to a bar near the beach and settled in for the day, happy to just relax. Sunday at 10 am is not the best time to be at a bar, but I made do. A few younger local guys plopped down next to me.

"Hey, man, why are you in that suit? You going to church or something?" asked the first.

"Oh, just working, not a big deal," I replied.

"So even though you're a big white dude in a suit," began the second, "you like to party?"

I just looked at him, confused. He looked back, nodded, touched his index finger to his thumb, brought them to his lips and inhaled. Not subtle. Ah, I got the message. I've never smoked much weed, and I sure as hell didn't feel quite right getting high on an official trip with the Democratic leader of the House just minutes away. But then again, I had at least eight hours to kill. If I smoked a little now, I would be sober by the time we left. So party we did.

We walked down a private quiet little side street and they handed me a joint. Between the beers, the heavy heat, and the joint . . . dammit all, it was about the greatest feeling in the world. After splitting the joint, my newfound party buddies had an offer for me: I could buy as much of this great stuff as I wanted.

I might not have been a regular user of pot, but I was sky high and had plenty of friends in DC who might want to share this amazing experience. One of my many quirks is that I always carry a lot of cash on me. Traveling with Gephardt, I had a fear that a global emergency might strand us somewhere and I'd need the money to pay our way back to DC.

So I took that emergency cash and added it to what I could get out of the ATM, cobbling together about $2,500. In the U.S. Virgin Islands marijuana market, that is a lot of money. They gave me two large bricks and a few extra joints for being such a good customer. Since we had a private plane back to San Juan and then DC, no worries about airport security. But damn, it stunk. I took the twenty bucks I had left and bought three cans of Right Guard spray deodorant. I doused each brick.

Eight hours in the sun smoking pot and drinking beers in my suit made for one long-ass day. My happy self jumped on the plane with a highly illegal smile. Dick and Jane told me they had a wonderful day shopping. I did my best to keep my mouth shut, as I had no clue what might come out. What an amazing flight. Everything seemed surreal and wonderful. I swear, glorious dolphins jumped as high as our plane, guiding us home to San Juan. We landed at San Juan and the plane taxied to the private hanger.

Holy shit. I didn't think I had to be worried about security, but damn. Over a hundred cops, lights flashing on their cruisers, pointed big guns at the plane waiting for us. Motherfuckers, they got me. How did they know I spent the whole day buying pot? I was going to spend the next twenty years in a Puerto Rican jail. I sweated through my suit, panicking. I tried to keep quiet.

I did the only thing I could think of: I took my two bricks of pot and stuffed them into Jane's large purse when she wasn't looking. If anybody was going to jail that day, it was Jane Gephardt . . . drug queen Jane Gephardt. Nice lady, drug dealer!

We exited the plane. Dick and Jane went left, I dove right. And then it hit me—the police escort! Shit. These cops had come to take us back to the Hilton, not take me to prison. That moment of clarity was the greatest high ever. I got into the car with Dick and Jane.

"Jane," I said, as calmly as I could muster, "I love that purse. Did you get it down here?"

"Oh, no. This old thing? I got it at Filene's at home."

"It's still very nice. Would you mind if I took a quick look at it? I might want to get something like it for my girlfriend."

I got my pot back and Jane got a purse that smelled like Right Guard.

16

I WAS TRAVELING NONSTOP BY 1995, DOING EVENTS FOR GEP-hardt, the Democratic Congressional Campaign Committee, and other candidates for Congress. Raising money was the vehicle back to the House majority, and we were focused like a laser. Members of Congress who had never been involved with party activities now got the message: Raise not just for your own campaign but help the DCCC too, or you will not be part of the next Democratic majority. After all, they could raise directly for the DCCC or transfer unlimited amounts of extra money from their own campaign account.

Everybody got involved, from the most liberal to the longest-serving members. Not only did they have to write checks, they had to raise money. One year prior, these same people didn't make calls, knew only the donors who came to see them in their offices, and spent a majority of their time with other members of Congress and senior staff, legislating.

If ranking House committee members—who hoped to be powerful committee chairs in the next majority—"owed" the DCCC $50,000 a year now, they had to get creative to reach new donors around the country. Party committees—the Democratic National Committee, Democratic Congressional Campaign Committee, and Democratic Senatorial Campaign Committee—faced no restrictions on the amount they could take in. Companies and union political action committees were restricted to giving only $15,000 in hard money to the party committees. Wealthy individuals could give as much soft money as they wanted to the party. Guess who got targeted?

Of course, members were still happy to take money from PACs, even with their limits. PAC directors scrambled to take credit for donations as often as they could. When a member of Congress called a lobbyist and asked for a DCCC contribution, the lobbyist would commit $15,000. When the next member called, the lobbyist would commit the same $15,000. Twenty members would end up claiming credit for the same $15,000, and the lobbyists who controlled the money didn't care. DCCC chair Martin Frost cut that game off quickly. If a member wanted credit for a check, the donor had to hand-deliver it.

It was tough to get rich people to care about Congress. The House of Representatives wasn't that sexy, but President Clinton was. The DNC started inviting rich donors to White House coffees for $50,000 a seat in soft money, which allowed donors to come sit around a table of ten people with the president for a few minutes. Wealthy donors thought it a better investment to give to him, and they were rewarded with White House coffees, stays in the Lincoln Bedroom, calls from Vice President Al Gore. Terry McAuliffe was behind much of it, and the Clinton team got a ton of bad press, like this:[1]

The documents show that Clinton scribbled his enthusiastic approval for the overnight stays on the McAuliffe memorandum, which recommended that major financial supporters be invited to meals, coffees, rounds of golf or jogging excursions.

"Yes, pursue all 3 and promptly—and get other names of the 100,000 or more," Clinton wrote, apparently seeking names of people who had given $100,000 or more to the Democrats.

It was an impressive way to capture the richest of the rich and give them access that nobody else had, access with which they could bend Clinton's ear on policy, tell him how to run his campaign, or instruct the White House how they wanted their money spent.

The DNC would aggressively sell these private gatherings, and by the summer of 1995—eighteen months before the next election—the DNC went up with TV ads for Clinton's reelection. It was revolutionary and marked the beginning of the permanent campaign. Before 1995, large amounts of TV time were usually reserved for the closing months of elections, not eighteen months prior.

The arms race for political money was on. Democrats had fired the first shot.

17

IN 1992, FUNDRAISERS GENERALLY TRIED TO KEEP THE COST OF raising money under 10 percent of what they brought in. By the time a member hired one of the few consultants to handle the single big DC event, then paid for the food, venue, and invitations, it might run about $15,000 a year while realistically bringing in $150,000. With the average campaign costing about $470,000, that $150,000 was a good chunk.

By 1995, costs were escalating. The full-time fundraiser or consultant cost anywhere from $2,500 to $5,000 a month in pay and benefits. To cover the additional event venues, food, and travel around the country, the gross costs could be well over $100,000. That meant you had to raise that much more to justify the expenses.

ONE WEEK A SUMMER in Duck, North Carolina, wasn't enough. David Jones wanted to expand the program, to get more donor-raisers involved with Gephardt. Almost everybody who had visited Duck had gone on to host a fundraiser for Gephardt, which meant the attention we lavished on them was working.

It was time for a winter trip in 1995. Gephardt had done a few other weekends on a smaller scale, but David was not much for the mild; he wanted to go over the top. We rented rooms at the Peaks Resort in Telluride for our winter retreat with Dick and Jane and began contacting as many potential big donor-raisers as we could find. We convinced a bunch to spend a long weekend in Telluride.

Dan Amos, the CEO of Aflac insurance, arrived on his private Gulfstream jet. Terry and his wife, Dorothy McAuliffe, came along. In all we had about twenty people plus David and me, Patrick Kennedy and his chief of staff, Tony Marcella. We had a few others from the usual crowd of donor-raisers from around the country, the most prominent of whom were John and Jane Huang.

John Huang was the Chinese American former head of Lippo Bank USA. He resigned and went to work at the Commerce Department early in the Clinton administration, then moved over to the Democratic National Committee to raise money in 1995. Jonesy knew of him and wanted to cultivate him so he'd raise money not just for the DNC but for Dick Gephardt and House Democrats too. I had met him on my first day when working for Nancy at the DNC. It's easy to say in hindsight, but he immediately seemed shady. In the run-up to the 1996 election, it turns out Huang funneled $156,000 in illegal foreign donations to the Clinton campaign and DNC. In 1999, he pled guilty, was fined $10,000, and faced a year of probation.

But first, he went skiing with us.

WE ALWAYS TOOK A GROUP PHOTO at the end of these trips, so the donors would have something to brag about to their high-powered friends . . . who, we hoped, would also want to get in on the act. Since we were in Telluride, we decided to ski up to the top ridge overlooking the city and take the photo there.

The next morning at 11, we arrived at the ridge, everyone in ski gear. Then we heard a couple snowmobiles shooting up the mountain behind us. Were we somehow breaking the law up there? Nope. John and Jane Huang had hired snowmobiles to ferry them up the slope. We were at one of the most exclusive ski resorts in the country, but two of our top targets were too good for the lift. And they were wearing business suits. So we snapped a photo of eighteen skiers and two Asian Americans in business suits.

THIS TRIP WAS EXPENSIVE. The hotel rooms, meals, flights, and ski passes added up. In 1995, campaigns generally didn't have official credit cards. For some of the bigger items, the campaign would get billed what you spent, and you'd send a check. But sometimes staffers like me had to put things on a personal credit card and get reimbursed by the Effective Government Committee. Normally this was simple enough; it would be a few dollars for day trips with Gephardt.

But our jaunt to Telluride landed over $80,000 on my American Express Gold Card. Most congressional campaigns were still in the realm of $500,000; we had spent more than 15 percent of that in *one weekend.*

When we got back to DC, Steve Elmendorf was pissed off at Jonesy for the out-of-control spending. On one level, Steve was right. I didn't understand why we spent so much to raise money; it always bothered me. I was concerned with our net profit. Couldn't we have just dropped $40,000 on our prospective donors and still made them happy? Steve refused to authorize the reimbursement. He may have thought he was punishing David, but I didn't have a spare $80,000 in my checking account. I defaulted, and my credit rating has never really recovered. A few months later, Steve paid the bill, but the damage was done.

IT MIGHT HAVE BEEN A COSTLY TRIP, but Jonesy talked John Huang into hosting a fundraiser for Gephardt out in Los Angeles. He could produce $20,000 for a breakfast, nothing to sneeze at for an hour of Gephardt's time while doing other business in California.

After that event, Jonesy stayed in California to go to some DNC events and raise more money. He FedExed me the checks for the Huang event, some of which I sent off to St. Louis for "Gephardt in Congress," maybe $25,000. Then I started to process a separate pile of about $30,000 made out to the Effective Government Committee, including more money from John Huang, Jane Huang, and a bunch of their friends that I put aside. In those days, there was no process for vetting donors to ensure they were upstanding U.S. citizens. It's a standard practice today, but nobody asked questions back then.

I forgot about the separate pile of checks for the EGC. A few months later I went to wash my car. As I pulled the trash out from under the driver's seat, I found about ten envelopes of checks. Some for Gephardt, some for the DCCC, and a couple for Patrick Kennedy. About $120,000 in misplaced checks were in my car, including those John Huang had bundled. Instead of 'fessing up to being disorganized, I tossed all them into the trash at the car wash. Money was everywhere in politics; nobody would miss that $120,000.

A YEAR LATER, the John Huang scandal broke to the press. Fundraisers right and left were hauled in to testify before Congress, including DNC finance director Richard Sullivan. After the Huang event in LA, our office was panicked that Gephardt might get caught up in the investigation, potentially ruining his chances at another presidential run. I was panicked for a different reason. The accountants and investigators might look for those missing checks and wonder why I had never deposited them into the Effective Government Committee's account.

We had only been using one old computer to track our donors, one of those with a yellow screen and a crappy database. It certainly wasn't hooked up to the Internet. Primitive at best, but it held all our information, including the John Huang California trip. We decided we had no choice. We waited for the sun to go down and took the computer into the back alley behind the office. I took a hockey stick, someone else grabbed a baseball bat. We pulverized that computer into a thousand pieces within a few minutes.

Two days later we get the call from our election attorney: The grand jury investigating the fundraising scandal would like all the documents relating to John Huang. We didn't have much left, but we sent over what we had.

Everything more or less blew over, though the Huang scandal was a sign of the times. And things were getting out of control. Neither Gephardt nor Jonesy was ever implicated, though we did end up returning three checks to John and Jane Huang, for $6,000, in March 1997.[1] Not that many; we couldn't refund checks that we never cashed.

18

ALTHOUGH PRESIDENT CLINTON WAS FOCUSED ON RAISING MONEY for his 1996 reelection and for the DNC, in the name of party unity, he offered to do fundraising days for both House and Senate Democrats. He could not raise for all the members and challengers for the House, so his time went toward raising for the DCCC. The president gave the House Democrats a day for New York, and we had to jump on it. If we knocked it out of the park, it might just be enough to win back the House! That's what we had convinced ourselves of, and that's what we sold to donors.

Our goal was $2 million. By this time, that was easy pickings in DC money, but outside of DC was more time consuming. We had two months.

I was assigned as the lead fundraiser for the event. I was pumped. I loved New York, and the chance to redeem myself from my early DNC

disaster was motivation enough. I went to work right away and pulled together over two thousand names who I knew could write at least $10,000
each. We booked the top floor of the St. Regis and decided that we should
have five hundred people in the room. Individual seats would be $2,500,
and $10,000 donors would get access to a pre-event private photo line
with the president. Fancy. We hoped to sell a hundred for the photo
line and four hundred for dinner, bringing in over $2 million for House
Democrats.

I put each of the two thousand names into binders; each name had one
page with the name, phone number, address, and as much giving history
as I could find. The idea was that I could keep handwritten notes on each
sheet of paper: called on this day, left a message on this day, or hopefully
committed $10,000 on this date.

DCCC chair Martin Frost—the fundraising machine—committed
four hours of call time a day, every day. Martin called and called. I sat with
him while he dialed, teeing up the next number as Frost neared the end of
the previous conversation. He left messages. If he did not get a call back
from his message, he would call the next day. And again. When he got to
speak to a potential donor, his script was direct:

> We can win the House back, Republicans are evil, we need you to be
> on the House Democrats' team. We need you to give $10,000, which
> will get you a photo with the president and a nice dinner with several
> members of the House.

It was refreshing because we got an answer right away, which all too
often was "I am focused on reelecting the president and I need to put my
money into his campaign." But Martin would not take no for an answer.

Of course, he was also raising for his own reelection, so occasionally
he'd modify his pitch: "Can you give me $1,000 and write $10,000 for the
DCCC?" Being the DCCC chair, he got to talk with more and more donors and hopefully could bring them into his own campaign's orbit.

And we had new tools at our disposal: committed time from members of Congress. Since Gephardt and Frost had made it clear that all caucus members had to help us win the House back, we got to take some to visit New York and pitch donors in person. A donor could say no over the phone, but what about sitting face to face? I divided that list of two thousand people and went to work finding meetings.

One of the first of these trips was for Frost. We hopped on the 7 am shuttle, had eight meetings (with a $10,000 ask at each), then grabbed the 9 pm shuttle back. We never gave this kind of attention to DC donors, going around town and spending an hour or two with each. I'd just call them. Welcome to the post-'94 realities of political money.

As soon as we boarded that morning, Frost pestered me for details about each donor. What does he care about? Which firm does she work for? Where do his kids go to school? Has he been to a White House coffee? What type of attorney is she? Who are her clients? I tried my best to answer his questions, but I had no clue about personal details. The only thing I cared about was their giving capacity. It was one thing to sit in a room and make calls with Frost, but spending the next fourteen hours running around New York was going to be a killer.

As the plane taxied down the runway, a gentlemen in front of us leaned back over the seat and said, "Martin, I know you have called me several times and I have just been too busy to call back, I am sorry. Here's my check." Super-lobbyist Tony Podesta had been avoiding Frost for weeks, but he was now stuck on a plane with him and he had no way out. Fearful he'd get cornered, he anted up and handed Frost a $1,000 check. This might be the perfect new way to raise new money: Let's just sit in the Delta shuttle boarding lounge and raise money all day!

Our first meeting was with David Stern, commissioner of the NBA. Martin tried to talk about basketball, but it was a struggle; he came off sounding like he was faking it. Stern shot me a few glances that said "Are you fucking kidding? Stop trying to bullshit me." I did my best to turn the conversation to winning back the House. That should connect with him—winning and losing—right?

But Stern had something he needed to talk about, the only reason he took the meeting. The NBA was in the midst of a fight with the Federal Communications Commission over broadcasting NBA games. The FCC wasn't blocking regional games from being shown on local cable networks. This was big money to the NBA; if it could not block local broadcasts of the games, they'd never capitalize on the national TV rights.

Frost wanted that check, so he agreed with Stern. Democrats were with the NBA! (They usually are. The NBA doesn't have a PAC but its players and executives give the vast majority of their money to Democrats.) Martin didn't have a clue what he was agreeing with, but he told Stern he'd make sure House Democrats on the Energy and Commerce Committee heard his case. That's how donor servicing works. Had the NBA headquarters been located in Washington, Stern would have gotten two minutes on the phone in return for $1,000, but because he was in New York, he got an hour for ten grand. I have no clue if it was because we sold him on winning the House back or that Frost promised him action from the committee. I didn't want to ask.

The day went along like this, meetings for an hour or two. Selling a message of taking back the House registered only if Frost talked about issues: tort reform, tax policy, TV rights. New York donors could not separate money from policy; it was their only reason to invest.

Frost got more and more intense with me as the day went on. He wanted more and more information about each donor. It was killing me. He basically started asking how many paces we had to walk to the next meeting. Not fun. We landed at 10 pm back at National Airport, Frost headed home and I went to 7-Eleven to buy my first-ever pack of cigarettes.

We ended up selling thirty tickets for the private photo line with Clinton and three hundred regular tickets. It was great for the DCCC to raise about $1 million. We missed our $2 million target, but it was still a solid event.

19

BECAUSE ALL MEMBERS HAD TO RAISE, I GOT TO SPEND TIME ON THE road with any member who wanted to go raise national money for themselves or the DCCC. I met Massachusetts congressman (and now senator) Ed Markey on a trip to New York, similar to one I had set up with Martin Frost.

What a difference. Ed was remarkably sane, laid back, fun, and although he never said it out loud, he hated these donors as much as I did. He made those trips because he wanted to be back in the majority.

We ran around New York that first trip: the president of USA Networks, David Stern again, executive David Shaw, and so on. They were typical big-money donors, but Ed stood his ground on his principles. I loved it. We had a dinner set up, but Ed had a different idea. The Big East basketball tournament was going on down at Madison Square Garden, and "Really, Lindsay, wouldn't that be more fun?" I agreed! It would! Ed made a few calls, and we ended up sitting in floor seats for the two evening games. That's my kind of fundraising.

Then Ed really figured things out. He wanted to go visit his wife's family out in Palo Alto, California. Perhaps he could do some fundraising on that trip? So I set it up, a week in California for us both, paid for by the DCCC. He wanted some "downtime," too, so I didn't over-schedule. Most of the meetings I did manage to wrangle ended up being canceled, so out of twelve meetings, we made five.

But don't worry, we justified our time. First we went down to the construction site of the new baseball stadium in San Francisco. Ed found a couple workers and asked them to show us where home plate would be. It was awesome.

The San Francisco Giants still played games out at Candlestick Park, so since we decided we were now fans, we went to the next four games. At one point we actually walked up to the Pacific Bell luxury box and knocked on the door. Who knew, maybe they would give some money? Nobody answered, but at least we tried.

Sooner or later, I started taking heat from the DCCC about how much I had raised. The committee was a little touchy, since we had spent over $20,000 that week on flights, car service, hotels, and meals. Surely one week in California would have brought in a couple hundred thousand? Nope. Nada. I had nothing to show for it. But no worries. I explained I needed to host an event to collect all the checks. So we set up a fundraising lunch for five weeks down the road with a goal of $250,000. I decided to stay in San Francisco and checked into a room at the St. Regis for the next month.

I went around town every day meeting with donors, kissing ass, and begging for checks. I didn't have anybody to help: no call time from a member, no more congressional visits. But I worked it, and I lined up Northern California Democrats to be honorary chairs of the event: Nancy Pelosi and Anna Eshoo. The former California Senate champion, Willie Brown, would be an honorary chair.

Willie was at that time the mayor of San Francisco. I didn't know him but I loved what I'd heard; he was a character out of a long-ago political novel. When I asked him about being an honorary chair for my event, he said didn't give a damn, all it meant was that he would have to show up to a lunch. He only had a few minutes to give me, but in those few seconds, he gave me his number one rule: "The Willie Brown dating rule of 70." If you take your age and you add the age of the person you are dating, it should not exceed 70. Willie was about fifty at the time, so guess how old his girlfriends were.

Thanks to Willie, my St. Regis event sold out, raised over $300,000, and probably saved my ass.

I RETURNED TO DC after that month on the road and was given one week to prepare for a day trip to Miami with Gephardt. Tired but ready to roll, I grabbed all the names I could and started making calls. One week wasn't enough time to set up a fundraising event, so I went for the wealthiest individuals most likely to write a check.

I was able to finagle four meetings for Miami but wasn't sure if they'd bring in much cash. Since I wasn't given that much time to prepare, though, I would be forgiven. Boarding the 7 am flight to Miami, Dick Gephardt in tow, I had an odd sense of calm starting out on what would be the strangest twelve hours of my young fundraising life.

Our first meeting was at the airport as soon as we landed. Vivian Mannerud met us at the gate and escorted us through the airport into a private office in the terminal. She handed over two boxes of Cuban cigars. Gephardt refused to touch them. Since not a single ethics rule pertained to a campaign staffer like me, I stuffed them into my briefcase.

Vivian went on and on about the need to open direct flights from mainland USA to Cuba. She owned a charter flight business that ran daily routes from Miami to Havana, but in order to comply with the law, her planes couldn't fly direct. They had to land in Honduras and take off for Cuba after a few minutes on the ground.

She handed over three $10,000 checks, $30,000 for the various accounts we funded. Thirty thousand dollars and two boxes of Cuban cigars seemed like a pretty good deal for forty-five minutes of our time. The moment struck me. Here was a wealthy individual who had just made a strong case for specific legislation that would benefit her business directly, and she had combined her request with a political contribution. Even the NBA commissioner, David Stern, who had asked Martin Frost to investigate an FCC ruling, had only *committed* to writing a $10,000 check; he hadn't handed it over on the spot. Willie Runyon had asked Gephardt to look into a Medicare audit, not change the law. Vivian Mannerud was putting in an ask with her money and clearly expecting something in return.

Rich donors get to spend real time with elected officials and make specific requests, yet the so-called influence peddlers in Washington never got the same opportunity: a direct quid pro quo.

WE JUMPED INTO OUR CAREY LIMOUSINE outside the airport and headed up to Palm Beach for lunch. Convinced our lunch date would result in at least $100,000, we arrived at an obnoxious mansion on the water, owned by a man I'll call Bob Walsh. I'd never seen such a place in my life. Bob lived primarily out of state and made a fortune in government contracting. I thought he might be our next Willie Runyon! All those folks cashing in off the government's dime seemed to have money to give.

The driver had to buzz just to open the gate in front of the driveway. Gephardt looked at me with his wry smile; clearly he thought we'd hit pay dirt. A burly older man greeted us in jeans and a blue sweatshirt. He walked us around the house; it took about thirty minutes. There were rooms for everything: a gym overlooking the ocean, three libraries, twelve bedrooms, and a TV studio. Every single one of them exceeded the size of my apartment. We sat down in one of his libraries to discuss his life, his business, and to get to the chase: How much was he going to fork over?

For nearly an hour, he explained that he was under investigation for contracting "issues" and he just was not in a position to donate, claiming poverty. Huh? It would be more productive for him to focus his efforts on the feds, not politics. He spilled his guts, trying to garner a sympathetic response from Gephardt and maybe an offer of help, though he insisted a donation was not on the table. He should probably not be giving when under suspicion, but he should have never agreed to meet with us in the first place either. The clock was ticking. He had now taken over ninety minutes of Gephardt's time, an amount of time nobody else in Washington would ever get to discuss their problems.

Bob suggested we have lunch. We couldn't really leave, although I wished we had, because it was obvious no money was going to come of this. I whispered to Gephardt that it better be the most expensive, best lunch we had ever had.

We walked into an enormous dining room with a table that could easily sit fifty. Four place settings were laid at one end. I became excited; four settings meant someone else was joining us. Maybe his wife? Maybe we could convince her to write a check?

A nice gentleman with long white gloves and butler tails came out to take our order. The choice was turkey or meatloaf. All three of us chose turkey, and Bob said that Poodles would have meatloaf. That was a cute name for his wife, I thought.

We chatted more about contracting and the prospects for future reforms while I salivated over the thought of a homemade Thanksgiving feast. It was not to be. Minutes later, the butler returned with four Hungry Man TV dinners, still covered in tin foil. He placed one in front of me, peeled back the foil, and explained that in this section was turkey, next was peas, and over here were the mashed potatoes.

What the fuck had I done?

The butler set the fourth meal on the table, and Bob called for Poodles. I heard a light clanging noise down the hallway and imagined his wife's expensive jewelry jiggling together. Then I heard his wife breathing somewhat heavily on top of the pitter patter of her four tiny feet. Wait, Poodles wasn't his wife but his French poodle, who happily jumped onto the table and tore into his meatloaf lunch.

To review, as I sat there with the Democratic leader of the House, potentially the next Speaker of the House, we were eating TV dinners with a dog. Fundraising at its best. I kept my head low on the return to DC, sure that this was not the best day Gephardt had ever had on the road.

JACK ABRAMOFF AND HIS ASSOCIATES ENDED UP IN JAIL FOR laundering political money from (and scamming) several Indian tribes and then for bribing members of Congress. Jack has maintained that he was just part of the system of lobbying. He is just plain wrong: He was a criminal who took the existing system of donating and lobbying to a new, illegal level. He is not, as he wants to imply, just one of many. Most lobbyists operate legally, but Jack was unique in exploiting the newfound thirst, on both sides of the aisle, for more campaign cash. His desire to bribe the likes of Congressman Bob Ney (R-OH) would not have been possible twenty years earlier, when the amount of money funding campaigns was so limited that Abramoff wouldn't have had access to enough cash to make a difference.

Through a men's ice hockey league, I'd been casual friends with Tony Rudy, one of Abramoff's associates who had gone to jail and had been a former chief of staff to Tom DeLay—the Republican leader whose conviction in connection with the scandal was eventually overturned. Tony and I played on the same team for a season or two. He was a smart, funny, good guy, and I liked him even more for despising some of the same people I did.

I was always clear to Tony that Jack was a complete scumbag. To this day, Tony tries to blame the lobbying profession for his mistakes. But in all my years of raising money, I've never met another lobbyist who was a criminal. Jack was, and he deserved to be punished much worse.

The one thing missing from all those congressional hearings, investigations, and sensational press stories was the fact that Democrats led the charge to get money from Native American tribal interests. It started slow in 1992, '93, and '94, mostly focused on Southern California tribes. We would take Gephardt out a few times a year, and they'd host a large fundraiser. Congressman Dale Kildee (D-MI) had introduced us to tribal money. Dale sat on the House Committee on Natural Resources, which basically had jurisdiction over Native American issues. The tribes had lobbied him, and he had become a champion of tribal self-rule.

But one of our first meetings was in Connecticut, with a few leaders whose tribes had established casinos on their reservations. Casinos provided jobs to long-suffering tribal members. And to protect their interests, they'd started giving the likes of Dale Kildee money. Tribes around the country that did not have casinos eventually got them, and we put the squeeze on for campaign cash for House Democrats. It was easy for us to make the ask: The federal government had granted you the right to have a casino, we represent the federal government, pay up. By 1996, we could get $150,000 to $200,000 a year from the tribes, their consultants, and their political friends. Some gave to protect themselves against competition, others gave to avoid or cut off the talk of federal taxes on casino winnings. It was easy to make the case for the tribal leaders to give; they had made so much money in a short period of time and we (Congress) had the power to cut that flow off.

By this point, we had taken on Patrick Kennedy as Dick Gephardt's political son. Dick's Hill staff watched over Kennedy's votes as a member, and we watched over his fundraising. In the summer of 1996, we decided to create a joint fundraising operation and do a little tour around the country. We started in Boston, then went to Seattle, San Diego, and Los Angeles. Boston was to capture the Kennedy money; Seattle and San Diego were all about Indian tribal cash; and Los Angeles was so Gephardt could appear as the first guest on the new Al Franken TV show.

We raised a decent chunk in Boston and flew to Seattle. There we spent all day with the tribes from lunch through dinner, with about fifteen tribal leaders from the three or four big Native American casinos in Washington State. They complained about the Interior Department's bureaucracy that prevented them from growing their casinos.

Both Patrick and Dick played nice all day and feigned interest in their concerns. Dick never asked how much we raised; he never ever cared. It's what I loved about the guy; he knew he had to do these meetings, but that didn't mean he had to care about the details.

We picked up over $50,000 that day, $25,000 for Patrick, $25,000 for Gephardt. Then Patrick, his fundraiser Jamie Whitehead, Dick, and I jumped onto a private plane to fly down to San Diego for the next tribal meeting. It was not the fastest plane in the world and had to stop in Fresno for fuel. We landed in San Diego at 12:30 am and got to the hotel at 1:15.

We had to leave by 6:00 to drive out to the tribes for a 7 o'clock breakfast. It was going to be a short rest, but you have to take money meetings when the funders are available.

PATRICK KENNEDY'S CREW took care of me in return, of course. Since they were sharing fundraising office space with us, I spent a lot of time with his staff, especially Tony Marcella. Tony was supposed to be Patrick's guardian, but he really just enabled Patrick's youthful indiscretions.

One afternoon, Tony was in the office doing some planning work with Patrick's fundraiser, Jamie. Tony came out and asked me for a favor. As I was an ever-eager liberal, any request from a Kennedy was hard to turn down. Tony wanted me to go to Georgetown to a bar called the Library on M Street and ask for Vinnie. Tony gave me an envelope of cash and said Vinnie would hand me a bag. I just needed to bring the bag back.

I was now a drug dealer. This deal went on for a few months, not every week, but more like two or three times a month. This was toward the end of 1996, and to thank me, Tony put me on retainer with Patrick's leadership PAC for $3,000 a month. I never saw what was in the bag, but I was pulling down a nice check for a few hours of work a month. Fundraising consulting can be fruitful at times.

21

AS THE 1996 ELECTION DREW CLOSER, DAVID JONES WAS UNDER pressure to produce more money for the DCCC. He told me to come up with $50,000 that week. I had only one person I could call, Willie Runyon.

"Willie, this moment is so important for House Democrats. We need to take back the House, and we could use your help. Can I count on you,

Willie? Can your friend Dick Gephardt count on you? Can I, your friend, count on you to come through for the sake of American democracy?"

"Fuuuuck no! Quit begging, it's pathetic. All you do is ask me for cash!" I had never met this side of Willie and I sure didn't enjoy it. I had no response. There's just not much to say when a powerful, wealthy donor is tearing into you, especially when, after all, I was asking him for money.

After Willie vented, he calmed down and started to cut a deal with me.

"Here's the thing," he began, "I've been cutting you so many checks that I've started to feel really bad when my staff asks for a raise and I can't give it to them." Point: Willie. "But if we can keep this hush-hush, I can probably still help."

Okay, I was listening.

"Drive to Baltimore and meet me on the corner of Pratt and Nelson Boulevard. Call me from one of the corner pay phones."

Shady corner drops and pay phones? I had no choice. Tapped out everywhere else and on a short deadline, I had to do it. I told David that if he never saw me again, I had appreciated all he had done for me. He had no clue what I was saying and went back to making calls.

I went up to Baltimore, parked, and made my call.

"Wait on the corner, and when an ambulance pulls up, get in the back."

Holy shit. But whatever, I'd wait.

Ten minutes later, one of Willie's ambulances pulled up. Everything looked safe, so I ambled up to the back door and knocked.

"Come on in!" It was Willie, all right. And there he was, lying on the gurney, smoking his pipe, in a suit. Great. I settled in to start begging for money in the back of an ambulance. Willie complained about his staff and their requested raises. He complained about Medicare, Medicaid, and anything else he could think of. I sat on the edge of the gurney and just soaked it all in.

He was paying for the right to get his speech out. He asked me how to make the check out, and I told him DCCC. He pulled out a blank check and wrote $50,000. I smiled, thanked him, and jumped out of the back of the ambulance, pipe smoke billowing behind me. I can only imagine what witnesses must have thought: that I had just spent five minutes in the back of a smoking ambulance, in my suit.

I had done my job.

22

DAVID JONES WAS THE NATIONAL FINANCE DIRECTOR AND I WAS the deputy national finance director. David thought it was time to make us sound more important. When a "finance director" calls, it's always to ask for money. But we could get our foot in the door more easily with better titles. David became chairman and I became chief of staff. Yep, my new business card had a picture of the U.S. Capitol and the title read "Chief of Staff."

It worked like a charm. I would meet with donors in New York, California, and Las Vegas, and no one outside DC knew the difference. Of course, Steve Elmendorf had just been promoted to Gephardt's chief of staff, so I didn't hand out that card in DC for fear of it getting back to Steve. One day, Gephardt saw what I was handing out and just burst out laughing. He knew what I was doing, but he didn't care.

I must have handed out several hundred of these cards over the course of a year. One day the phone rang at my "Chief of Staff" office on 7th Street. It was the Commonwealth of Puerto Rico's Senate leader and he became quite insistent that we meet, today. Puerto Rico had some serious budget issues, and the Senate leader wanted to make his case with Leader Gephardt's chief of staff.

The smart thing would have been to direct him to Steve, but I played the role I had put myself in and gave him the address to my office. He showed up with a ten-person entourage and pleaded for budgetary relief; I nodded relentlessly, no clue what he was talking about.

Eventually, a member of his entourage asked a very simple question: Why was the leader's chief of staff's office not located in the Capitol? Good question! I responded that my office was under construction and I was using this temporarily.

Steve found out about my new business card—well, he found out after one year—and in an angry call told me to destroy them. After that, I just kept them at home and handed them out on the road only.

DAVID JONES WOUND UP hiring one of our young, eager Georgetown students who started as an intern. In week one, we gave him the task of tracking down some checks from Richard Medley in New York. Richard was one of the outside financial advisors for George Soros and others and had helped make Soros a very, very rich man through currency trading. I had actually met Richard as a kid when he worked with my father on the House Banking Committee.

This young fundraiser was supposed to see Richard to pick up about $10,000 for Gephardt. When our colleague called Richard's office to set up the meeting, Richard's assistant said that he would not be in that day. Richard had mentored and supported a poor neighborhood kid, who had been hit by a car and died that day.

A tragic moment for anybody. But being young and not wanting to disappoint Jonesy and me, our colleague was not convinced that Richard's excuse—death—was valid enough. He thought Richard might have been trying to give him the slip to avoid making the donation. So our colleague called Richard back and left a voicemail: "I am sorry for your loss, if he really did die, that is. I would like to still come by and pick up the checks, perhaps later today?"

Richard never gave the money. He was not happy.

WHEN WE DID ROAD TRIPS FOR MONEY, we had to send the schedule to Mr. Gephardt's Capitol Hill office days in advance. This was both so the staff knew how to prepare him for the upcoming meetings and so we could prove we had filled the time. I had one trip upcoming to New York, but the afternoon time slot still said "to be announced." This set a panic through Gephardt's office.

When the staff pressed me to fill the time, I tossed out names: Bloomberg, Felix Rohatyn, Ed Koch—any name I could come up with for that 3 pm slot. Truth was I had already arranged for a meeting with Geoff Bible, CEO of Philip Morris. Tobacco had become toxic for Democrats and the scapegoat for many corporate bad actors. But thanks to Martin Frost's neuroses, the staff knew I loved tobacco of all sorts and had become friends with Philip Morris's chief lobbyist. I knew Gephardt wouldn't care if we met with them.

Elmendorf called every few hours; what's up with that meeting time? I kept repeating that I was just waiting for a response from Bloomberg. Off to New York we went, and the schedule still said "TBA at 3 pm." We walked into Mr. Bible's office. The fruit bowl was filled with packs of cigs, and I helped myself to a few. We chatted about how insane the hearings against big tobacco had gotten. Mr. Bible reminded us of how many jobs big tobacco provided. It was an honest conversation, much more so than sitting with a wealthy liberal person who couldn't relate to the working class. Philip Morris employed the working class, and its leadership actually understood their needs a lot better than you'd think. Tobacco companies and employees had been strong supporters of Democrats up until that year. They never would be again, and I am almost certain this was the last meeting ever between a Democratic leader and a big tobacco CEO.

The DC office was not pleased with me. It was a matter of time before I would be shown the door. I still had David Jones to protect me, but he was inching his way out also. Steve made a change to Gephardt's travel after this; he hired a young kid, Charles Jefferson, to always be with Gephardt. It was solely so Charles could tell Steve everything we did, whom we met with, and what was said.

I didn't really have an issue with that, I knew I was on my way out. But what really bothered me was the cost: We now had to pay for another plane ticket, another hotel room, another meal. Over twenty-five trips a year, that added up to over $100,000 in new campaign costs, just so Steve could keep his power.

23

WE PUT EVERYTHING INTO WINNING THE HOUSE BACK IN 1996. WE sold the new class of rich donors we'd discovered on that idea, and we promised them we could pull it off. We raised a lot of money from them. We didn't win back the House, but we kept on working them. They gave money because we spent time with them and gave them access to the top party leaders; they gave because we told them we would win. This new band of donors was not well-organized, yet.

Bill Clinton won handily that fall. A big part of that win was the early money Clinton raised and spent right away on TV advertising. His campaign had been able to "define" Bob Dole (that is, tell the public what they should think of him) before Dole had raised much money. This was a lesson that all candidates have since learned: Raise early, define your opponent, and win. President Obama's campaign used that strategy perfectly in 2012 against Mitt Romney, a playbook the Clinton/Gore team designed in 1995.

Terry McAuliffe was still running the money show for the DNC. Raising money is what he knew, and he used his access to the White House to create a reason for wealthy donors to give early. The scandals linked to him have been covered well: the White House coffees, stays in the Lincoln Bedroom, Chinese money through John Huang, and so on. What hasn't been covered well is the brewing behind-the-scenes frustration among elite liberal billionaires. They didn't have much in common with Terry and didn't like the more centrist tone coming from Bill Clinton. Most of them had taken the opportunity to go to White House coffees or other private events, but they didn't feel embraced by Clinton.

For many of them, Terry was the problem. He had opened fundraising up to pro-business Democrats. The elite liberal donors would show up in a room with eight or nine other people from the business community, industry leaders who happened to lean left but who didn't share the ideals of a utopian liberal government with the likes of George Soros and other billionaires. It wasn't enough to have a Democratic president if the White House didn't push for a liberal utopian agenda. The billionaire takeover of the Democratic Party started in 1996 because they didn't like being a part of the corporate class of donors Terry built.

So they pulled back in the years following the 1996 election and reassessed how to take over the Democratic Party. Some helped Gore in 2000, but only a few. They had been meeting behind closed doors to come up with a way to drive the Democratic Party toward their personal agendas. It would take them ten years to figure out how to organize this effort, but by 2006 they would succeed.

More on that later.

24

WE HAD BEEN DOING SO MUCH FUNDRAISING THAT IT WAS GETTING harder and harder to get people to show up for Gephardt's big event every year in DC. Yet again, we had to get creative. I wanted people to still think the event was special, just like back in early 1995 when the entire Democratic DC community showed up. The president was grabbing all the attention. It was now 1997, and I knew I was about to leave Gephardt. His staff was going the wrong way, and any future run for president did not look bright.

How could we stand out? We had raised so much money and didn't have much left to squeeze out of the DC crowd. The maximum amount a Democrat could get from every political action committee in town had swelled to $1.2 million, but that upper limit was mostly confined to senators who really worked for it. House members could squeeze $300,000 to $400,000 out of two years of fundraising from PACs and another $100,000 in direct checks from lobbyists. Still only half of what senators got, and with a House campaign running around $700,000[1] by the 1997–1998 cycle, that was a lot of money to make up through rich folks.

Since Gephardt was the leader and because he had worked the community so hard, he could garner closer to that $1.2 million out of DC PACs. We had raised over $1 million of it already by the winter of 1997. I was stuck on how to hit my previous high-water mark of $500,000 for Gephardt's one big annual event. Worried there weren't enough dollars available in DC, I had to step up my game. The president was embroiled in the Lewinsky scandal, but still he was the president. The DC donor community loved a good party and still wanted to see Bill Clinton. His most loyal friends at his lowest point in political life were the DC Democratic donors.

Following the Lincoln Bedroom and John Huang fundraising scandals of 1996, the president demanded background checks on all his donors. Everyone who attended a private event with him had to supply their Social Security number and date of birth. The White House and DNC had set up a compliance office, and they ran checks on each RSVP. Not that it really prevented any scandals, but it suggested the president was at least trying.

There's no reason President Clinton would show up for one event just for Gephardt. Dick had no challenger, didn't need the money, and the relationship between the Hill and the White House was frosty. But to raise more money from DC donors, I decided to imply that the president was coming to Gephardt's event. That would surely get some extra donors to turn up. At the bottom of the invite, I added: "VIP to Attend, Social Security number and date of birth must be submitted three days prior to event for all guests."

It worked like magic. I sold tickets to folks I'd never known to give money before. Typical donors who'd shown up in years past bought two tickets: one extra for the spouse, significant other, or mistress. Not many asked who the mystery VIP guest was, but they all assumed he lived in the White House. I sold out over five hundred $1,000 tickets in a matter of two weeks. The event would be packed.

Now I just needed to come up with my VIP. Convinced I'd be quitting soon, I decided to make my statement about how ridiculous the fundraising game had become. I got my VIP.

The event was at the Navy Memorial museum on Pennsylvania Avenue. I thought the proximity to the White House would continue the charade that President Clinton would make the quick walk over. The place had two large rooms next to the exhibits. We set up the food around the outside next to the exhibits with a photo line into each room. The first room featured Dick and Jane Gephardt. Stand in line, have a picture with them, and then proceed to the next room for a photo with the VIP.

My VIP got some laughs, caused some consternation, and aroused some pure shock.

I had hired an Elvis impersonator. Everyone got a picture with him, but you had to wait until he sang "Viva Las Vegas" first.

25

BY MID-1997, DAVID JONES LEFT GEPHARDT. HE WOULD STAY IN-volved as a consultant (the wave of the future!) but not run the show full time. Jonesy sensed I was never going to stick around, so he hired a few fundraisers under us, including a young surfer kid from California, Noah Mamet. From day one, Noah, with his slender face and jet black perfect hair, exuded the unique quality all good fundraisers share: bullshit.

Noah had no clue about what was important to a movement that had gotten Gephardt to the leadership position: the working class, and a well-honed partnership between unions and business. Born and raised in LA, Noah had cut his teeth as a West Coast liberal elite, working in California Democratic politics. He only wanted to go after big money, Hollywood donors—people like him. He was the poster child of the new money game. It's who he was, where he was from. It wasn't his fault. But Noah's donors wanted influence, so they sucked up the most precious quantity of politicians who begged them for money: time.

With David leaving, Steve Elmendorf had to decide who would take over for David Jones and run the money machine. Steve set up separate meetings with Noah and me; we'd each get one hour to make our pitch. Noah did his song and dance about building a national big donor network. Hollywood types, trial attorneys, and business executives in cities like New York, San Francisco, LA, Chicago, and Miami. He wanted to spend time and grant access to a small group of 100 or 150 people, with the hope that each would write and raise $50,000 or $100,000 for the next big campaign, whether that was Gephardt for president or another run at the majority, which would make Dick Speaker of the House.

Steve's watch must have been broken, because my hour was twenty minutes long. I knew Steve wanted Noah, but I wanted to use my time to make a point about how to change a fundraising system that had spun out of control. My pitch went something like this:

Dick Gephardt is the champion of the middle class, but he understands business too. Together, that's what makes America tick. Incredibly rich donors understand only themselves, what they need to get ahead. Gephardt isn't one of them, but we—the Gephardt team, and others—have helped give the super-wealthy more control over the system than they've ever had. They needed to be put in check. Gephardt can relate to them only because he understands how to use power, and he wants to use it to help the middle class and the companies that create strong relationships with their employees.

If Gephardt still wants to be president, he doesn't need a hundred mega-donors but a million union members and middle-class Americans giving him a hundred bucks each. Raising $100 million for a presidential run from average folks would be the greatest statement in politics, and the one guy who could pull that off is Dick Gephardt. So let's spend the next few years working the 14 million union members and the corporate leaders who have productive relationships with them, and we might just build the ultimate national partnership, one that checks the power of big donors.

It wasn't much of a decision. Steve had no clue what I was talking about. He wanted the big money. Steve wanted Noah. Noah would do Steve's bidding. That's the only thing Steve seemed to care about—his own success, not his boss's, or what Dick Gephardt represented. I knew I wouldn't win him over, but when he didn't even spend some time thinking about the prospect of small donors delivering a winning team, I was sad. Not for myself but because I knew at the end of those twenty minutes that Dick Gephardt, my hero, would never be President of the United States and he would never be Speaker of the House.

Noah got the job and Steve had his puppet. Dick would run for president in 2004, but he would not raise much money at all, "just" $21.6 million, least out of the four main Democratic candidates in the primary. For somebody who had run before and had raised so much for House Democrats, it was a pitiful showing. I could have told you in 1997 that his next presidential run would flame out. Gephardt didn't understand what he was doing by surrounding himself with the likes of Noah and Steve, operatives who didn't understand what Gephardt represented. I did, and that's why it was clear Dick Gephardt's career was on the downslope.

Now I had to figure out how to make a difference and find a new horse. Gephardt was finished as the champion of the little people.

PART 2

LAS VEGAS AND THE AFTERMATH

26

MY ASSOCIATION WITH DICK GEPHARDT ALLOWED ME TO BE PER-
ceived as one of the biggest fundraisers in DC. But after six years of the
Washington game, I despised the thought of calling another lobbyist for
another $1,000. The thought of doing it four hundred times a day made
me sick to my stomach.

In six short years, the black sheep of the political family, the fundraiser,
had gone from the outhouse to the House. Cash was now king for the
Democratic Party: When I started in Gephardt's office in 1992, a candidate for Congress had to raise less than $500,000; by the 1998 to 2000
cycle, you needed $840,000, a 66 percent increase in just six short years.[1]
For years, I'd believed that I made a difference by raising the money that
would help Democrats take power. But I was just making politicians focus
more on money and less on the middle class, and I'd come to realize how
unfulfilled I was.

As my days of servitude as a staffer in the Gephardt fundraising machine were coming to an end, the political fundraising consulting industry
was exploding. These events were related. Instead of relying on a monthly
paycheck from one member, my fundraising colleagues and I realized that
as consultants we had the ability to get multiple retainers. I decided to strike
out on my own. To me, the only question was how hard I wanted to work.

Sick to my stomach though I might have been, fundraising was my one
marketable skill, so I might as well make it profitable and have the freedom
to choose my clients. After I quit and started as a freelance consultant, my
loyalties started to change. For my own survival, I had to care about my
top one hundred donors more than any member of Congress I might be
working for, and certainly more than your average middle-class American.
My donors' happiness was critical. No longer would I call once a year to get

a check for Dick Gephardt; I was now calling constantly, asking them to donate to my client of the week. I depended on them so much, my ability to say no to a donor was disappearing.

In 1992, there were a handful of independent political fundraising consultants in DC. By 1997, there were over forty. The fundraiser's power was growing too. In the 1970s and '80s, the path to power in DC was direct: A staffer worked for a member, who gradually climbed the leadership ladder and one day became chair of a committee. The staffer became powerful too.

On a Tuesday night in Washington in 1970, a powerful Hill staffer hung out with the few lobbyists in town at the Monocle Restaurant, talking about the next day's markup of a bill. By 1997, the staffers were drinking alone, but the lobbyists were down the street with the member and the fundraiser, having the same talk.

As an independent consultant, my first client, not so coincidentally, was Dick Gephardt. My second client was a young congressman named Patrick Kennedy. My third client was an older man named Senator Ted Kennedy. Even though I was disappointed that I'd failed to take Gephardt in a different direction, I was happily making more money as a consultant while doing half the work.

MY FIRST EVENT was to raise money for Patrick's leadership political action committee. I arranged with Jamie Whitehead, Patrick's full-time fundraising staffer, to get Tony Bennett to come to DC for a concert. The Cafaro family—mall magnates from outside Cleveland who we called the Addams family—wanted to extend their political ambitions and influence beyond Ohio, so they had purchased a gigantic mansion on Chevy Chase Circle. Tony Bennett would be their first event.

I arranged for a 6 pm reception and a 7 pm concert, and then we'd walk down the street to a little French restaurant for a private dinner with the top donors, staffers, and Patrick. The peculiar Cafaro family wanted to protect their new estate, so they removed the entire first floor of furniture and set up a ridiculous number—and I mean fifty—of Port-A-Potties in the backyard, complete with outdoor heat lamps along the path and a violinist. J.J. Cafaro and Captain Smith of the *Titanic* had many things in common.

Getting Tony Bennett for a private concert would squeeze more money out of donors. The trick would work for a few years—the PAC directors could take husbands, wives, or mistresses/girlfriends for a nice night out, paid for by their organization's political contribution. It would stop working as donors discovered the real scam: It was not a *concert* by Tony Bennett, as I may have sold them on the phone, but at best a two-or three-song tease.

After Tony Bennett's blistering three-song set, we left the Cafaro family to deal with the aftermath of disappointed donors, and took their daughter Capri and nine other big donors to celebrate the performance at the French restaurant.

Patrick spent the entire dinner trying to hook up with Capri. We had to get him out of there. So Patrick, his chief of staff Tony Marcella, Jamie, Jonesy, me, and the Shahs—a nice Indian doctor couple—jumped in the Shahs' stretch limo and sped toward downtown DC on Connecticut Avenue. With wine still flowing through his veins, Patrick opened the sunroof and climbed out to the waist, screaming at anyone who'd listen that he was in a limo with Sgt. Pepper and His Lonely Hearts Club Band, who were trying to prevent him from getting laid. And he could prove it because Dr. Shah was Sgt. Pepper.

If all of my fundraising consulting days had been even close to the thrill that Patrick and Sgt. Pepper had provided me, I may have stayed in the business. Unfortunately, very few nights were like this.

Oh, and in 2010, J.J. Cafaro was sentenced to three years' probation for making illegal contributions to his daughter Capri's congressional campaign.

BY 1998, AS A CONSULTANT, I didn't have to be in the office at 9 am, and I sure didn't have to stay until 8 pm. I was judged solely on the amount of money I raised. It was a clarifying measuring stick. The ease with which I raised money for Democratic leader of the House Dick Gephardt was how I viewed the world, a world in which David Jones and I pretended to work hard for four years. But really, few donors could say no to the Democratic leader.

Then in early 1998, I discovered something. It filled a void I never knew I had. It gave me purpose, it gave me pride. It let me compete against the best of the best, bringing joy when I won, heartbreak when I lost. EA Sports' *Madden NFL '98* was my lover. I couldn't get enough of that game. I'd spend hours upon hours on my couch playing and playing and playing. It didn't matter, I was in love. More important, I wasn't spending my days calling Kate Moss, Don Kaniewski, Tim Scully, Tommy Boggs, or any of the other lobbyist-donors who would just cut me a quick check and not make me bullshit my way through another story about how the world would end if they didn't give to my candidate of the week.

After my roaring success with Sgt. Pepper, Patrick apparently told his father, Senator Ted Kennedy, about his tremendous success at the Cafaro event. The senator must have interpreted Patrick's comments as a fundraising victory, which would explain the call from Jill, the senator's full-time fundraising staffer: Would I work for the senator and pull together a large DC event in the spring of 1998?

I was intrigued by the offer. I'd spent the previous summer high as a kite at the Kennedy compound and wanted to be invited back, and, come on, Senator Kennedy was the liberal champion I'd grown up with. But I didn't understand why the liberal lion of the Senate—who would never face a real campaign ever again—needed to raise so much money a full three years before his next election. My standard pitch to a donor—"the world might end if you don't contribute today!"—was harder to sell three years out.

I agreed to do it, with three months to set it up. I had to find fifty to a hundred hosts in the first month before sending out the invitations. I picked up the phone and called my first slam-dunk donor, the National Committee to Save Social Security and Medicare. Barbara Canelli, a former member of Congress who now ran that very successful PAC, gasped on the phone.

"Of course I love Senator Kennedy. But why," she wanted to know, "would I waste this money three years before the senator's next election?"

I had no response. I couldn't tell her the world would come to an end if she didn't give. She virtually cried. Kennedy was her champion, but she couldn't justify contributing three years before the election. It was 10 am on a Tuesday, and I had a good eight hours of calls planned that day. I thought I could leave messages for at least a hundred people, but Barbara had a point. So I hung up my phone and waited for my PlayStation to boot up.

I started a new season on *Madden NFL '98*—sixteen full-length games—at 10:30 am that Tuesday. The season ended 5 pm on Sunday afternoon. I hadn't left my apartment and had made only one phone call for Senator Kennedy. I had lost the Super Bowl to the San Francisco 49ers and felt sick about my loss. I slept on it. I woke up Monday morning and my choice was clear: I could make those calls for the senator or aim for a rematch with the 49ers.

At 8 am on Monday morning, Season 2 began. By Thursday at 4 pm, my New York Jets had won the AFC East with a remarkable 12–4 record. They started the first playoff game against the Patriots. My phone rang, but clearly it wouldn't be a Kennedy donor calling back because I had tried only one. I was perturbed; the call was interrupting my rhythm. It was Jill from the senator's office, checking to see how many hosts I had for the fast-approaching event. I scrambled.

"Give me a couple days. I've called a lot of people, we'll make it happen."

I was a fundraiser, bullshit was my game. Jill was a fundraiser too and knew bullshit when she heard it. She demanded the list of hosts by Monday morning. I told her I'd send it over. I unpaused the game, and three hours later I defeated the Patriots in overtime. It was now 8 pm and I couldn't really call anyone to host the event. So I made a few calls Friday morning and got the same response Barbara had given me: "I can't justify donating to the senator now."

I couldn't worry too much. I was more concerned with the AFC championship game. When Monday morning rolled around, the 49ers had defeated me again on Sunday night in the Super Bowl. I didn't have much to say to Jill that morning, except to give her the best update I could: "We have zero hosts, no money committed, and I have no excuse." Thus ended my consulting agreement with Senator Ted Kennedy.

SENATOR BARBARA BOXER of California hired me to do an event later in the spring of 1998. That cycle, the maximum amount of PAC contributions available for Senate Democrats was about $1.4 million. By this event, she had already collected well over $1.3 million in PAC money. My job was to find the last $50,000 or so.

At least she was on the ballot that year, but she still wouldn't have much of a race. But I'd do the event for the paycheck, and got a room at the Monocle near the Senate offices. With Boxer, the rejections were different: "Why do fundraisers keep calling me when I've given all I can?" It wasn't so much about finding the needle the haystack for that last $50,000; the needles were poking me in the eye telling me to stop calling.

Six U.S. Senators agreed to attend, including Joe Biden, all of whom wanted to send a powerful message about their support for Boxer. At the event, everyone was a little surprised why there were four more senators than donors. I'd gotten a grand total of two to show up.

BEFORE I HEADED TO VEGAS to work full time for Las Vegas mayor Jan Jones, my last big contract was for Gray Davis, running for governor of California in 1998. I didn't care about Gray or California, but it was a fat contract for one event. The fundraising team in California had worked out the ultimate business model. His chief in-state fundraiser wasn't paid a salary. She got paid a 10 percent cut of what she brought in. Gray raised over $50 million, so she took in $5 million while I was getting a $5,000-a-month check. When I heard about this, I sat at my desk with tears in my eyes and counted my career total: For Gephardt, his PAC, other members of

Congress, and the Democratic Congressional Campaign Committee, I had directly raised over $40 million. I only had $500 in my checking account.

After a crazed gunman killed two Capitol Hill police officers in a July shooting incident near Gephardt's office, Gray Davis called to ask if I was all right. I was shocked. Why did he assume I worked in the Capitol? Is this how everyone outside of Washington viewed fundraisers? Like I was stepping off the House floor, dialing for dollars on a break between votes? I flashed back to a moment in 1993, as I sat in Dick Gephardt's fundraising office and listened to David Jones cuss out the Verizon representative on the phone for not giving us a "225" extension—the extension that would make it look like we were calling direct from the Capitol.

Of course, Gray was only paying lip service to my health. After "Are you all right?" his second question was, "What'd we raise today?"

Gray Davis is probably best known for losing a recall election in 2003 to Arnold Schwarzenegger. In the 1998 primary, Davis was a well-liked lieutenant governor, a local politician who'd worked his way up through the California Assembly and become his state's controller. Davis was schooled in professional government, considered a competent manager who'd paid his dues at lower levels, someone who would make a respectable governor. In those days, if you were a wealthy self-funder, it was tough to beat a local politician who'd put their time in.

By 1998, no longer could a candidate like Gray Davis rely on his resume to get ahead. Fixing stoplights and filling potholes wasn't enough to win in California; now it was more important to spend your day at the country club or union hall with guys who could write $100,000 checks.

He faced off in the Democratic primary against Representative Jane Harman and Al Checchi, both with tens of millions of potential campaign dollars at their disposal. Harman had represented California's Thirty-Eighth District for five years and had her husband Sidney Harman's billions to fall back on. Al Checchi was the co-chairman of Northwest Airlines and had been a bigwig at Marriott after leveraging a fortune out of Disney. Net worth? Six hundred million. He cut his campaign a $40 million check.[2]

Checchi and his millions would have fit nicely in the Republican Party in the 1980s, but he was running as a Democrat. But what does a guy driving a Rolls-Royce have in common with a Democratic primary voter, like Grandma who's missing her Social Security check? Just think about the kinds of candidates who had run for national office in Democratic primaries in years prior—Clinton, Dukakis, Gore, Biden, Gephardt, Harkin, Mondale, or Gary Hart. Even if they had a small personal fortune, none of them threw in their own money to run. Democratic candidates were long-serving politicians with strong bases of local support—teachers, firefighters, middle-class families—but a new type of candidate was starting to appear at the state level, and the poster child was Al Checchi.

Gray had to raise $50 million just to keep pace. He would rejoice at call time, spending hours on the phone raising money. He just loved to do it, and that was fine with me. He raised a ton of money from the usual suspects in business and unions. With no limits on campaign donations in California, he had to spend all his time with people who could write him million-dollar checks. By the end of the campaign, Gray spent so much time with the president of the firefighter's international union (donation: $1 million), I was convinced he had the ability to put out a fire in any home in America. The new test of credibility for a candidate was money, and Gray Davis passed with straight As.

Checchi took the bullet for the rich white men of the 2000s in the Democratic Party. He thought he could simply pay for a bunch of TV ads that would put him over the top. But he failed to tell his personal story, thinking his resume and millions would shine through. In the end, he failed to connect with Democratic primary voters.

Things started to change around 2000, when ex–Goldman Sachs CEO Jon Corzine of New Jersey put his personal $34 million campaign war chest to better use. In that Senate primary, Corzine developed a message and then invested as much in building a constituency within his party as he did on TV advertising. Checchi's failure taught rich, self-funding Democratic candidates like Corzine how to get over the hump.

27

AS A CONSULTANT, I HAD THE FREEDOM TO BE ANYONE I WANTED TO be, and after making many trips to Vegas to raise money with Dick Gephardt, I decided I wanted to be a Vegas insider. So when the call came with an offer to help a Democratic candidate in the Nevada governor's race in 1998, it was the easiest, most joyful *YES!* in my life.

Pure adrenaline—I was on my way to Vegas in August 1998. Coastal elites always looked down on Las Vegas—you know, "What happens in Vegas . . ." and all that. They had no clue what that valley could mean to a middle-class family. I love that town. Sure, I loved gambling, but I had also fallen for Vegas's unique concept of middle-class success. Unionized workers built the casinos and resorts, then worked at them. Then they stayed and built the houses they lived in, the restaurants they ate at, and the schools their kids went to. In no other American city could a single parent buy a large house—probably with a pool—for $100,000 while pulling down $80,000 a year as a blackjack dealer. And thousands of them did. It was my "Go West, Young Man" moment.

State-level politics mattered, and to me, it seemed like local officials were still interested in serving their constituents, not raising money all the time. I wanted out of DC, and a Nevada governor's race run out of Vegas seemed like a hell of an out.

In mid-1998, Senator Harry Reid's (D-NV) staff asked me to move to Las Vegas to help a long-shot candidate for Nevada governor raise enough money to help get the senator reelected. Senator Reid was up for reelection that year against good-looking Republican representative John Ensign. Reid was in trouble. Not only was the Lewinsky affair hurting Democrats all over the country, but the Nevada governor's race was causing Reid problems too. In a topsy-turvy field, State Senator Joe Neal was the most likely

Democratic nominee for governor, and that scared Reid. Neal's big campaign promise was to raise taxes on the casinos, a topic Reid didn't want to go anywhere near. Reid desperately wanted Las Vegas mayor Jan Jones at the top of the ticket to help his cause. As a dynamic female candidate, Jan would energize the party, soften the blow from the Lewinsky scandal, and motivate Democratic women to go to the polls. And while they were voting, they would also pull the lever for Reid.

And for me, DC was a painful experience by now, and I thought local politics might have a bigger, more direct impact on people's lives and the race would be cleaner, honest and goal oriented, even in the City of Sin. Toss in twenty-four-hour bars, sports betting, and great food, and it was going to be a blast. It didn't disappoint.

BY THE TIME I'D LEAVE VEGAS ten months later—not exactly by my own choice—it had beaten me. Not the gambling, drinking, or drugs (though there were plenty of all three), but the politics beat me. I ran two major races there, one for governor of Nevada and the other for mayor of Las Vegas. The politics of the 1970s and '80s had always been about endorsements, from unions or community groups. The 1998 Nevada governor's race showed the changing landscape in American politics: Early endorsements (and money) from donors built momentum.

Early money allowed candidates to get on TV faster, following the Clinton model of 1996. In the 1992 cycle, just six years earlier, most candidates blitzed their district with thirty days of advertising, and many House Democrats didn't bother to run any. Based on the Bill Clinton 1996 playbook, the question for Democratic candidates had become which would arrive first: opening day of the baseball season or your first TV ad. The problem? TV's expensive. To really saturate a market to the point where ads impact voters, you need to buy a bare minimum of fifteen hundred "points" worth of time (points are how TV channels measure value to sell advertising). In laymen's terms, buying fifteen hundred points means the average TV viewer would see that ad fifteen times in a week. Campaigns work to hit that magic number for each demographic. If you want to make sure that a young voter sees an ad ten or twelve times a week, you will buy more ads on Comedy Central or repeats of the *Simpsons;* if you want the seventy-year-old voter, you might buy all the ads on *Matlock* reruns to hit that number. Every TV market in America has this demographic break down, so campaigns will also air ads on shows that everybody will likely see—those for the local news, for example—as part of specific demographic targets. Ad buyers will purchase a mix of timeslots across programs to reach fifteen hundred points. In Vegas in the late 1990s, those fifteen hundred points cost $140,000.

28

JAN JONES WAS RUNNING TO BE GOVERNOR FOR THE SECOND TIME. In 1994, she made the ambitious decision to challenge incumbent Democratic governor Bob Miller in the primary. She had one chance to dent Miller, during the state-wide televised debate. She spent weeks preparing for that moment and thought she could crush him with her smarts. Jan and her team hadn't focused on four-page glossy campaign pamphlets; they'd spent a year producing binders worth of policy ideas.

She decked herself out, piling on way too much makeup. The Miller team got to the set first and cranked the heat up (this is Vegas—it was already hot) knowing that Jan was disposed to slathering on foundation and rouge. Her face melted on stage—literally—and any chance of Jan winning was finished in one big sloppy mess of eye shadow and lipstick for the entire state to see. That's how you play politics, Vegas style.

In 1998, some of the state's power brokers were still pissed at her for creating a headache four years earlier—they had been forced to pick between supporting the incumbent governor and the sitting mayor of Las Vegas. Jan was truly brilliant and had real potential to be a new leader for Nevada's future, but she had jumped the gun and forced the city's Democratic power brokers to choose between two powerful incumbents. The pain she caused these money players had lingered for four long years, and even her smarts could not overcome the hurt feelings in the casino mogul crowd.

Jan and I had met a few years before when Dick Gephardt and the Democratic Congressional Campaign Committee tried to convince her to run for Congress in a recruit-the-rich drive (i.e., people who could fund their own campaigns) during the 1996 cycle. We wanted her to challenge freshman congressman John Ensign, who was now running against Harry Reid for Senate. But after her meltdown on stage in 1994, she had no desire to go to Washington.

That's why I liked her. She was genuine. She'd been the spokeswoman in a series of TV ads for her family's grocery store chain and her ex-husband's car dealerships, real local Americana mom-and-pop businesses that were doing well. That made her someone who knew about real-life struggles and who had a stake in her community, not a schmoozer in DC. I enjoyed just kicking back and drinking wine with her, which we did often at her home in Summerlin, and having a good conversation.

I'd been to Vegas many times with Gephardt and the DCCC and knew many of the folks who'd give to federal candidates. I was looking forward to bringing them over to Jan. However, there was one major problem. I couldn't tell her why I was coming, but she must have known: She had no chance to win.

SHE DIDN'T HAVE A CHANCE because Republican Kenny Guinn was "The Anointed One," as Vegas political journalist Jon Ralston wrote in the book of the same name on the race. Guinn was a former bank president, interim head of the University of Nevada–Las Vegas, and the shoo-in establishment candidate. He'd been unofficially running for years. Guinn was running the blandest of campaigns, but he got away with it because he'd been "anointed" by the state's elite years earlier, and already raised a ton of cash. Almost two years before the election, Kenny Guinn had nearly $600,000 on hand.

Then by January 1, 1998, Guinn released a massive list of contributions showing he'd hauled in $2.5 million—about half from casino moguls. They were huge numbers for the time, and would leave Jan in a hole. The race was already all but over. The endorsement of campaign cash was now more important than any yard sign or endorsement from a union, and the Guinn campaign embodied this brave new world of political momentum.

That January, politics was the farthest thing from Jan's mind. She had just announced she had breast cancer. While Kenny Guinn had locked up every Republican operative and funder—and a fair number of Democrats—a full year before the election, the candidate I'd soon work for was undergoing chemo.

Then a couple funny things happened. Jan got better. By April, she was talking about her breast cancer in the past. Then in May, a private poll showed her that she might actually have a shot at winning. That was it, she'd run. It was typical, impulsive Jan. Reid was the happiest guy in Nevada—he told her that the race wouldn't be that hard and that she'd only have to raise $750,000. Yeah . . . right. Reid knew that Jan couldn't win, but he didn't care—he had a superstar woman at the top of the ticket, one who would motivate women to the ballot box to vote for him, too.

Jan filed her candidacy the second-to-last day she could, in mid-May 1998. With the election just five months away and Guinn so far ahead in the money game, she was screwed from the start. She pledged to raise $2 million for the race, enough to make her competitive. Jan had a pretty good month in June where she took in $112,000 in contributions. But Guinn had $3 million already on hand out of his $3.5 million budget. He started buying TV ads that month and was out talking to voters while Jan was still making desperate phone calls to raise money.

And there was one other problem. Candidates in financial trouble often lend their campaigns money to get them off the ground (and the ones who raise a lot of money on the back end often repay themselves with interest!). She had lent herself $300,000 when she ran for governor in 1994 and ended up losing $250,000 of it.[1] She didn't want to lend herself money at the beginning of this campaign, which put her in an even deeper hole.

Jan's campaign imploded before I was hired. It was so bad that she ended up crying on stage at an event. She had lost control and was twenty-five points down in the polls. So that July they called in outside help: Harry Reid's former press secretary, Susan McCue (who would soon become more important than campaign manager Denise Rawles), media consultant Roy Behr, and me.

Susan was Harry Reid's narc, his tall, red-headed informant who funneled intel back to the senator's camp about how things were going in Jan-Land. She'd go on to be Reid's chief of staff and then run Bono's One Campaign. Susan was a good, competent, Machiavellian sort of political operative, loyal to her boss—Reid—over anyone else. She was a good leader, and couldn't be more opposite to Steve Elmendorf, my old colleague from Gephardt's staff.

I couldn't figure Roy out. He was a savvy TV guy whom I'd hire later for the Las Vegas mayor's race. But he was a cagey oddball. At one point he went to Rome and tried to arrange to be the marketing lead for every piece of Vatican memorabilia sold in the United States.

Susan and I would regularly go to this awesome little Tex-Mex place on Paradise Avenue, where politicos from every camp went for happy hour. We'd go to be seen and get drunk. This is how local politics works: Political operatives of all stripes hang out together no matter who they work for, to drink, get shit done, and search for the gossip of the day over a couple of drinks.

MY JOB WAS TO HAVE Jan reach her $2 million goal and make it a single-digit loss that would allow Harry Reid to return to the Senate. We had a real shot at hitting our target, and for one good reason. Technically, Vegas had a $10,000 contribution limit per donor. It had just been reduced from $20,000 at the end of 1997, which only encouraged Guinn to get as many $20,000 donations in as possible before January 1998. But at $10,000 or

$20,000, limits were easy to ignore. Vegas's staple industries are tax-averse, cash-intensive businesses and keep plenty of money on-site. So who cared if I took $10,000 or $100,000, so long as it was untraceable cash? We could essentially hide the money on campaign finance disclosure forms by creating names or attribute the money to donors' kids.

We could never raise $2 million, a thousand bucks at a time, in just four months. So there was no way I could build a network of average Joes to support Jan Jones for governor, like I'd have preferred. So I did what I'd been taught to do, and I knew I had enough time to raise $2 million in $10,000 chunks, or more, in cash. It was a fascinating problem, one that illustrates the central trade-off in modern politics: Just as any other business, in politics time is money. Why should Guinn get to waltz to the governor's mansion just because he got in the race so early and had more time to raise money? With big donations, Jan could spend less time raising money and more time talking to voters, crafting her message, and preparing for debates.

Of course, taking vast sums of money from just a few sources poses a different problem. If you take, for example, $1,000 from twenty thousand donors, you can afford to piss off a couple and not lose much money. But what happens when you piss off one of the only two hundred donors who's given you ten grand?

I'd soon find out the relationship between a donor and a fundraiser in Vegas was not a numbers game, as it was in DC. Sending out five thousand invitations to Washington lobbyists and following up with five thousand phone calls was tedious, and getting a 5 percent response was a huge success. But since there are only a couple hundred Democratic donors in a town like Vegas who could give $10,000, a 5 percent success rate doesn't cut it.

The die was cast: one hundred twenty days to raise $2 million. That's $17,000 a day. I would do anything to make it happen.

Let me show you.

29

MY FRIEND AND SENATOR REID CONFIDANT PAUL HENRY PICKED ME up at the airport that July. Paul was a great guy, thoroughly enjoying life as a young Vegas power broker. He drove me to the Golden Nugget, the Steve Wynn–owned hotel and casino where the Jones campaign was putting me up for a few weeks. He gave me one hour to unpack, shower, and get ready for dinner with him and another political operative whom I'll call Mike Palmattir.

Paul and I drove out to old-school Vegas beyond the Strip, through neighborhoods I had never seen before or knew anything about. We got to this little Italian restaurant, one of those places that had been around since the Eisenhower administration, which was probably the last time it had been professionally cleaned. The place even had the pictures of the Rat Pack on the walls, although it was so dark I could barely see them . . . not that I really wanted to know what the floor looked like. The place smelled like Dean Martin's corpse was rotting under our table.

We went into the back dining room with sliding doors, set up so you could have a private conversation. I thought it was nice of Paul and Mike to throw me a Welcome-to-Vegas dinner. But this had nothing to do with being happy to see me. I was about to be baptized into Vegas politics.

We chatted about Vegas, Jan's campaign, and Reid's tough reelection fight. At first it was cordial dinner conversation for political hacks. I knew almost nothing about Jan's campaign, hadn't even gotten to the campaign office yet. But these guys knew the lay of the land, and anything I could learn from them would help.

The conversation turned to Senator Reid. His reelection campaign had apparently gone off the rails and needed new leadership. Mike wanted a new manager for the senator's campaign, but he and Paul couldn't convince Reid to make a change. The senator worried he'd look desperate only a few months before the election. But Paul and Mike had just one thing in mind—protecting Senator Reid—and they thought the current guy, Larry Werner, couldn't do it. If the senator refused to make the move, they wanted to force a change, Vegas style.

The next fifteen minutes were one of the most amazing conversations I've ever had. I was unnerved but was gaining a deep, sober appreciation of the world I'd entered.

They needed Jan Jones to back them up. If I could get Jan and her team to support their plan, they would execute it that week. All Jan had to do was create some sort of media drama to cause a deflection. A few days of bad press for Jan was not going to make a difference in a race she'd surely lose, but it would deflect attention from the Reid campaign. Would I talk to Jan about the plan? Sipping my coffee, inside a private room of this old Vegas restaurant, I had to say the right thing.

The plan was simple. The Vegas cops would pull over Larry and magically find a large amount of cocaine in his car. Easy. Senator Reid would have to fire him on the spot, and a new person would take over as campaign manager. My heart pounded, adrenaline ran through my veins, and there wasn't a drug in my system . . . yet. My new high was Las Vegas politics.

DC Beltway politics was rough-and-tumble for all the wrong reasons, a kiss-ass cesspool of fundraiser climbers begging for $1,000 checks from every lobbyist in sight. Vegas politics was rough for all the right reasons, underhanded but oddly straightforward. It was about working-class families building and running an industry from the ground up . . . and the politicians who'd stop at nothing to represent them. Fake drug busts somehow seemed more honest than pretending to care about an issue just for the check.

I stood up, smiled, shook their hands, and told them I would get back to them. They seemed overly appreciative that I was even open to the idea. I was not, of course, but I wanted to get back to my hotel in one piece. Paul drove me back and we talked about baseball. I never mentioned the idea to Jan, and they never brought it up again. *Ever.* Was it a loyalty test, old-school style, to see if I was on their team? I never wanted to find out, but I never wanted to leave this town. For the next ten months, my heart pounded any time I saw a cop car.

Who knows if the plan was real? It was at a minimum a test embedded in a night of drinking. Paul had a sly sense of humor, and he had—at the very least—put me in my place. I respected him out of fear for the next few months.

30

I ARRIVED EARLY THE NEXT MORNING AT "JONES FOR GOVERNOR" headquarters, a used car lot storefront a mile or two from the Strip. My absolute favorite thing about Jan's office was the twenty-four-hour Mexican bar next door, complete with slot machines. My previous trips to Las Vegas had always been to the Strip, but I soon realized that every 7-Eleven, grocery store, and gas station had slots. The Mexican place was a little hole in the wall, with maybe twenty seats. They didn't seem big on security or on making people show up to work in the morning. The owners would just leave the doors wide open with a jar on the bar next to a menu and a note: "Please help yourself to any drink you'd like, just leave the money in the jar." I'd drop two bucks in there every day for my 10 am can of Miller Lite.

Next door at the campaign office, ten people sat around, eight of them local women, friends of Jan's who were trying to help out. Denise Rawles had come out from Philly to be Jan's campaign manager but was clearly in way over her head. She would be sidelined soon enough.

I didn't know what Susie Lee's role was, but her husband was Allen Foreman, who served as Steve Wynn's comptroller. It seemed like she joined the campaign just because she was desperate to be a part of something.

Sloan Arnold, a nice, young twenty-something, would go on to be a successful fundraiser in her own right.

Then there was Bubba. Bubba Grimes, a hulking, sweat suit–wearing old huckster, was the former chair of the Nevada Democratic Party and had raised some money with Jan Jones when she challenged Governor Miller in the '94 primary. He stuck around Jan's race making sure his presence was felt. We'd go on to open a consulting firm together in Vegas—Grimes-Lewis—to try to make some money later on. Bubba had some sort of disability and had convinced Jan to give him a handicapped parking tag to hang from his rearview mirror.

Jan didn't tell Dan Geary, her fundraiser, that I was coming. My arrival was a little bit of a shock, though I just told him I was coming to "consult." It really wasn't my place to tell him he was no longer needed. He was about to take care of that himself anyway.

DAN HAD SET UP A MEETING that first day at somebody's home for dinner. He had met some rich guy on a flight recently who offered to raise money for Jan.

I figured out what was going on in the first two minutes of a five-fucking-course dinner. I've just developed a sixth sense about money meetings—this crew wasn't going to raise us a dime or at best would write a puny check . . . just like David Bender and Poodles. They were rich folks who were happy to surround themselves with important people like a candidate for governor but would keep their checkbooks tight. I was no longer in DC, the golden land of political money where everyone understood the deal. I had entered the bizarro world of Vegas chumps.

Dan fucked up. *Never* agree to a full dinner. If it goes badly, you're trapped, wasting time talking to weirdos who won't give enough, if any, money. Dan didn't research these people. If he did, he would have found that they hadn't given much to other candidates and wouldn't give us much either. And he didn't set expectations for our hosts about the dinner's goals: Prepare them for how much Jan would ask for, and ask what issues interested the host. At the dinner, Jan's job was to make the ask, then explain to the host that she is "very busy and can only stay a few minutes."

The food wasn't even that great. I glared at Dan, seething with contempt that I was stuck courting people who just weren't going to give nearly enough to make our time worthwhile. The three hours we spent at this tacky home could have been spent doing something useful for the campaign. Sitting on Las Vegas Boulevard with a tin can begging for money would have been more productive. Instead, we sat and listened and flashed fake smiles of appreciation for their thoughts on the campaign's direction. Jan shot me that look, the candidate look I knew well, the what-the-fuck-am-I-doing-in-this-room-and-get-me-the-hell-out-of-here look.

Oh, but they had advice, typical advice that rich powerful folks give when they've got political candidates cornered. The entire discussion was about the campaign's color scheme. The colors. That's right, if Jan would just start wearing more purple and put purple into her ads, she would win. Simple! We're saved! And it wasn't just a suggestion, they had samples of the shades of purple. And they used their samples against Jan's face, then looked at me and Dan for approval. I played along. This is the bullshit you tolerate (and ignore) from donors who bundle hundreds of thousands of dollars, not jackoffs who aren't giving much beyond the salmon on my plate that night. That was it for Dan. He was on his way out, but Jan had to find the excuse to fire him. She got it soon.

IN ALL MY TIME of raising money, I have never threatened a donor. You can turn up the pressure a bit, but it's not good to outright threaten them. If a prospect tells me no or makes a direct appeal for something in return, I stop. The *Las Vegas Review-Journal's* Jane Ann Morrison got hold of a voicemail that Dan had left for a donor, a prominent local home builder who'd have to get approval through city government for new projects. Dan wanted to make it clear that being on the mayor's good side would help. Here's part of the message as reported:

It's Dan Geary with Jones for Governor. She feels pretty strongly that just out of friendship and the fact that she's either going to be mayor or governor at the end of this election cycle—it's not really whether she's going to be in office or not—that she wants to sit down and talk with [the donor] . . . and feels pretty strongly about the fact that their friendship really, as far as she's concerned, transcends the party boundaries. Or if he just flat out doesn't want to meet her at all and talk with her at all about this, then I guess just let me know that, too, and I'll make sure she knows. But give me a call when you get a chance.[1]

Not the worst call ever, but just plain stupid. Even though Dan apologized for being "overzealous," it was enough to have him move along. I was in charge now.

31

KENNY GUINN WAS WAY AHEAD OF JAN IN THE MONEY CHASE, BUT at least he had an opponent in the Republican primary. Our hope was that Aaron Russo would at least beat him up a little and force Guinn to spend some of his millions. Russo was the Tea Party before there was a Tea Party: radical, insane, crazy, and endlessly entertaining.

If the name Aaron Russo sounds familiar, it's because he was a famous Hollywood producer, with credits like *Trading Places, Wise Guys,* and *The Rose.* While making *The Rose* in the late '70s, he dated Bette Midler, one of the movie's stars. As of 1998, Ms. Midler still had a restraining order against Aaron, for abuse. "My manager [Russo] was beating me and I decided I couldn't take it any more," she told her biographer.[1] I am sure that the Guinn campaign wished they could have gotten Bette to spend time in Las Vegas in the summer of 1998 to keep Aaron away.

Nevada had no income tax and still relied on a high car tax to balance its budget. Aaron's pre–Tea Party platform was to get rid of the car tax, period. He had no plan to replace the revenue, but that was never his concern. Russo spoke for the people! He was a pain in Guinn's ass, and we all loved it.

As the primary approached, Russo was actually going after Guinn by playing his Hollywood card. Jack Nicholson came and did a few appearances and taped one of the worst political ads ever, but it was pure Aaron. He was a wacky candidate with a terrible message, but at least he understood the value of having early money up front. By July 1997, he was already self-financing his campaign to the tune of $1.27 million, and that bought him 26 percent against Guinn in the primary.[2] Guinn had sewn up so much early money that the only way Republican voters were given a choice in the primary is because crazy Aaron Russo was a self-funder.

He had achieved his goal. In the weeks after the primary, Russo had such hatred for Guinn and his puppet masters that he begged us to let him endorse Jan. He would show up at our office, he would call all the time, he would make us meet him in public, he would go on radio and talk about Jan. Finally, we let him.

IN THE MIDDLE OF AUGUST, Jan's campaign was a joke. It was run as if we were in the 1950s, when putting up yard signs and a big poster at the grocery store were keys to swaying voters. Her staffers were simply not political professionals who knew how to use TV, radio, and mass mailing outreach to reinforce a specific message to a defined universe of voters. It had the feel of losing House campaigns, chaotic and dysfunctional. The public polls had her trailing Kenny by over twenty points. If we had any chance of making this race close and helping Senator Reid, we had to do it now.

I was determined. Not to win the campaign, I wasn't that crazy, but to win the money battle and make this race competitive. I wanted Jan to hit her $2 million target for the race—which would be a hell of an accomplishment in just a couple months—so we could buy enough TV ads to get close.[3]

I went into fundraising overdrive. Every time I walked into the office, I'd yell "BATTLE STATIONS!!! BATTLE STATIONS!!!" to keep the staff excited and on their toes. We didn't have eight months to pull together a budget and lay out the incremental targets, as for a congressional race. We had a few weeks to plan a budget, raise it, and spend it.

I set up in the corner office, just a desk and two chairs, two phones, a poster board on the wall with goals for the day, for the week, and for each call. I put together my target list, which grew to two hundred people Jan needed to call. Some friends of mine, some who cared about Senator Reid, some filthy rich folks that I figured visited Vegas often, and the Vegas money elite. And we went to work, dialing for dollars. Vegas journalist Jon Ralston thought I was the only thing keeping it close:

> If Jones hadn't hired Lindsay Lewis, she would have been even worse off. . . . "Lindsay would just pick up the phone and start dialing numbers," Jones remembered later. "He would say, 'Mayor, it's Marvin Davis.' I'd say, 'What do I say? And he'd say, 'Just tell him Gephardt told you to call him.'"[4]

Like most politicians, Jan hated call time, the scheduled amount of time a fundraiser makes a candidate raise money on the phone. Think about it—how horrible is it to ask people for money, all day, every day? It's mind-numbing to make the same pitch, over and over, for hours on end to people you don't know. The fundraiser is there to keep the candidate going, as the candidate calls down a very long list of names. If you're running for office for the first time, it's literally all you do for months and months until you get close to election day.

Jan would make excuses about not calling this person or that person, or she'd delay. Her excuses were the standards I've heard from almost every candidate I've worked for: "I think he's sick," "We should wait a week to call," "I will see her at that event next week, let's wait," or "I think it's better if my friend calls first to see if he is interested." It's just uncomfortable to ask friends and family to write you a check. If a candidate is calling a friend, often they'll chitchat for as long as they can stay on the phone. Call a few of your friends, have prolonged conversations with them, and before you know it, call time is over!

To be fair, Jan was better than most. She still believed she could win this race, bless her heart. I was not going to dissuade her from that line of thought.

32

ONE OF JAN JONES'S EARLY CALLS WAS TO RICK RIZZOLO. IT WAS clear they were friends, and as they chatted, I was worried Jan would drag out the call too long. Then out of nowhere, she told Rick to get off his ass and pony up, it's the least he could do. I was impressed. It was my dream as a fundraiser to have candidates be so direct and clear: "I want $50,000 from you, Rick." That was $40,000 more than the legal limit, but he agreed without a second thought. For that kind of money, I'd even let her chat a few more minutes.

Rick wasn't a lobbyist, a union guy, or a corporate donor—you know, the folks I had been dealing with in Washington. Rick was the owner of Crazy Horse Too, the biggest, most successful strip club in Vegas.

Jan hung up the phone and told me to go pick up the money; Rick would be giving it in cash and had it on him right now. Since he was also giving us so much more than the limit, we'd have to get creative when we declared it. Chills went through my body, I was in love with Las Vegas. I was about to drive my little white Saturn over to a strip club to pick up $50,000 in cash. Hot.

I got over to the Crazy Horse, parked, and walked in. The bouncer didn't bat an eye when I told him I was here from Mayor Jones's office to see Rick. He checked me out, did a little pat down, and made a phone call. I was nervous. I'm a blue-collar kid from Maryland—I had never, ever put my hands on that much money. Just five years earlier, I was making $18,000 a year working for Dick Gephardt. Now I was about to collect more than twice that, in cash.

The bouncer came back out about five minutes later and told me to walk through the dance floor and down the hallway to the wood door. Rick was in his office. It was my *Goodfellas* moment, a slow-motion Scorsese clip where I imagined "Street Fighting Man" playing in the background. I walked with purpose through the club and gave the thumbs-up to the girls working the poles. I was twenty-eight, and this was life.

I knocked on the big office door. A slit in the door cracked opened, and a pair of old eyes asked me what the fuck I wanted. I told him the mayor had sent me to see Rick. The eyes told me to wait and closed the slit.

Two in the afternoon must be a busy time for the strippers' union. I could hear a few girls arguing over shifts and complaining about custom- ers. They didn't have prime dancing slots and they wanted better. I found it fascinating that these women had the same concerns as any grocery store employee or blackjack dealer. I wanted to recruit them for Jan's campaign.

Ten minutes went by. I waited. A few dancers stopped to ask me if I was the new security guard. I smiled and explained that I was just waiting to meet with Rick. Not that I was in any hurry, I was happy to take in this glimpse of the inner workings of this high-specialized middle-class industry.

Finally, the old eyes opened the door and apologized for the wait. See, when Jan told Rick that "Lindsay" was coming over to pick up the money, he hardly expected a twenty-eight-year-old, six-foot-five ex-hockey goalie. With fifty grand on the line, they got worried it might be a stickup, a sting, or something worse. They called Jan to clarify that Lindsay was, in fact, a large man.

I walked into Rick's massive, seedy, smoke-filled office, with leather couches and a big wooden desk at the far end. The walls were covered in security TVs, at least fifty different views of the dance floor, the bar, and the entrance. Ten young girls lounged away, clearly going through the "interview process" with Rick. The eyes behind the door slit belonged to Rick's personal assistant, a sixty-five-year-old gentleman with long white hair, decked out in a white shirt and dress pants. Rick presided over the scene in a wifebeater, his Air Jordans kicked up on the desk to reveal a pair of ratty sweat pants. My kinda guy.

I was in a daze. Piles of cash, booze, slutty women, and banks of security cameras were things I had only seen in movies. I was amazed a place like this actually existed, much less was playing a part in the democratic process. Rick asked if I wanted to stick around and hang out. Of course I did! But I had to take a rain check; I was running this campaign for governor, and if I started the three Ds—drinking, drugging, and dancing—at 2 pm, I knew myself well enough that I'd still be there at 2 am.

Rick handed me a manila folder stuffed with five hundred hundred-dollar bills. I said a quick thank you and ran to the car. I wanted to be careful, so I placed the envelope in the trunk and triple-checked to make sure it locked. I quickly considered taking my pile of cash and hitting the casino. I thought better of it. In Vegas lore, there was a mobster who supposedly laundered a million bucks cash for his *capo*. On his way to deliver his boss's money at the Egyptian-themed Luxor casino, he decided to try to turn a quick profit and bet it all on black. When the roulette ball landed on green, he promptly headed up to the tip of the Luxor's pyramid and landed nine hundred feet below on a blackjack table.

I drove back to the campaign office with windows down, the music cranked, and the biggest this-is-what-being-alive-means smile from ear to ear. If we could find twenty-five more Rick Rizzolos, we'd have the money we needed!

Rick was rumored to have ties to the Chicago mob and other notorious types in the Las Vegas underworld. The FBI staked him out that year, which always made me wonder if my giddy excitement in Rick's office was captured on FBI tapes. Eventually the feds nailed him. In 2006, Rick agreed to a plea bargain on racketeering counts, which led to jail time, almost $16.5 million in fines and back taxes, and an agreement to sell the Crazy Horse and get out of the adult entertainment business. In return, the feds agreed not to go after Rick's father, sister, or brother. Last I heard Rick was working some minimum-wage job in the valley; he had lost his strip club and much more . . . but I had his $50,000, which we reported as a $5,000 donation from him and another $5,000 from Bart Rizzolo. We hid the rest of the money under other names, which I don't remember.

JAN CALLED CASINO OWNER STEVE WYNN. Steve had given $40,000 to Kenny Guinn, so there was concern that maybe he wouldn't donate to us. But he told Jan that he would give her the same amount he'd given Guinn because he didn't believe that Guinn should just walk away with the election. And either way, Jan was going to be the mayor of Las Vegas, win or lose the governor's election, so he was just protecting his business interests.

Wynn understood how to use power and was happy to give an equal amount to Jan. He basically didn't have much of an ideology, but he knew what was important to him—keeping gambling taxes low—and built an entire political operation to protect his empire: the Mirage, Treasure Island, the Golden Nugget, and, about to open in January 1999, the Bellagio. But it was also about playing nice with Harry Reid. Reid was a senior senator, and when you're a small state like Nevada, a senator high up the seniority ladder was something worth paying for, and that meant supporting Jan.

Wynn's political operation extended well beyond just donating to candidates. He'd get his employees—thousands of them at four major casinos—to go into the community and build grassroots support. He'd have his employees do everything from cook pancake breakfasts at senior centers to run car washes at high schools. Everyone would know the Wynn empire and understand it was there to help the community.

I couldn't argue. Wynn's casinos employed tens of thousands of people, usually at decent wages and working decent hours. I'll never forget the conversation I had with a valet at the Mirage, who bragged that he pulled down $140,000 a year working just four days a week. He played golf on his days off. If Wynn fought to keep gaming taxes low and could continue to employ people who could make even half as much, that was okay by me.

Regardless, Wynn's donations were a critical part of his strategy, and it's no coincidence that the Mirage, Treasure Island, the Golden Nugget, and the unopened Bellagio all donated $10,000 each to Jan's campaign on the same day.[1] He had used each member of his casino empire to donate the legal maximum to Jan.

33

WITH FIVE WEEKS TO GO BEFORE ELECTION DAY, THE REID CAM-paign was pulling away from Jan. They had thought she could be their savior, but her collapse in the polls was now hindering the senator's victory. Kenny Guinn was solidifying his twenty-point lead, and we weren't taking in enough money to close the gap.

Reid's team might not need us anyway because his campaign was effective at exploiting a soft-money loophole, and that worried me. As a candidate in a federal election, Reid could accept unlimited amounts of soft money. "Hard money" referred to contributions used to support a candidate's campaign—to run ads that said "Vote for Me!," to pay staff, to print yard signs. Soft money could not be used to support a candidate directly. Instead, it had to go to "party-building activities" or "issue advocacy," such as generic advertising around policies, like lower taxes or clean energy.

Legally, federal candidates couldn't even touch a soft-money check, though in the '90s they all had soft money accounts. Fundraisers, however, weren't regulated. So a candidate could go to lunch with a donor, who'd hand over a $5,000 hard-money check for the candidate's campaign account. Then the candidate would basically close his eyes as the donor handed the candidate's fundraiser a much larger one for the soft-money account. It was back-asswards but somehow made federal regulators feel good about themselves. But they were really just giving candidates a legal roadmap to accepting unlimited donations.

"Party-building activities" were rarely on the mind of any senator or member of Congress. So, candidates would advertise a two-for-one deal. The candidate's campaign would transfer, say, $100,000 from a soft-money account to, for example, an out-of-state party, like the California Democratic Party. This organization would transfer $50,000 in hard money back to, say, the Nevada Democratic Party, which would then run TV ads directly in support of the candidate. And since there were no limits on hard-money transfers between parties, it was all perfectly legal.

In other words, the Federal Election Commission was forcing more hard money into the system. With its wink-wink feel-good regulations, federal candidates had to double their fundraising efforts. In 2002, the McCain-Feingold reforms would eliminate soft money given to the parties by putting a cap on donations directly to party committees. This would just force money outside the system by encouraging billionaire donors to find new ways—527 organizations, then super-PACs—to go around the parties, as we'll get to in the coming chapters. Is any of it really an improvement over G. Gordon Liddy's Watergate envelope stuffed with cash?

MONICA LEWINSKY'S BLUE DRESS had stoked fear in the Democratic Party. Bill Clinton was dragging down the Democratic brand, and the Reid camp had begun a nonstop whisper campaign to keep the president away from Las Vegas. I wanted Clinton—he might have been wounded, but he was still the President of the United States, and for Jan, the opportunity to raise money was the best of the best—that's an automatic one-million-dollar night. The Clinton team offered, and I begged Jan to accept. She wanted to. Two hours later after a few harsh and somewhat direct conversations between her and the senator and the senator's team, we had to reject the offer. The Clinton team understood and came back with a backup plan. They could send Al Gore for one event and Hillary Clinton for another. That's not too shabby of a consolation prize.

Hillary would come first for a "women for Jan" event at the Fashion City Mall Chinese Restaurant. That's how they roll in Vegas. At $1,000 a head, we sold out in a few hours. I would have loved to charge $10,000 a head and take in cash only, but with the first lady, we had to keep the books tight and aboveboard. It would not be a gangbuster grab-all with the president, but it would help a ton.

Al Gore visited next, another great opportunity. We only had ten days' notice, but I needed a plan to make sure this would bring in every dollar possible. I started upping the pressure in private. I made a list of everyone who had said no to Jan and told them they had to make a choice: Saying no to Jan in a tough race is one thing, but would they say no to an opportunity to be in the same room with the next president? Plus, this wasn't about Jan or Kenny Guinn, it was about showing Al Gore that Vegas appreciated a high-profile visit. And that was an evolution in itself. Back in the '50s and '60s, an entire city would get a makeover when Eisenhower or Kennedy would show up for a speech. Now leaders just showed up to raise money.

We went to work, working every single donor in Las Vegas who could afford $1,000 or more. Jan made calls, her friends made calls, we went after it all. We absolutely packed the ballroom at the Stardust Hotel. Packed. You could not find an empty seat.

Oddly enough, I was supposed to hate Gore with a passion. Something had happened during the 1988 presidential campaign when Dick Gephardt and Al Gore were both candidates, and they had essentially not spoken since. I never knew the details, but when Clinton picked Gore as his running mate, Gephardt staffers' anger was intense. It continued through my years working for Gephardt.

Even though I had given up on Gephardt's future, I still liked the man. So I did what any loyal soldier would do. I put Rick Rizzolo, that strip club business leader and cash contributor, at the front of the ballroom with all his friends, at the main table, right next to Gore. And I snapped away with my disposable camera. I probably took a hundred pictures of Gore shaking hands with the Vegas's gambling kings and strip club owners. I appreciated the help Al Gore was giving to Jan, but I was going to make sure he was tagged with the strip club emperor of Las Vegas in case I needed it.

Between the first lady and vice president, we'd raised over a million dollars in just ten days. We couldn't keep that pace up, but it was a hell of a start. We started to spend a decent amount on TV and in direct mail, and the campaign was coming alive. As we raised money, we bought ads, and our visibility increased. As voters heard from us, the polls started to go our way. And when it looked like we might have a chance, donors started giving us a second look.

That twenty-point lead was now damn near single digits. Kenny Guinn's camp was starting to panic. The calls flooded in from the big donors, casino executives, all kicking the tires of Jan's campaign. Could she really win? And if she could win, could they hedge their bets against all the money they'd given to Kenny? It was fun to be on this end, and it was satisfying to know that the "battle stations" over the past five or six weeks had worked. We had made something out of the shambles of that summer.

We needed more. We needed $500,000 for the last ten-day TV buy. If we could buy over forty-five hundred points on TV, it just might close the gap. Vegas was a relatively cheap market and half a million bucks would go a long way, but we wanted to saturate the market by buying every slot we could.

34

BY THE END OF THE SUMMER OF 1998, IT LOOKED LIKE JAN MIGHT actually have a small, but definite, chance. She had a few more Rick Rizzolos up her sleeve, including Teddy Binion of the Binions casino fortune. He had been the highly visible manager of Binion's Horseshoe Casino, which he ran along with his siblings, Jack and Becky. Together with their dad, Benny, they'd started the World Series of Poker, a tournament Teddy ran himself. Their casino was one of my favorites, if only because every fifteen minutes they'd make a PA announcement that a call was holding on line one for Benny . . . who'd been dead for years.

Jan had already received $5,000 from Jack Binion and $10,000 from the Horseshoe. Teddy, round-faced with what was left of gray hair, was no longer speaking to his siblings; he'd become the black sheep of a family that embraced the American dream. They had come from nothing and were filthy rich. But with money came trouble. Ted's easy access to drugs proved too tempting in the middle of a twenty-four-hour-a-day Vegas party. He had struggled with addiction for years, heroin specifically, and once shaved every hair off his body to avoid a hair-based drug test. He was arrested in 1986 on trafficking charges and rumored to be connected to organized crime. I'd only meet him the once, but I admired and appreciated his struggles. If I'd had rich parents, I would have lived his kind of life.

By 1998, he had pushed the Nevada Gaming Commission too far. Thanks to his drug problems and association with mobster Herbie Blitzstein, the commission stripped him of his gambling license and banned him from even entering the Horseshoe, which suited his family just fine. Because Ted couldn't enter his own casino, he asked Sandy Murphy, his blonde bombshell ex–exotic dancer live-in girlfriend, and Rick Tabish, a trucking contractor, to inventory and remove millions of dollars' worth of silver bars hidden in the casino's basement. Rick's company moved them out to an underground vault Binion built near his desert ranch in Pahrump.[1]

JAN CALLED TEDDY, and it was clear that they had been friends for years. Their relationship wasn't based on political donations; they'd bonded because of who they were and what Teddy had gone through. Teddy invited her over to stop by his house in the city at 3 pm and have a few glasses of wine. He would donate $40,000, in cash. We were so much closer to that last TV buy. Later the *Las Vegas Tribune* reported that there had been speculation that Jan had promised to reinstate Ted's gaming license if she won, but I wasn't aware of that deal.

Over the next forty-eight hours I would not sleep, convinced that I was about to die or end up in jail. At 3 pm, Teddy handed over the cash, Jan gave it to me, and I put it in the trunk of my Saturn. I headed back to the office, about an hour drive through traffic. I walked into the office and everybody was huddled around the TV. They turned to look at me. Every single one of them was stone-faced. A few women cried.

Breaking news: Teddy Binion was dead, found wrapped in a sleeping bag in front of his TV. The news speculated a suicide/overdose . . . or murder.

Look, fundraising is not the most honest profession. I might have done some pretty questionable deeds in my political life, but murder is definitely not on my list of sins. Anyway, I liked taking care of good donors, and this guy was great. He just gave $40,000! I would never murder a *good* donor. Plus, Binion's money had brought us within $200,000 of our goal, a hell of a load in a very short time.

Questions raced: How could this happen? And within an hour? What if Jan or I got caught up in the investigation? We'd lose by seventy points if she was implicated in the slightest. What if Teddy's killers thought Jan witnessed it . . . or maybe me? Was there a hit out on one of us? Both? And what the fuck were we going to do with the forty grand Binion had just forked over? What exactly had we seen?

I smoked a full pack of cigs. My heart pounded, but I didn't completely understand why or how I was still breathing. Ted Binion, God rest his soul, was dead, but my political career was becoming more exciting every day. Never once had a fundraising call to a DC lobbyist resulted in death. Susan McCue and I needed to blow off some steam, so we went and got drunk as shit. We took my Saturn and drunk-drove all around Vegas. I couldn't tell you why we had coconuts in the back of the car. She took all four of them and tossed them out the sunroof, trying to hit other cars as we drove down Flamingo Avenue. She missed. All of them.

I decided to never mention that Jan was anywhere near Teddy's house that day, at least until the election. We had come so far in making the campaign close, I couldn't let a front-page story kill our momentum. I made an executive decision: I'd conceal Binion's money. Since it was cash, I would just declare the money under other folks' names. Standard practice.

I decided to declare that we'd received the legal limit, $10,000, from Ted on September 15, two days before his death. Long after the campaign, Jan told the press that Binion had given her $40,000, all but $1,500 in cash. She'd later say that Ted told her that $10,000 of the $40,000 was from him, $10,000 was from his son Damien, $10,000 was from his daughter Bonnie, and $10,000 was from his girlfriend, Sandy.[2]

Sure, we put Ted's donation on the fifteenth, before he died, but waited until September 25 to declare the others.[3] And even though his kids couldn't vote, that didn't mean they couldn't give to our campaign!

That was that. Except that I was not sure about how Teddy died. Was it a mob hit? I let my imagination run wild with scenes from *Goodfellas*. I did not want to end up in Joe Pesci's trunk.

The night of his death, I grabbed a case of beer, a carton of cigs, and went home to the Golden Nugget. I got into the room, put the news on, moved the love seat against the door . . . if anybody was going to come in the room, I had them blocked. I turned the lights off and sat in the bathtub with my case of Budweiser. To be clear, I wasn't taking a bath, I was hiding in the tub. It must have been the safest place—if the tub in *Lethal Weapon 2* could protect Riggs and Murtaugh from a bomb under the toilet, maybe mine would at least deflect a bullet? I unplugged the phone, turned off my cell, and settled in for a night of safety in the bath.

At 10:30 pm, I'd been in the tub for over three hours and had crushed about half the case of beer. Then: BANG BANG BANG BANG BANG . . . BANG BANG BANG BANG BANG. Somebody was pulverizing my door. Nonstop. BANG BANG BANG BANG, double-fisted drum rolls. I tried to slink lower in the tub, not easy when you're my height, and hoped the love seat would hold. They got me. This is it. My last moments on earth would be spent in a Golden Nugget bathtub with crushed beer cans scattered across my faux Venetian tile and acrylic bearskin rug.

The pounding carried on for a solid three or four minutes, though it seemed forever. I sat there and half drunkenly whispered to myself, "It's been a great ride and if it's my time, then it's my time." The banging stopped as quickly as it started, but I wasn't convinced my hit man had left. I stayed in the tub for another seven brutal hours. I finished six or seven more beers, convinced that tying on a strong buzz was the only way I was going to "sleep" at all that night. What if the door knocker set up camp and was just waiting outside my room?

Around 7 am, the couple in the next room headed out, and I didn't hear any gunfire. Perhaps my hit man took off? I showered in my bed, got dressed, and tried to pull myself together. I ran through mob movie scenarios. My Saturn was in the valet lot, little chance of a car bomb. What would Ray Liotta do? I grabbed a towel and moved the love seat away from the door. I cracked it open and tossed out the towel. If the hit man was going to shoot me, he would shoot at the first thing he saw, the towel. It floated to the floor. I got on my knees, not to pray, but so I could peer around the corner. Nothing, nobody in the hallway. I was safe! For now.

My phone had eight voicemails. Did mob hit men leave messages? I was intrigued. Every single one was from Paul Henry, advisor to Senator Reid who'd asked me to get involved in his little fake drug bust. Can you believe that it somehow slipped my mind that Paul and I had tickets to the 11 pm all-nude review at the Riviera? He couldn't get hold of me, so he figured I must have passed out in my room and came to find me.

I needed a change of scenery, so I moved out of the Golden Nugget and into an apartment a donor had lent Susan and me.

35

WITH THE HELP OF DEAD TED, WE HAD RAISED $300,000 OF THE last $500,000, but time was up. We had to place the ad buy or we would lose that air time over the last two weeks. The pressure from Senator Reid's staff had restarted. They needed Jan to make the campaign even closer if he was going to win.

At that point, I figured Reid would owe Jan, a lot. She had made the campaign competitive, she was no longer dragging him down but was unquestionably building excitement among women voters, just like Reid wanted. So I asked Jan to lend the campaign over $200,000 for the TV ad buy and other expenses. I could not lie to her. I told her that at best she was still a five-to-one shot of winning, but that I was sure that Senator Reid would help her raise money after the campaign to pay off the debt, win or lose.

Jan was not happy. She was in a bind and faced a real risky move. Don't make the loan, save $200,000, and have almost no shot at winning. Make the loan, still lose, and hope to raise it back after the campaign. (That's a very difficult prospect if you come up short. How many donors want to give money to a failed candidate?) Or make the loan, win, and easily raise it back.

In tears by the end of the conversation, she told me to make sure Senator Reid appreciated it, and we hoped for the best. I could not imagine the ability to write a $200,000 check on the spot. She did. And we purchased the air time.

In the end, we lost, 51 to 42 percent. It was a respectable nine-point loss, not bad for a late start and against a well-funded competitor. Harry Reid beat John Ensign to retain his Senate seat, however . . . by 428 votes. I'm sure they were all women.

Ted Binion's murder became a national case in 1998–99. Sandy Murphy and Rick Tabish, Ted's girlfriend and his vault builder, respectively, were arrested as Rick dug up the silver bars from Ted's vault in the desert. They were charged with Ted's murder too, when prosecutors alleged that they forced Ted to swallow massive amounts of Xanax and black tar heroin. Swallowing drugs like that is known as "chasing the dragon." Their lawyers got a retrial in 2003 and Sandy and Rick were later acquitted of murder, though convicted of larceny and burglary. After Jan stated to the press that she'd received $40,000 from Binion, she testified to the same effect at the retrial, adding that Binion seemed optimistic even though he had recently lost his gaming license.[1] But no one has ever asked where I was at 2:59 pm.

36

LARRY WERNER, REID'S CAMPAIGN MANAGER WHO MIGHT HAVE wound up with a baggie of blow in his backseat, should have gotten a ton more credit for helping Senator Reid get reelected by 428 votes. But he was out of a job within minutes of the final count. As a weird going-away party, he invited us all over to his place for movie night. We watched *Wag the Dog;* how creepy is that? The Saturday after the election, Susan McCue and I cleared out the apartment we'd been sharing on Flamingo Avenue, and I took a red-eye that night back to Washington. Susan was on her way to be Senator Reid's chief of staff, I was heading back to DC with no clear purpose.

I had made enough money off the Jones campaign that I could screw around until the next one popped up. I still had a consulting contract with the Gephardt team, but I was finished with them: It was clear to me that the likes of Steve Elmendorf and Noah Mamet didn't understand what

Gephardt really stood for and would mismanage his career. But I was lucky, because Gephardt was so powerful, and since I helped him raise so much, I could always find work as a fundraiser. So I was on my way back to DC. Most of the new fundraising consultant class back then was not so lucky—they'd raise money for six or seven months during the campaign, then be unemployed immediately following the election. In 1998, fundraisers were starting to create more opportunities for themselves, expanding their industry. If they pushed candidates to raise more money earlier in the campaign, fundraisers could create jobs for themselves. It's one of the key reasons why campaigns today never seem to end.

I did have five hours before my flight. So I went to my favorite casino, the Las Vegas Hilton, with five hundred bucks. The Hilton had donated $5,000 to Jan, so I was happy to return the favor. My goal was to make that last for four hours of great entertainment before heading to the airport. I sat down at the $25 minimum double-deck blackjack table. Some of my regular gambling buddies told me you could count cards playing double-deck. Rain Man, I am not. I had no clue how to count cards but what the hell, I'd give it a shot. All I wanted was $500 in free cocktails.

A FUNNY THING HAPPENED with my little experiment. I could not lose. I won hand after hand after hand after hand. Then I won some more. And again. Every hand . . . I won. I built up a stack of $1,000 casino chips, and that was just in the first thirty minutes. A smart person would take the ten grand or so sitting in front of him and walk away. I stayed. I loved gambling, and I loved winning. I'd stop to take a piss, or get a drink, and I'd sit back down and win again . . . and again.

In hour two, I had a pile of $5,000 chips, little pink pieces of pure plastic pleasure. And I had lots of them. The pit boss roped off the table so I could play in private, like I was some celebrity. I embraced it. I was a winner!

In the middle of my run, Susan stopped by to wish me a good flight. She couldn't believe it. She had a few drinks and enjoyed the ride. By this time I was playing two hands at once, each with either a $5,000 or $10,000 bet. Susan would proclaim for the masses to hear, "Do you know how many pairs of shoes you could buy with that chip!?!?!?!" and hold up one of my pink disks of glory.

By hour four, it was clear I wouldn't make my red-eye back to DC. I had close to $300,000 in front of me. Stacks of chips. Chips, chips, chips, chips, chips. Casino bosses were trying to figure out how I was cheating. A cheering audience of about a hundred people I didn't know gathered around. They wanted me to take the casino for all it was worth. Power, money, excitement. All the things I loved and hated about politics were right in front of me, in chip form. All that money could be a way out, a means to a different end in my life: Save a little, invest a little, and just take some time to figure out how I'd get out of politics for good.

I rode it out for two more hours and fell back to earth after hitting a few snags . . . but not too bad. Susan left, too nervous and disgusted when I lost $30,000 on one hand. That's gambling, babe! But I walked away from the table after six hours with $165,000 in cash from that $500 beginning. I was in love with Vegas.

I made a choice that night: Fly back to DC, pack up my Jeep Cherokee, and move to Las Vegas. If I could win that much in one night of blackjack, imagine what I could do every night! What a simple game!

I got back to Washington, went into Gephardt's office, and announced I was ending my consulting gig. I was done with shitty DC political fundraising, and I was about as happy as I could be. Nothing had ever felt like that surreal moment—my family never had much money, and now I could do just about anything I wanted. That little run of blackjack gave me the chance to get away from DC forever. Let the new generation of young fundraisers suffer; it was a new show and fundraising was the center of politics. I wanted nothing to do with it.

It took me one day to pack, and I was on Route 40 for the cross-country drive. I was ready for a new chapter in life.

37

BE CAREFUL WHAT YOU WISH FOR.

It was December and I wanted to enjoy the spoils of my gambling victory with my friends. I invited about fifteen out from DC—and paid for about half of them—to welcome the New Year in style. I booked the penthouse suite at the Las Vegas Hilton and had a day or so to kill until they started showing up.

Big-time gamblers have big-time appetites, so the first morning in the penthouse, I ordered the breakfast menu. The entire breakfast menu: six different kinds of pancakes, French toast, oatmeal, bacon, sausage (links and patties) and Spam. I got every kind of egg you could imagine: the Benedict special, scrambled eggs, poached eggs, sunny-side up, sunny-side down, hard boiled, soft boiled, medium boiled. Who cares, I wanted it all. Fruit Loops, Frosted Flakes, Cheerios, Honey Nut Cheerios, Raisin Bran, granola . . . and the fruit plate. It came with a free carafe of coffee, and the room service waiter was thoroughly confused when he asked how many mugs I wanted with it and I responded, "Just one."

New Year's was ridiculous. We gambled, we limoed all over town, we partied, we drank. A lot. Things got pretty hazy. Olivia Newton John was playing New Year's Eve at the Hilton, and I got us front-row seats. After the show, we headed back up to my penthouse and the rager carried on. At one point, Sir Richard Branson walked in . . . or maybe it was the guy Olivia Newton John was dating? Who the fuck knew—they kind of looked the same, and I was in no condition to tell them apart. And I didn't care, and I paid for everything. It wasn't quite like I forgot I'd met Mike Tyson and the tiger in *The Hangover,* but it was one hell of a week.

After the holidays, I moved into the Desert Inn Country Club Towers, on the eighth floor overlooking the Strip. It was my *Jeffersons* moment, I was moving up to the East Side, and now I definitely had a deluxe apartment in the sky! This was it, just a little different from Maryland's middle-class suburbs where I'd been raised. I decked out my place with over $15,000 in furniture and another couple grand on electronics and settled in for my new life as the world's greatest blackjack player.

I had spent the first six years of my career raising money from rich people around the country, and now I thought I was one. My first morning at the Desert Inn, I sauntered into my living room in my tightie whities. Floor-to-ceiling windows overlooked my new empire. It was just about the biggest apartment I'd ever been in.

That night I hit the tables and got up over six figures again, but fell back to earth as quickly as I got up. Oh well, I figured it was a minor bump in the road. Then I got into a big fight with Bubba Grimes, my business partner. I'd called him from DC the week before New Year's and told him to put ten grand on the Broncos. Sure enough, they covered, and Bubba just got around to telling me he forgot to make the bet. I missed out on a $10,000 payday.

As a highly paid political consultant and blackjack king, I had to keep up my image. I wore a suit—everywhere—to make sure people knew how important I was. I tipped valets and bellboys hundreds of dollars just because I could. I threw around money at strip clubs because I wanted to spread the wealth.

By January 1999, I had spent over $150,000 of my winnings. All my friends had left, and as I sat on my balcony with a bottle of Jack Daniel's, I stared into my Vegas kingdom and wondered what the fuck I was doing with my life. Two months, and almost all my money was gone. My new lifestyle was unsustainable, and I'd blown the chance to do something productive with my cash. Oh well.

38

MY LIFE WAS BECOMING INSANE. IT WAS TIME TO FIND A JOB, AT least to supplement my blackjack career for a few months. Jan Jones had decided not to run for reelection as mayor in 1999, so the field was wide open with the election six months away. I decided to go work for one of the candidates. By the time the last vote was counted in June, I would be escorted out of Nevada across the Hoover Dam by my business partner, Bubba Grimes. Bubba was at times this lovable, big-boned man who looked like a former NFL lineman. And at times Bubba was a ruthless money grabber.

Would you believe Vegas politics, not gambling, beat me? Bubba was a political hanger-on, that guy who offered very little but put the time in so he could take credit for anything good that might occur: Say a big donor calls and wants to give. Bubba would just be around and could chime in, "I talked to him last week, I knew he was going to give." Every campaign has one.

The illustrious Grimes-Lewis consulting firm hung out its shingle. Bubba and I decided we'd split up and work for the two strongest candidates in the mayor's race. If we played our cards right and at least one of our horses won, we would be sitting pretty, controlling access to the new mayor. In the meantime, we scored a few contracts to kick things off.

Jay Bingham was the Mormon choice and early front-runner, a former member of the city council, family values–type father of five. He was an ex-fireman and ex-rodeo rider.

Mark Fine was a clueless real estate magnate who'd been developing most of Vegas as the economy soared. We met to see if I could work for him, and I wasn't impressed. He was that typical rich-guy candidate, the kind who started cropping up more in more in politics with the mentality that "I am successful at business, I can fund my campaign if I want to (or have to), and I can run my campaign my way, like my business." Fine gave his campaign $100,000 to get it off the ground.

Then there was mob attorney Oscar Goodman. Goodman represented many notorious organized crime bosses in Vegas, was charismatic as hell, and was ready to talk to anyone about anything. It was clear Goodman was a natural campaigner with plenty of tie-ins to people who'd feel safer if he was mayor and would probably give him plenty of campaign cash along the way. But most important, Goodman cut his campaign a $140,000 check straight out of the shoot.

Arnie Adamsen, a long-serving and pretty boring city council member, was the final candidate. He was probably best known for leading the Sister City program, which meant he took a lot of trips to Asia to promote Vegas to rich Asian tourists. I liked Adamsen's background—at least he was a real middle-class guy trying to work his way up through the political system. Arnie had come from nothing, an Iowa grain farming family that had lost everything in the Depression. His father was a drunk and took off early. His mother, also an alcoholic, abandoned him and his five siblings to their grandmother. Then he ended up in an orphanage. He moved to Vegas, became a craps dealer, then a loan shark. He got involved in local politics leading a protest against rising energy costs. Not a penny of his own money went into his campaign war chest.[1]

Fine and Goodman were part of an expanding breed on the new frontier of big-money politics—rich, self-funding candidates who run for office simply because they have money, need a new challenge, and think they have a right to the job. *I succeeded in business, why not give politics a shot?* It doesn't matter how ridiculous a candidate's background or platform, a few of their own dollars give them a huge leg up.

Three things about self-funders. First, early money attracts more money. Self-funders can use the first check to build an image of themselves as a serious candidate . . . and it shows other donors that their investment in you isn't a waste. Second, self-funders raise the price of a campaign. If you're a local prosecutor or member of the city council, you might steer clear of a race if the barrier to get in requires spending hours and hours to match a check the other candidate can write in two seconds. Third, self-funders often make shitty candidates and shitty officials. The I-have-money argument rarely plays well in American elections, since voters are always looking for the candidate they can have a beer with. Then ask yourself whether you'd rather have your city managed by a responsible five-term member of the city council or a lawyer from the mob. Fortunately, just having money doesn't guarantee you'll win.

Jan nudged me toward Arnie. He was the best of a bad lot, and I had to work for one of these guys to pull in a paycheck. I met with Arnie for a short get-to-know-you meeting and he offered me the job on the spot. I accepted. At least I could respect his tough childhood. I was now his campaign manager.

Let me be direct. I had worked for Senator Tom Harkin, Representative Dick Gephardt, hundreds of members of Congress, and Jan Jones. All smart, ambitious people. And now I was working for Arnie Adamsen, a nice guy but someone who'd never be mistaken as a member of MENSA . . . hell, I am not even sure he could spell MENSA. Arnie was more fit to be an extra on *The Beverly Hillbillies*.

Jay Bingham—the Mormon family-values candidate—had a solid lead in the early polls, registering somewhere in the high thirties. Arnie floated around the mid-teens. As a long-serving member of the council, he was a known, dull quantity. Oscar was considered a joke and Fine was unknown, and both sat around 2 percent in those first surveys. Las Vegas holds nonpartisan elections, so if anyone broke 50 percent in the May 4 primary, that candidate would win outright. If nobody did, the top two would go to a runoff on June 9. My goal was to make the runoff.

Arnie had a few amateur staffers, nice old ladies from the glory Vegas days. It was January; we had time to get our act together. We just had to keep Bingham under 50 percent and avoid the perception that he was going to run away with the race.

That problem took care of itself, and fast. We woke up one day in the middle of March with a shock announcement in the *Las Vegas Review-Journal*.

Jay Bingham was dropping out. His spokesman said he had a heart condition and in the last few days his heart had been beating "extremely rapidly . . . and his physician advised him that running in the mayor's race is ill advised."[2]

Oh, but the rumor mill knew why his heart was beating so fast. A private eye had snapped some pictures of Bingham with a mistress several times a week. Once Bingham saw the photos, the family-values candidate agreed to quit.

OVERNIGHT WE HAD GONE from a distant second place to the leading candidate for mayor. A great feeling to be sure, but one that would last only a few days. We had no money, and we had to raise a ton quickly because Goodman and Fine had given so much to their own campaigns.

The race was on, and Goodman saw his opening and started making his moves. First, he hired Bubba, my business partner, as we had planned. Then he used his early money to turn himself into a serious candidate. He went up on TV first with lots of feel-good ads. As a mob lawyer who'd even had a cameo appearance as one in the movie *Casino,* he needed to build a nice, soft, personable image of himself as the common man's champion. First his four kids cut ads talking about how they, not millions of dollars in mob money, were Goodman's "real success story." Then every cop and fireman Goodman could find endorsed him on TV. Then his eighty-four-year-old grandmother told voters what a nice man Oscar was. His strategy worked; Goodman's early advertising blitz made you like him.

Meanwhile, we had no money, either to tell Arnie's story or to remind voters that Goodman was hardly the man he portrayed himself as. Initially broke, our campaign let Goodman build his story with several weeks of television all to himself. Goodman won the race in those first weeks. That doesn't mean we weren't trying, we were just late.

BEFORE THE RACE SLIPPED too far out of my hands, I decided to take a few stabs at some rather specialized constituent outreach. For that, I went back to my friend, strip club king Rick Rizzolo. He'd forked over $50,000 in cash to Jan the year before, and of course I just wanted to hang out at his joint again. He told me to swing by the Crazy Horse Too.

Convinced the FBI had bugged his place, I went through the club to the door with the eye slit, but I didn't have to wait this time because they knew Lindsay was not a woman. As I approached Rick in his office, I looked around and thought how easy it would be for the feds to have hidden microphones. So as the brilliant criminal mastermind I was, I suggested it was better to step out the back door into the alley to discuss our business. I felt extremely smart, I was outdoing the feds in my fundraising career.

We stood outside his back door in the bright sun on a hot day in the valley, me in my suit, Rick in gym clothes. I looked up and down the alley to see if two G-men might be watching us. I was protecting myself, Rick, and my candidate.

"Rick, you're a great citizen of Las Vegas. It's important to our future that Arnie is elected mayor. I hate to ask you, Rick, but, man, I need twenty-five grand. Cash. Today. We're going to win."

Rick looked up at the glaring sun, trying to not make eye contact for about ten seconds, then looked at me. Rick gave an answer no political fundraiser ever wants to hear: "Let me think about it and get back to you." As I fundraiser, I would have preferred a simple no.

I felt less smart than I did five minutes before. Not only had I not gotten the cash I needed, now I may have been recorded by the feds asking for an illegally large contribution. A double whack to my pride. Defeated, I went back to the campaign office and pulled Arnie aside. I lowered my number.

"Arnie, we need fifteen thousand in cash within the next twenty-four hours."

I don't know where he went or what he did, but the next day Arnie showed up with $15,000 for me. He probably took it out of his bank account. It didn't matter; now I was ready to be the kingmaker of Las Vegas.

In downtown Vegas, there were only four African American Baptist churches. I set up appointments with each. I met the first pastor, who invited me back to his office. He sat behind his desk, and I was blunt.

"Thank you for taking the time to meet with me, your honor." Is that how I should address him? Church wasn't really my thing. "I am running the political campaign of City Councilman Arnie Adamsen, and Councilman Adamsen wants to be mayor of this city. I just know, your honor, Councilman Adamsen is a good man and will be a great mayor. We'd like your blessing for his campaign."

"Arnie is a good man," he responded. "We like Arnie."

His honor, who could speak for hours from the pulpit on Sunday mornings, had little to say to an East Coast, non-churchgoing political hack. I didn't know what to say next; I knew nothing about his congregation. I could have brought up baseball or food, but God spoke to me, and I brought up the weather.

"Ooh, it's a hot one."

I removed from my suit coat jacket fifty $100 bills and slid it across his desk. I said, "Praise the Lord!" as I did, thinking it was the most natural thing I could come up with. I asked him to pray with his congregation for Arnie that Sunday. He agreed.

As he escorted me out of the church, there were about twenty-five women in the pews. His honor stopped and told them that I was working for Arnie. The women stood up and blessed me, telling me that the Lord would be with me and Arnie on election day. I felt the power of the moment and wanted to dance. I threw my arms in the air, like the wave at a sporting event, and praised Arnie myself.

I went around and had basically the same conversation three more times that day. But since I only had $15,000 on me, I had to lower the token of my appreciation down to $2,500 for the last two.

The second pastor invited me to a Wednesday night service. He hugged me when I arrived and personally escorted me down to the front pew. The place was bursting with folks. He started his sermon off slowly and gradually built to the crescendo.

"We all know it's tough times in Las Vegas right now," he intoned, shaking his head back and forth.

"Amen! Uh-huh!" the masses responded.

"And we have an important election coming up here in this city. . . . We need to choose a leader who is going to represent our needs, and do what our community needs a mayor to do!"

"I know that's right," came a small old lady's agreement from the back.

"Now," he continued, "I can't tell you how to vote. I'm just not going to do that from up here, that'd be breaking the law. But we can pray, certainly, for our brother, Las Vegas Councilman Arnie Adamsen. I know Councilman Adamsen to be a good and decent man. A churchgoer. A family man. A man who cares about our community, a man who will fight for this city, and this church."

"Mmmm-hummmm. Amen."

"So let us extend our hands up to the Lord our God and pray for Councilman Adamsen, that Jesus keeps him healthy and happy throughout this campaign, and that he continues to work for the needs of our community. Can I get an AMEN?"

Case closed.

39

WE GOT SOME HIGH-QUALITY ENDORSEMENTS FROM THE POLICE and fire unions. The all-important Culinary Union—which represents the casino workers and could pledge its super-charged grassroots network—endorsed Arnie next.

Arnie had put in his years on the city council and had a great local net-work of donors. He called donors like he was owed. He was a pure animal. Either he had Martin Frost blood in him or he wanted to avoid actually talking to voters. He called all day, every day . . . and I just sat back and watched in amazement. I was focused on finding enough votes to ensure we'd get through to the runoff and maybe win outright with 50 percent in the first round. At the very least, I was putting together the winning coalition for the runoff.

I couldn't believe that Vegas voters would fall for Goodman's bullshit. This guy was bad news, not what the city needed heading into the twenty-first century. Of course, Arnie wasn't what Vegas needed either, but that didn't mean that I wouldn't try to sell Arnie to voters.

We started to raise some real money and began to close the financial gap with Oscar. We could finally run ads on TV. We started to expose who Good-man really was and fight the nice-guy image he'd built. But we'd gotten in so late that we needed a distraction, a way to open a new front on the battlefield. Arnie had to make the campaign's big debate about the future of the city, not about who Goodman was. What would Vegas be in ten years? I wanted Vegas to diversify its economy beyond casinos and strip clubs while subtly remind-ing voters that Goodman represented those kinds of shady clients. It was the simplest argument that I felt confident Arnie could grasp. And by "grasp" I mean remember his talking points. More ads went up. The direct mail went out, ads went on TV, and I was even quoted in the *New York Times*:

> Lindsay Lewis, who as manager for Mr. Adamsen's campaign has run advertisements recalling some of Mr. Goodman's unsavory mob clients, said, "The issue now for Las Vegas is diversification beyond casinos, and it's going to be harder to sell that to the outside world if we get pushed back 50 years to the old days."[1]

Mark Fine had run some ads but fell into a self-funder's trap: thinking his business success would work with voters. He had one of the worst, most nonsensical messages I've ever heard, summed up with, "I built houses and I will build Vegas." Clueless. I mean, really?

We were walking a very high tightrope. We needed Fine to stay viable and get 10 percent of the vote because he'd steal those votes from Oscar. That would keep Oscar under 50 percent so Arnie could get into the June runoff. But we couldn't let Fine get much more than 10 percent, because that would drive down Adamsen's numbers.

After about one week of running ads, we went out with a poll. The numbers actually came back better than expected: Oscar and Arnie were basically in a dead heat.[2] With a month to go, we clearly had a real chance. Another poll a few weeks later was less positive, but not terrible. Goodman stood at 36 percent, with Arnie and Fine both at 20 or 21 percent.[3] As I confidently told John L. Smith of the *Las Vegas Review-Journal* just before the primary:

"The race is ours to win," Adamsen's campaign manager, Lindsay Lewis, says. "We weren't sure how we could compete money-wise with two guys who could write checks. But we've done a great job."

We just had to keep Arnie on task, no flubs.

GOOD CAMPAIGN MANAGERS look at polling numbers very differently from the press or the average voter. It's not a horse race. The important numbers are way down in the weeds, where voters' preferences are broken down by gender, age, race, religion, location, ideology, and more. Political staffers read polls looking for very distinct cross-sections of voters, say, African American women under forty, to target with a variety of messages.

In the Las Vegas mayor's race of 1999, one of the unique cross tabs in the polling was that women had no clue how they'd vote. About 25 percent of all voters were undecided, normal for a local race a month out. But the number of undecided women voters was closer to 40 percent. That told me they didn't like the mob lawyer, but they weren't sold on Arnie either. It was time to turn on the charm.

Going through some of Arnie's votes on the city council, I found a gem. He had pushed for funding for an abused women's shelter downtown. It was pure gold that I'd use to make a pitch to undecided women voters— they should like the candidate who funds a women's shelter, right?

I pulled together an event with a few of the shelter's leaders and several women who'd tell moving, positive stories of their time there. This had to put undecided women in our corner. The women stood up at that podium and told stories that would put a lump in your throat, all of which ended with how Arnie's shelter had helped them through tough times. Arnie stood next to them, nodding in sympathy. It was the best political theater I had ever created.

After the women wrapped up, Arnie gave a quick speech and turned it over to the press for questions. Fucking reporters. Vegas was a cesspool of weekly rags, mixed in with professional journalists at the *Las Vegas Review-Journal* and *Las Vegas Sun*. Arnie got through the normal questions and kept the political theater humming along.

Then a reporter from one of the Las Vegas weekly rags raised his hand. To this day, I cringe thinking about what happened over the next four minutes. Yes, it took him four minutes to ask the question. Well, it wasn't really a question, more like a rambling statement that became our crushing moment. As the reporter droned on and on and on, I felt myself sliding to the back of the room trying to hide. I wished I was back in the bathtub at the Golden Nugget. The reporter's statement basically prodded Adamsen for a response to an accusation of sexual impropriety from some years ago.

What. The. Fuck. This was the first I'd heard of it, and the reporter never offered evidence to substantiate his claim. Every campaign manager asks their candidates to bare their souls in private, just so the campaign can defend itself against anything negative should the opponent use it against them. Arnie sure never mentioned a word to me about this. It was what you'd call a worst-case scenario.

I left and went to have a drink. A few drinks. I went with my gut and my gut told me to win. My political mind immediately cast back to the Bill and Hillary Clinton interview in 1992 on *60 Minutes* about Gennifer Flowers and how it saved his campaign.

That kind of response was too tame for this moment.

I frantically dialed every respectable reporter at the event and went into protect mode. *You have no proof, it's all made up. If you run the story we will sue you. And you won't have time to research the story just days before the election.* It worked. At least it worked insofar as the story never made a mainstream paper like the *Review-Journal* or the *Sun,* but the rumor mill had started.

It called for a response. And respond I did. As part of our opposition work on Goodman, we had identified a few over-the-top statements he had made on a local newsmaker talk show. Goodman had waxed about his opposition to Megan's Law, the statute that required a convicted sexual predator to notify neighbors when he moved into a new street. We focused on the following Goodman quote:

> Do you realize how tough it is for somebody who's getting out of prison
> to get back in society and become a productive citizen? . . . Let them
> become a part of the community. Don't brand them.[4]

Goodman claimed he was playing a role arguing issues on the show, and he didn't believe many of the things he said on it.[5] But whatever, this is politics. *Thanks, Oscar, I got you now.* I decided to use his position on Megan's Law to counterattack, insinuating that Goodman had relationships with children. I hoped it would muddy the waters in voters' minds, and they wouldn't know who, exactly, had the sex problem. You can debate about the merits, but Goodman opposed Megan's Law and that made him a "monster."

First, the campaign went up with an ad on TV highlighting his opposition to the law. Then the campaign put together a piece of mail, a simple piece that would tell all the voters of Las Vegas that Oscar Goodman was a "monster." We arranged a photo shoot with an old man with a child on either knee. We blurred out the old man's face. If you looked quickly you just might just happen to get the idea that Goodman was raping a kid. That was the cover. You had to open the piece of mail to read a few of the finer points about Goodman's opposition to Megan's Law, but that was not my goal. This was payback. This was war.

The campaign mailed it to over 150,000 households in Las Vegas. I think 148,000 of those people called the office the moment they opened it, and they were not calling to say *great piece!* They all called to complain. Joe Gelman, a political operative living in Vegas, wrote an opinion piece in the *Las Vegas Review-Journal* about my little stunt. Here's an excerpt:

I opened my mailbox the other day to find one of the most disturbing pieces of political mail that I have ever seen. This was definitely a new low for politics in Las Vegas, or anywhere else for that matter. . . . As a long-time political consultant from California . . . I have crafted many myself. But the political mailer I received recently at my Las Vegas home was so far over the top that it deserves to be exposed for what it is: a sick, perverted political assault that should be illegal.

When the brochure is opened, a large photo appears . . . The man is wrapping his arms around a little boy who is looking down innocently. The photo is clearly designed to imply sexual intent on the part of the man toward the little boy, but just in case the readers don't get it, a loud headline spells it out: "There are monsters among us."

The opposite page then goes on to strongly condemn candidate Oscar Goodman . . . for "welcoming" pedophiles and sex offenders into our community because he opposed Megan's law on a TV show a few years ago. The back page then returns to the smiling children with a strong message: "On May 4, vote as if your kids' lives depend on it." It was paid for by Friends for Arnie Adamsen. . . .

What is deeply disturbing to me is that Adamsen's political handlers thought that it was OK to use a real child in a photo session to subtly simulate sexual abuse. These political strategists actually conceived of the idea of putting a man and little boy together in a photo session to carefully stage a visual image that will suggest sexual misconduct of the most sinister kind.

It was perhaps the worst piece of mail ever sent in American political history. It backfired, fast. We dropped like a rock in the polls. Goodman didn't have to do anything. He just let us suffer and wallow in our self-inflicted pain. On election night of the primary, we got slaughtered. Oscar got 49.8 percent, just a couple hundred votes shy of winning the race outright in the primary. Arnie hit 29 percent, and Mark Fine scraped home at 16 percent.

I HIT ROCK BOTTOM. What had I done? Now, Goodman opposed Megan's Law on the record, and voters deserved to know it. What had I become? I would have done anything to trade places with the valet at the Mirage who made $140,000 a year and played golf constantly. I was desperately hoping the local election board would find a couple hundred more votes to push Goodman over 50 percent so I didn't have to run my pathetic, self-destructing campaign for another three weeks into the second round. I didn't want to do this anymore, it was too painful.

I handed Arnie his election-night speech after scraping through the primary. As he walked up to the podium, he opened his notes and looked confused and lost. All I had written was, "We have Oscar right where we want him." What else could he say?

We were done—we barely raised a single dime from that point on. Our donors knew it was over, and they didn't want to waste their money. Let's be honest: If you were a donor, would you want to help fund the next piece of pedophile mail? We didn't even have enough money to run a single TV ad between the primary and the second round. I trudged though the next few weeks. Goodman won the runoff easily, 65 to 35.

Want to know the kicker? Adamsen actually won the money race. We hauled in $665,000, more than Fine at $595,000 and Goodman with $571,000. Adamsen spent the most on TV ads, at $285,000, compared to Fine's $260,000 and Goodman's $248,000.[6] The lesson is that even with the most money, it wasn't the earliest money. You can outraise and outspend, but Oscar owned the airwaves for about three weeks in the beginning of the race because he cut himself a big check. No matter how much we raised, the voters were bombarded with images of nice-guy Oscar, and we spent a lot of money to fight to change that. But by that time, Oscar had defined the terms of the election, and we couldn't do much about it.

Goodman let me know he wasn't happy with my little stunt. Well, "wasn't happy" is really not the way to put it. He was absolutely furious. He sent Bubba Grimes, my business partner and his advisor, to let me know. Bubba had a few thoughts: It was likely a good idea for me to leave town, I had overstayed my welcome in Las Vegas. Sure seemed like a threat to me. Although I didn't really know what the threat implied, I thought back to my first dinner in Vegas with Mike and Paul. I had no wish to get busted on cocaine charges.

Not only was I getting kicked out of Las Vegas, my business partner was screwing me. Bubba and I had managed to put together a few contracts and had collected several thousand bucks. He informed me he'd be keeping all the money. I didn't exactly have a lot of leverage—so I didn't say anything.

I went back to the glorious Desert Inn Country Club and packed everything I could into my Jeep Cherokee. I was the blackjack king of Las Vegas six months ago, now I was dead broke, coasting out of town on fumes and failing brake pads, with my former business partner Bubba following me out to the Hoover Dam and across the state line. I could even see that handicapped tag hanging from his rearview mirror in the dark.

40

THE DRIVE ALONG INTERSTATE 40 FROM VEGAS BACK TO DC SNAKES through some of the most fascinating territory in the country. The scenery is unreal, and the towns dotting the highway scream classic Americana. The trip gave me a few days to roll the windows down, smoke cigarette after cigarette, and take stock of my life and my career. Was Vegas my Alamo?

The Big Texan Steak Ranch sits along I-40 in Amarillo, Texas, but billboards start advertising it every couple miles along the highway back in Arizona. At first, they're confusing as hell, completely random. But then I realized that the billboards are slowly telling a story and advertising a free 72-ounce steak (if you can eat it within the hour). They go on for miles and miles, hours away from the place. If you're driving by yourself and thinking about life, it's a welcome distraction. When I pulled into Amarillo, I couldn't wait to stop.

The Big Texan Steak Ranch has a motel, where I stayed for the night. The place was run by a nice family who'd built their restaurant and hotel business from the ground up. I started working in politics for these folks. I wanted to engage them, to get them involved in the democratic process, and help them understand that they had a voice in their government too. I wanted to give them a seat at the table, one that was quickly filling up with rich donors, lobbyists, and special interest groups. Their work seemed so much more honest than mine. I briefly considered applying for a job. I'd already lived in Section 8 housing in Baltimore during my first year of college, so working at the Big Texan in Amarillo would be cake!

Instead, I was headed back to DC with my tail between my legs. Vegas should have been my escape from Washington, a place where I could have seized the opportunity to achieve real political change at the local level, or at least become the king of double-deck blackjack. But here I drove, in a Jeep Cherokee whose reverse gear didn't work, practically broke. How far I'd fallen. My dad was now so worried about me that he Western Unioned me a hundred bucks, just in case I needed gas.

I HATED RAISING MONEY, I crossed the line with Oscar Goodman, I was disillusioned with politics, and I was dying to try something else . . . *anything*. But I didn't have any other marketable skills. So I shuffled along as a fundraiser, trying to put on a happy face on what was fast becoming a career I couldn't escape from.

Political fundraising was becoming a self-sustaining industry. In the early 1990s, a handful of fundraisers were happy just to be on staff somewhere, either at the Democratic National Committee or in a presidential race. But we began to spread ourselves throughout the country, finding paydays in DC with new candidates and elected officials who weren't yet aware that they needed us, promising candidate after candidate that money was the only path to victory.

It was a huge scam. A fundraiser's pitch is simple: raise more money to win, and every minute a candidate wasn't raising was one that the competition definitely was. Candidates raised money to get their message out, but they were also raising money to make sure their fundraiser got paid.

While fundraisers were spreading themselves throughout the country, even established figures who didn't need the money were raising anyway. Political money was no longer a means to an end, it had become the end itself. The 1999–2000 cycle was just past the tipping point of when fundraising to win became fundraising for show. Fundraisers were pushing candidates to raise more, and elected officials were pushing fundraisers. The total amount of money raised was skyrocketing, and an infant industry was learning how to walk.

SENATOR KENT CONRAD, a Democrat from North Dakota with a seat on the powerful Budget and Banking & Finance Committees, hired me to be his finance director in June of 1999 after I returned from Vegas. Gephardt was a renowned money man in the party, and Conrad clearly thought that with me he was purchasing a little piece of Gephardt's success. Before he was a senator, Kent Conrad was North Dakota's tax commissioner, and that made him a numbers guy, an accountant. He lacked any sort of common touch with regular people trying to make a decent living, like those motel workers in Amarillo. He would be the perfect guy to staff a senator, but I wasn't terribly proud to call him an elected official from my party.

I did not know him from a hole in the wall, and it was quickly apparent that ours was a mismarriage of needs: I needed a paycheck and he wanted to raise money he didn't need.

The difference between a guy like Dick Gephardt and a guy like Kent Conrad was clear. Gephardt was a real middle-class champion. The money I'd raised for him actually meant something, at least at first. Sure, we raised more than he needed, but Dick used it for a purpose: He spread the wealth to other campaigns to solidify his position in leadership, but we were also really helping Democratic candidates run for Congress. That helped the party, and—in my mind anyway—had been a forgivable sin along the way to changing the world. But Kent Conrad raised money just to raise money. It was about him and only him. It had no effect on other candidates or a greater cause. Add up more numbers, a means to an end.

Working for Kent Conrad was a death sentence. My little basement office on C Street in Capitol Hill even felt like a tomb. Conrad was a barometer of what politics was becoming: Now C Street was lined with these fundraising coffins because virtually every Democratic senator had a full-time fundraiser working somewhere on the block.

At first, I thought it would be simple. As a member of the Senate's Budget and Banking & Finance Committees, Conrad had influence on every major piece of financial legislation that moved through Congress: banking, taxes, defense, real estate, healthcare, you name it. His position allowed him to raise a lot of money, easily, from all the lobbying groups that wanted connections to his committees. I understood what I was getting into, but I accepted my fate and just hoped for a 9-to-5 normal routine. He fired me ten months later.

Everything started off well enough. We came up with a $2 million budget. Two million bucks would scare away any serious opponent, in either the primary or the general election. That was part of the new game: Reelection is easier without a serious challenger. Conrad was right, of course, and reminded me of Kenny Guinn, who'd all but sewn up the race for Nevada governor a year in advance. The fear of having to raise $2 million just to be on par with an incumbent senator was enough to scare off many good people. But is spending all your time raising money to keep out potential challengers really what democracy is about?

Senator Conrad was spending too much time raising way too much money, given his historically weak competition. He was first elected to the Senate in 1986 in a tight race and then declined to run in the general election of 1992. But then Senator Quentin Burdick passed away and Conrad comfortably won a December 1992 special election by thirty points over Jack Dalrymple. He won a full term again in 1994 by sixteen points over Ben Clayburgh. By that time, Conrad was a known quantity in North Dakota, a political stalwart whom no opponent would touch for the next fourteen years.

Conrad also wanted to keep up with the Joneses. To be considered a player in the Senate in the year 2000, raising money helped show how powerful you were, it helped get the press's attention, and it made the other kids in the playground—your Senate colleagues—want to be associated with you. Senators were buying higher profiles, spending valuable time raising money when they could be getting to know their colleagues or writing legislation.

KENT CONRAD IS A QUIRKY guy when it comes to raising money. Neil Brown, the senator's other fundraiser, had been around for a year or two and had experienced the senator's odd ways. But it was Neil's first job, so he just thought all senators were like this. No way.

If I wanted to settle into a comfortable daily routine and still haul in $2 million, I had to start fast. The plan was to get a lot of money in quickly, then relax. I stayed late that first week, usually till 9 or 10 pm, preparing call sheets, following up with donors, and planning the next day.

After a few days, I began to notice a car pulling up every night, usually around 8:30 pm. It would just park right in front of the building, but the windows in my basement tomb went only two feet above street level so I couldn't really make out who was driving. Like clockwork, every night at

8:30. At first, I thought maybe it was the undercover Capitol Police checking on the light in the basement. The driver never got out, never did anything but park out front for five minutes, then drive off.

It was Senator Conrad, checking on me. To play by his rules, I would make sure I stayed late every night until I could see those wheels. Now, I didn't really raise money those extra few hours; I mostly watched TV, surfed the Internet, drank a six-pack or two.

When I actually did try to raise money, it was painful. I couldn't justify in my head why raising money was necessary and started referring to myself as a "dead fundraiser walking." The senator had plenty of cash, enough to purchase every single TV ad slot in North Dakota and probably most of them in South Dakota too. The money would never have any other purpose than sitting on Senator Conrad's balance sheet, scaring off anyone who'd think to challenge him.

He would come up with odd excuses to spend money. Maybe he would visit a town and one person would not be nice to him. Maybe someone wouldn't wave back from across the street . . . *Gotta spend more on TV there! They don't know me well enough!* A few meetings in his state would have taken care of the problem. But this was how you campaigned for Senate in 2000—in a few short years, it had gone from raise enough to win to raise as much as you can.

Conrad hoarded his money. The year I worked for him, Democratic Senate candidates Brian Schweitzer in Montana and Chuck Robb in Virginia were in tight races. Power in the Senate hung in the balance, and a win by either one would swing control to Democrats. With Conrad's stockpile of over $2 million, he transferred just $20,000 to the Democratic Senatorial Campaign Committee, less than 1 percent of his take. Schweitzer lost his race by three points; Robb lost his by five. Conrad might have given a lot more to the DSCC—transfers to party committees aren't subject to limits—and helped push maybe one over the edge. Both could have still come up short, but we'll never know.

I TRUDGED ALONG. I set up a lunch event to raise a few small checks at the Monocle Restaurant on the Hill. In the middle of lunch, someone suggested we should go around the table so that everyone could say a few nice words about Senator Conrad. The assembled lobbyists bullshitted their way through a few sentences. Then it was my turn.

Senator Conrad looked in my direction. "So, Lindsay, what do you most appreciate about me?"

"Well, Senator"—I shot back a shit-eating grin—"you sign my paycheck."

The room erupted.

I didn't like doing small events. The smaller the gathering, the more one-on-one time lobbyists got to twist the senator's arm over specific language in a bill. My skill, my motivation, was the big event, a cattle call of every donor I could think of. It seemed like a much cleaner form of collecting money. I'd pack as many checkwriters into the room at once, and nobody will get to spend much one-on-one time to exert influence. Just like how Fraioli-Jost did it in the '80s and early '90s. Each donor would maybe get two minutes of happy talk with the senator.

The buffalo meat lobby had offered to cut me a deal on a massive amount of, well, bison. I immediately set up the "Join Senator Kent Conrad for Some Meat" event on the Hill. Neil and I hit it out of the park, packing the room with over five hundred folks, who handed over lots of checks and got in lots of happy talk with very little arm twisting.

"Hey, Senator, how are you? Good to see you!"

"Not sure if you remember, but I'm Bill with the aerospace industry."

"Nice to see you, Bill!"

"Senator, I'd like to talk to you about . . ."

"Ooooh, sorry, Bill! Gotta run and say hello to my good friend Susan, but let's talk soon!"

I had done my job and enjoyed some delicious grass-fed bison in the process.

AS MEMBERS WERE BECOMING more like the new Kent Conrad and less like the old Dick Gephardt, the lobby community started to change too. Conrad, like most of his Hill colleagues, started to raise more money by exploiting the new dynamic on K Street.

In the early '90s, lobbying on K Street was different. Lobbyists would donate a few bucks to attend your event, but they knew the issues their organizations cared about inside and out, were paid a reasonable salary, and developed long-standing relationships with members of Congress and their staffs. In turn, lobbyists produced measured results over time.

Now the lobbying industry was adapting to the drive for campaign cash. New firms cropped up all over town as lobbyists previously employed by companies (and ex-members who were becoming lobbyists) realized they could leverage their political relationships. The new firms were hired guns, more loyal to their next payday than their clients' missions. They had to produce results to justify their contracts. So they started throwing their firms' money around to solidify relationships with the Hill. These relationships were based on campaign contributions, not their clients' interests. That's why many hired-gun lobbyists were happy to switch sides on any given issue, provided a larger paycheck was attached.

Kent Conrad, and to be fair many other senators and members of Congress, was happy to take the new DC for all it was worth. He'd encourage his staff to take meetings with as many lobbying firms as possible, spreading his network of loyalists throughout town so long as a thousand-dollar check was attached.

There were also guys like former Representative Charlie Wilson of Texas, later made famous by the movie *Charlie Wilson's War*. He was my favorite, caught between the old DC and the new DC. After he left office, he needed to make money and signed up with a new lobbying firm in town. He was part of the "revolving door" of former members of Congress who'd leave office and lobby their former colleagues on the Hill for whoever happened to be paying them that day.

Wilson hated the new DC, and it showed. He'd turn up at every event his bosses asked him to go to, where he'd drop off his $1,000 check and be gone in three minutes without saying a word to damn near anyone. But he could say he was there. The new lobbyist was more akin to a factory worker. It wasn't that the lobbyist had loyalty to the one issue he was paid to work on. It was much more important to show up at seven or eight fundraisers a night and clock in for two minutes of time with a representative, then clock out and move along to the next one.

41

THE SENATOR KEPT UP THE PRESSURE. HE WANTED MORE AND more, and more, and more . . . and more. So I went to raise more. The West Coast swing it would be, to California and Seattle. Senator Conrad was far from a liberal champion, and I knew Los Angeles would be tough. Just after special prosecutor Ken Starr had released his report on the Lewinsky affair, rumors had flown that Conrad might actually vote to impeach the president. Conrad had told Greg Craig, Clinton's special counsel, that a mutiny was brewing among Democratic senators, who were on the verge of asking for the president's resignation. Then Conrad had a huge fight with the Left of the party when he threatened to endorse a constitutional amendment to ban the burning of the American flag. It had been a heated war of words, and the senator had led the charge to make it a crime before doing a last-minute about-face.

Norman Lear of *Sanford and Son, The Jeffersons,* and *Fried Green Tomatoes* fame produced an advertisement for People for the American Way featuring a Vietnam veteran who opposed the flag-burning amendment. Lear and Conrad had sparred several times over the flag issue, but they had a good, honest debate. On some level, they respected one another. Lear was one of my first calls.

"Mr. Lear, I know you and Senator Conrad have had your differences, but he would really appreciate it if you hosted a fundraising event for him in California in a few weeks," I said, putting on my best kiss-ass voice.

Remember, having people host events was important because they commit to writing a check for or raising a certain amount of money. In this case, I asked Lear to either write or raise $20,000. His job was to call his friends, and friends of friends, to make sure the room was packed so he didn't have to write the whole $20,000 check himself.

He agreed on one condition. "I don't want to be the only host. Senator Conrad's a decent guy, but we've butted heads. I'm happy to show up with a check, and if you need to list me as one of the hosts, that's fine."

"Got it, Mr. Lear. Our goal is to have twenty to twenty-five hosts for the event. You won't be the only one."

Sounded like a green light to me. This was a multiday West Coast swing, so I had to arrange several events. We had the big one with Lear, but then a smaller one with Kathleen Brown—former California governor Jerry Brown's sister—and then another smaller event with some corporate types. Then I set up a lunch in Seattle.

WITH SO MUCH ON THE SENATOR'S SCHEDULE, I had to send out invites to literally thousands of people, and it would be tough to keep track of who was RSVPing for which event. If someone called my office and said, "I'd like to RSVP for Senator Conrad's event," that didn't help very much. I could hardly ask "And which event would that be?" because Conrad would look like he was grubbing for money. But I still needed to know how many fruit cups to order for breakfast!

So I used that old trick from Fraioli-Jost, and put a different fake name in the "please RSVP to" line on each event's invitation. That way, if someone called and asked for "Wayne" or "Chip," I would know which event they were talking about. I stuck "Please RSVP to Wayne Stephenson" on the invite for Lear's big event in Los Angeles. Wayne Stephenson is one of my favorite old hockey goalies for the Philadelphia Flyers and Washington Capitals. I always tried to give a little respect back to my favorite sport.

Then I ran into a little problem. Between the rumored impeachment and flag-burning votes, LA's liberal donor community hated Senator Conrad. My twenty-five cohosts just didn't materialize; I only had Norman Lear. Two weeks before the event, I couldn't wait another day to get a second host. I had to send the invites. I couldn't really cancel—*my boss needed his $2 million!*—so I swallowed hard, stuck "*Norman Lear Invites You to an Evening with Senator Kent Conrad*" on the invite, and sent out 2,500 to people on Los Angeles donor lists.

I figured I would still be able to raise $40,000. Surely folks would show up to see the senator if Norman Lear invited them, right? Out of 2,500 invites, a 2 percent response rate would be fifty people, a good event.

I waited three days. Then I started following up with donors to make sure they'd received the invite and to ask if they'd like to attend. I would stay late in my office/tomb, just like the senator wanted, to try to catch people at the end of the day: 9 pm in DC was only 6 o'clock in Los Angeles. I called and called down my donor list, and the overwhelming response was *No! No chance! No way in hell I am helping Kent Conrad! The FEC only lets me give so much money every year, so why should I spend it on him?* This wasn't DC. In Washington, any lobbyist would find that thousand bucks. (The Supreme Court struck down the cap on individual giving per year in 2014's *McCutcheon v. FEC.*)

But this crowd was California's billionaire liberal donor community, and they gave money only because they felt a personal connection to a politician; they didn't need to establish a business relationship with the politico. I respected their reasons for not giving—Conrad had no real opponent, was too conservative for them, and they wanted to spend money on competitive campaigns. I left a lot of messages, talked to a few administrative assistants, talked to a few donors, and got nothing . . . no one was coming.

Then at 8 pm, the phone finally rang. Finally an RSVP! I tried to play it cool . . . waited for it to ring three times. I answered.

"Is Wayne fucking Stephenson there? I need to talk to him right now!"

Uh-oh. "Sorry, Wayne is not in, can I take a message for him?"

"You tell Wayne that I am pissed off. This is Norman Lear, and I have a real problem with this invite he sent around. I never agreed to be the only host for Senator Conrad, and he needs to fix this right away."

Wayne never returned Mr. Lear's call.

SENATOR CONRAD DIDN'T WANT to pay for a staffer to fly with him, so he traveled alone. He was the only senator I knew who would go fund-raise by himself. Fundraisers play roles on the road: They chitchat with donors, protect their boss from odd requests, take care of last-minute problems, and work the phones to make sure people show up at events. Not with Senator Conrad. So off to Los Angeles and Seattle the senator went alone.

Norman Lear produced a few folks, Kathleen Brown produced a few folks, and Wayne Stephenson drew lots of heat. Of course, the senator had no clue what Norman Lear was talking about, but Conrad, in typical senator customer service mode, told Mr. Lear that he would look into Stephenson-gate and take care of the problem. At the end of the Wayne Stephenson reception, the senator picked up a handful of checks.

Then it was off to Seattle. I had sent over two thousand invites to donors for this little lunch. No hosts, just a grab bag. I was pretty fed up and didn't exactly do a great job following up the invitations with phone calls, but surely twenty would show up to see the senator. I arranged for the lunch to be set for thirty. Ken Alhadeff joined Senator Conrad for lunch that day. Ken is the chairman of Elttaes Enterprises, a Seattle-based holding company. Alhadeff has been an active philanthropist and supporter of Democratic causes. "I love my democracy," he's said. Contributing "doesn't come from my company as much as it comes from my heart."[1]

Ken was the only one to show up that day. The table for thirty was lunch for two. Conrad walked out of the restaurant, called John Van

Heuvelen, his chief of staff, and told him to fire me. I was actually relieved, happy even. Van Heuvelen was the nicest guy and liked me a lot personally. Neil Brown, the other fundraiser, liked me too. So I told him, "Here's the deal. Conrad's never going to know . . . don't take me off payroll yet," so I got an extra paycheck out of the good senator.

I raised a good chunk of the $2.4 million Kent Conrad brought in for the 2000 campaign. He would have won easily if he'd just raised $240,000. I was leaving the senator with $2 million on hand, and I no longer had to pretend to raise money he did not need. In 2000, Republican Duane Sand stepped up to challenge Kent Conrad. Raising excessive amounts of money had achieved its goal and prevented serious competition. Duane was a first-time, no-name candidate and didn't have a chance. He would raise $399,000 for the campaign, or six times less than Senator Conrad, who won 62 to 38 percent.

42

MILLIONEYES.COM WAS MY LATEST WAY OUT OF FUNDRAISING AND politics for good. After I was fired by Kent Conrad in 2000, I got a call from a friend who thought I might be able to help one of his firm's deals. MillionEyes was a free Internet service provider that was going to compete with paid dial-up services offered by AOL and others. All I had to do was set up meetings with the powerful people I knew to try to get the company on its feet.

I was convinced I'd never have to raise money again. I was out. I was moving on to the next chapter in my life by democratizing the Internet, giving access to the information superhighway to everyone, for free. I met Tim Scully and Don Kaniewski—my old labor lobbyist friends—for lunch and told them that they were "dinosaurs," that I was on the cutting edge and about to be an Internet tech tycoon. They laughed in my face, but that didn't stop me. I spent my days surfing the Internet for $10 million beachfront properties that I was going to buy when my stock options went through the roof.

Of course, that was the problem. MillionEyes.com paid me in stock, not cash. Three months later, the tech bubble of 2000 burst. Tim and Don call me "Dinosaur" to this day. My career was Hotel California.

43

THE DAVID JONES FUNDRAISING BUSINESS WAS BOOMING. HE WAS doing an event for Dick Gephardt, and he asked me to help Dick raise money out of the new high-tech industry sprouting up in northern Virginia. Sure, at least it would be a quick payday. So I went into David's office every day and started making calls.

But after calling the same people over and over—donors I'd been calling since 1992—I was miserable. I knew who would say yes and who wouldn't even pick up the phone, so why bother with the formality of actually calling? So I did what a "dead fundraiser walking" would do: I made hours and hours of fake calls. I would call the weather line, I would call the date and time line, I would call the sports update line, I would call my home line, any line I knew nobody would answer. This is how I got through the day.

I was supposed to gin up excitement because Kevin Spacey was going to headline the event. Spacey had struck up a relationship with Gephardt, and they bonded over Democrats' struggles to regain the House. The two-time Oscar winner staged a performance of the play he was starring in, *The Iceman Cometh,* in New York for donors, and he gave the party a hundred tickets to the premiere of the movie *American Beauty* to reward its top givers.

Doing an event with Spacey was supposed to be about engaging Hollywood stars in political giving. It was a giant pain in the ass. We had to find a five-star hotel that accepted his huge dogs, not an easy task in DC. After a lot of convincing, we finally got the Jefferson Hotel on 16th Street to take them. He complained when I asked him to sign a bunch of *Usual Suspects* posters for donors. I sent over a list of about fifty names. I knew I'd pissed him off because I slipped my own name on the list, but did I get a cool signed poster from one of my favorite movies? No, but he did leave me a *K-PAX* poster, from his new flick about a crazy guy who talks to his shrink about space aliens for two hours.

But Gephardt was trying to solve a problem with Spacey, one he was pretty explicit about to the *Washington Post* and which us fundraisers had known for years.

> For all their political activism, most stars and studio execs are fairly parsimonious when it comes to writing checks. As Gephardt put it carefully, "People in show business have strong feelings about issues, but they don't always step up to the plate and help you.[1]

That article says the entertainment industry gave $488,000 to the Democratic Congressional Campaign Committee in the 1998 cycle. Thanks to Gephardt's drive to take back the House, the industry gave $966,000 by the end of 1999. By 2000, Democratic fundraisers started chasing the allure of Hollywood's political money as their next big hit, convinced there was untapped gold in its hills.

Gephardt was right—getting the entertainment industry to pony up, both then and now, is usually excruciating and inefficient and allows stars a disproportionately large seat at the table. Wringing money out of liberal entertainment moguls is political fundraising at its worst. Some entertainment big shots, like George Clooney, Leonardo DiCaprio, and David Geffen, do give hundreds of thousands of dollars. But most use their star power to entice several hours out of a politician's schedule without writing much of a check. And politicians, happy to meet stars, let them.

That didn't change the fact that we were still putting on an event with Kevin Spacey at a rich donor's mansion in Great Falls, Virginia. We packed the place that day—even with my calls to the date and time number—and earned nearly $100,000. Spacey no doubt attracted some donors and raised some money on our behalf. While it might be fun to spend a few hours with someone you see on the silver screen, why spend so much time with just one person? It would make tons more sense to spend that time with the people who elected you.

AFTER THE EVENT, David Jones and I had to "steal" $128,000. There was always competition among fundraisers to hit targets and get the most money in the door. Noah Mamet, Gephardt's full-time staff fundraiser in those days, was going too far. Jonesy would raise money for Gephardt for this event and others and have the checks sent to the Effective Government Committee's office. Noah would intercept the mail and take Jonesy's checks so he could get credit with Gephardt. About $128,000 was missing by Jonesy's count.

We knew when Noah went for lunch every day, so we waited out on the street until we saw him leave. Then we went up to the office, prepared to tear through everything looking for the money. But dammit, Adam Olson—a young guy on staff—was still in the office, "guarding" money he probably didn't even know was there. So Jonesy started chatting him up about some bullshit, and he gave me a nod. And then another. Finally, I got it. While Jonesy kept Adam distracted, I darted into Noah's office and started going through his desk. There they were—all $128,000 in checks—in Noah's bottom-left drawer. I snuck them out and returned them to their rightful owner.

44

BEFORE A BILL GETS A VOTE IN FRONT OF THE ENTIRE HOUSE OF Representatives, it has to pass out of its relevant committee first. When a

Democratic member who serves on a committee votes to approve a bill, it often sends a signal to other Democratic members not on the committee that they should vote for it on the House floor. Why would a member of Congress who's not on the committee bother to study the details of a bill when he or she could just look to see if a strong majority of Democrats on the committee voted for it?

By early 2001, many members of Congress had fully started to use their committee assignments as tools to raise money. They leveraged their committee seats to squeeze money out of lobbyists, often by threatening to advance legislation that would hurt an industry's bottom line. Lobbyists would simply donate to kill off bad legislation. The lists I'd first learned about after the 1994 election—those that set fundraising goals for each piece of legislation—were alive and well. Democracy at its finest: Instead of lobbying *for* something, lobbyists were now giving money out of fear to prevent their industry or company from getting hurt. The members of Congress had reversed the relationship, they had the leverage.

Sometimes it worked the straightforward way, of course. I knew of one member of Congress who offered to sell a committee vote to a lobbying association in exchange for a $5,000 donation. This was the first time I had direct knowledge of a "sale." Worse, this member never faced serious competition and didn't need the money. How dumb. I was disgusted.

I quit fundraising that day.

I SAT AROUND for a few months, unemployed. Drank a lot, played a ton of PlayStation, watched movies, and went broke. Twelve years as a fundraiser and I had made not an ounce of difference in the world. I was miserable. I could go raise money again, but what was the point? I was sinking lower and lower, depressed at the thought of continuing to raise money for politicians who didn't need it and in a game I didn't want to play anymore.

I was dead broke, living in a shitty apartment in the Mount Pleasant neighborhood of DC. The power company cut me off. My apartment turned dark and cold. I ran an extension cord down the hall of my building to a hallway plug to steal power. I plugged my refrigerator, TV, and cable box into the power strip. I would only do this after 6 pm, because I didn't want the building to know that I was borrowing some electricity. Living life on the edge, my way.

THE LOBBYIST FOR KRAFT had given me a holiday gift bag a few weeks before. It included ten tins of Altoid mints, some cinnamon, some plain white. The local news on Channel 5 just ran a big story on the youth drug culture on Friday nights at Nation, a dance club. Suburban kids were apparently coming into the city and spending money to party and buy drugs. The drug of choice was new: ecstasy. I may not have had power, but a light bulb went off in my head!

If you look at an Altoid in the right way, you could imagine it kind of looked like the ecstasy pill I'd just seen on the news. I went to work. I got some 7UP and started "cooking." I splashed 7UP on the mints but did too much and they dissolved. Slowly I got the hang of it. With just the right amount of 7UP and water, I dissolved just enough of the Altoid to turn it into a beautiful little "ecstasy" pill. Then I dipped the pills in a little blueberry Pop Tart jelly for a blue tint. Game on.

I had never been to a rave and wasn't much of a club guy, but I did have a yellow visor from a Laurel Park racetrack give-away. At age thirty-two, I put on a wifebeater and my yellow visor, and packed two hundred pills into little sandwich baggies. Off I went to Nation.

Mental note: Don't show up at a rave the minute the club opens. No one was there, so I waited. I walked around looking cool, smiling at everybody I could make eye contact with. I wanted them to know I had stuff. I wasn't too worried or nervous. If the cops busted me, how much time would I get for selling breath mints? By 11:30 pm, hundreds of suburban kids packed the place. I set up camp near the bathrooms. I had no clue how a drug dealer advertised himself, so I improvised. I stood by the door to the bathroom and slowly pulled a baggie out of my pocket, just enough so a potential buyer could see it.

It was like playing with a cat on a string—dangle just enough of it in front of a cat's face and it's mesmerized. This young guy took notice and slowly approached. "Whoa. How much, man, and what is it?"

"Best damn ecstasy pills on the East Coast," I smirked, staring straight ahead to make sure no one would pick up on our transaction. I flipped my visor backward. "Just in from a lab in PA, quality shit. Twenty bucks a pop, three for fifty."

Marketing at its best. The kid passed me two twenties and a ten and told his friends. Within a half hour I had sold every single damn pill, all two hundred, and had $3,500 in my pocket. And I ran out. I paid the power bill, I paid the rent, and I never went back to Nation.

This was what I'd sunk to. I'd rather sell fake ecstasy pills than a vote in Congress. And those kids had some great breath.

45

CHRIS VAN HOLLEN HAD BEEN RAISED OVERSEAS WHILE HIS DAD was in the Foreign Service. He went to nice schools, traveled the world, that sort of thing. But he was down to earth and got into politics the right way: He paid his dues over twelve years in the Maryland State House, then the State Senate. He ran for Congress in 2002 because it was the next evolution of his career, the next logical step as he needed a new challenge.

And he was in for a challenge. First, he had to get through Mark Shriver—a Kennedy—in the primary. Win that, and he'd be up against incumbent Republican representative Connie Morella in the general. Morella had represented Maryland's 8th congressional district since 1986 and had won reelection fairly easily every time. The 2000 election had been her closest in years; she'd snuck through by six points after her opponent, Democrat Terry Lierman, outraised her by over a million dollars.

I stretched my ecstasy payday for a few months but had no intention of making it a steady revenue stream. Tom Fahy, an old colleague from my Gephardt days, called me to let me know that his buddy Steve Jost was running Van Hollen's campaign. Jost had started his firm, Fraioli-Jost, in the '80s and knew how to raise money the right way: in big events that raised a lot of money and didn't take too much time. Steve was bitter, disillusioned with DC power politics, but a political operative who knew how to win.

Since the district was trending Democrat, the DCCC sensed a bit of weakness and made Van Hollen's one of their highest-priority races. Unfortunately for Jost, the DCCC's priority was also backing the presumed nominee, Mark Shriver. Nobody had ever defeated a Kennedy in a congressional primary, and while Mark Shriver was a decent guy, he didn't deserve a congressional seat just because of his last name.

Jost tried to sell me on the idea that Van Hollen had tons of grassroots support in Montgomery County. If a few things broke our way, Jost thought Van Hollen might stand a chance in the primary and could win it just like Gray Davis had won in California. I definitely needed the paycheck and may not have had much choice, but I was actually excited about this race. Working for an underdog, fighting for the little guy, that's why I had gotten into this business. If I could help enough Van Hollens get into office, maybe that would be how I might make something of my career.

DC INSIDER MONEY was backing Shriver. Senator Ted Kennedy was doing events for him, and the old guard was excited to have a new Kennedy join the family business. In the end, Shriver would raise $2.7 million for the primary.[1] We couldn't compete dollar for dollar with the Kennedy machine, but that didn't matter. We just needed to raise enough to run high-quality, well-placed TV ads, do some smart direct mail, and use this army of grassroots volunteers Jost had bragged about. It had to be a methodical, efficient campaign . . . just what I liked.

Even though Van Hollen had been in the State House for over a decade and had been on the ballot several times, a congressional election is a bigger deal. He was a rookie, and that has disadvantages. Van Hollen didn't trust anybody but himself and would have run his own campaign if he could have. Of course, he didn't know how to run a big-time campaign, and his wife was way too involved.

Being a rookie also has some advantages. I started with the typical first-time candidate fundraising: college alumni, colleagues, neighbors, relatives, and good friends, people close to Van Hollen who had no political agenda other than to care about his success as a member of Congress. Unfortunately, this always works only for first-time candidates. After the rookie wins, his friends and family get sick of getting hit up again and again for campaign dollars. They slowly disengage. At the same time, members begin to discover the ease of raising money in DC from lobbyists, PACs, and rich donors, so there's no need to keep bugging that college roommate when coddling a lobbyist could bring in five times as much.

By February 2002, Shriver had $1.2 million in the bank, more than double Van Hollen's $560,000.[2] Then Shriver's campaign headed downhill. He ran an amateurish race, typical of a candidate who thought victory would come easily. His staff mailed it in, literally and figuratively, sending out a direct mail piece on "smart growth" with a background picture supposedly of Montgomery County but actually a stock photo of the Chicago Skyline. Oops.

We began to capitalize on that grassroots network Jost kept talking about. After years of campaigning for the State House, Jost was right that Van Hollen had built up an army of volunteers intensely loyal to him. As we got closer to the primary, more and more would show up at the campaign office, practically begging us to send them out to knock on doors for Chris. On primary day, we had six thousand volunteers getting out the vote for Van Hollen, a number absolutely unheard of in a congressional first round.

Luckily the race was in Montgomery County, one of the wealthiest in the country. A fascinating thing happened on the way to our fundraising goal. Our army of volunteers started returning to the office with checks,

$250, $500, or $1,000 at a time. I was amazed—these were local citizens who believed in a candidate and a cause, who wanted to fund a campaign from the bottom up. And best of all, since these checks were basically appearing out of thin air, raising the extra money didn't take an extra minute of Van Hollen's time.

The Van Hollen campaign was not without its hiccups, though. Did you, for example, know that *Time Magazine*'s Man of the Year in 2002 was Chris Van Hollen? That's what you might have thought if you'd read one of Katherine Van Hollen's direct mailers, which she mocked up (without our knowledge) to replicate the iconic magazine cover featuring her husband. Time, Inc. sued that day. Katherine had no idea what she was doing. What would the message be? Would it connect to the TV ads? Would it work? Anybody with basic knowledge of campaigns could have told her to hold off, but nobody knew what she was up to.

Things started to turn around when we picked up critical endorsements from the teachers' unions, the *Washington Post,* and the *Baltimore Sun.* The campaign felt good going into the primary, but no question it was still up in the air. Would folks vote for a Kennedy in numbers that didn't show up in the polls? Would they win just on name ID? I had more faith in the voters of Montgomery County, but who knew?

We spent every single dime we had, but we funded most of the campaign not with mega-donors from New York, or California, or DC lobbyists but with voters in the district. We squeaked by and beat Mark Shriver and the Kennedys 43 to 41 in the primary. Do you know how good it feels to win the right way?

Now we had to get our act together for the general election, but we had major financial issues: We were $150,000 in debt.[3] Jo Becker of the *Washington Post* wrote about our successes and challenges in October.

> Democratic congressional candidate Christopher Van Hollen Jr. woke up the morning after his come-from-behind primary victory ecstatic— but nearly broke. [H]is exhausted moneyman brushed aside the dirty

coffee cups littering his desk, ignored the hurricane of papers strewn across the floor and began to take stock.

By Lindsay Lewis's calculations, Van Hollen had about $99,000 left after spending more than $1 million in a tough, late battle for the party nomination. Their Republican opponent in Maryland's 8th District, eight-term Rep. Constance A. Morella, had nearly $1.7 million in the bank. . . .

A look behind the scenes shows just how relentless the push for money has been—as well as how successful. By yesterday, Van Hollen had brought in more than half a million dollars for the general election. . . .

Amassing enough started with Lewis identifying donors who had given in the primary campaign but who had not reached general election contribution limits. He put those names into white binders. His next focus: the list of people who had declined to write a check during the primary because they were committed to an opponent. Those names went into blue binders. Yellow books were for Washington givers such as labor heavyweights and Democratic-leaning political action committees that could be approached for help. . . .

"This isn't a question of trying to find people in New York who could write a check," Lewis said. "The majority of the folks we need are right here. It's just a matter of how do you get it in the door." . . .

Lewis has just one rule: No one can tell him the campaign's running total. "I raise and I raise and I raise, and if at some point, someone wants to tell me the goal, I'll tell them if we can meet it," he said. "But I don't want to know if we had a good day, because I don't want to get overconfident."[4]

The one thing Jo Becker didn't mention is how I paid down some of our debt. I used an old trick. The third guy in the primary, Ira Shapiro, raised $900,000.[5] We arranged a debt swap with Shapiro's finance director: I had a bunch of donors who had maxed out to us and were legally prohibited from giving more but still wanted to help. Shapiro had the same problem. So I'd call our maxed-out donors and tell them that if they wanted to help Van Hollen, the best thing they could do is write a $1,000 check to Ira Shapiro. Shapiro's finance director told theirs to write a thousand bucks to Van Hollen. I raised around $50,000 that way.

Connie Morella eventually took in over $3.8 million for that election, to our $2.9 million. Van Hollen's campaign filings tell the story of our success: 76 percent of the money was from individual contributors, mostly from donors living in Maryland who gave less than $500. We were outspent by $900,000, but we were ruthlessly efficient with what we raised. By the end of the campaign, we had $3,886 in our account. That's how to win an election the right way. It's the model I wanted to use for every candidate for Congress.

46

I STUCK AROUND WITH VAN HOLLEN AFTER HE WAS SWORN IN. I hoped he would be a new kind of member, one who built a grassroots-led, small-dollar, local financial powerhouse with an incredible opportunity to set a new tone in how campaigns were run.

It took three weeks for the system to change him. *Three weeks.* The underdog outsider transformed himself into a DC insider before I knew what happened. He was showing up in the call room at the DCCC with all the other members, calling and calling and calling for dollars. He carved out twelve hours a week to make calls to rich people far beyond his district, directors of political action committees, and lobbyists. He was raising for no reason: He never raised less than $1.5 million for any of his races through 2012, and none of his opponents ever raised more than $353,000. No one ever came within twenty-nine points of him.[1]

CHRIS VAN HOLLEN and Kent Conrad were typical of a growing trend in politics: the increasing cost—in dollars and time—of raising money. Every member of Congress was spending more of both to raise additional funds. Cost and time are the two variables in political fundraising, much like every other business. If a candidate wants to raise more, she or he must invest more of one or both to do it.

First-time candidates are cheapest. For his Senate race in 1986, Kent Conrad raised $994,000, a big haul for sparsely populated North Dakota, especially at the time. He employed two fundraising firms on a temporary basis and flew occasionally to New York, Houston, or California to host fundraising events. He spend just over 5 percent of what he took in to raise that money.

By the time I worked for him during the 2000 election, Kent Conrad had two full-time fundraisers on his staff. He maintained an office for his fundraising staff just off the Hill because it is unethical and illegal to raise money from your congressional office. With full-time employees and an office, that meant adding salaries, health insurance, employee taxes, rent, utilities, phones, computers, mass mailings, and office supplies, none of which he had to pay for before. He traveled constantly all over the country to raise money, throwing fancier events in more expensive locations. It all added up, quickly. He raised $2.4 million for his 2000 campaign and was now spending nearly 13 percent of his budget to do it.[2]

When I worked for Chris Van Hollen on his first race in 2002, we ran an efficient campaign focused on small-dollar donors. He employed one fundraiser for the majority of the campaign—either me or the person who had the job before me, who joined the race less than a year before the election. Late in the race, a fundraising assistant joined me. We raised $2.9 million and spent only 5 percent of our budget on bringing in money.

As soon as Van Hollen decided to make a play for party leadership, his fundraising costs escalated. He began employing full-time fundraisers on staff for the entire two-year cycle and started spending on all the same things Conrad had: offices, insurance, mass mailings, events, travel, fancy hotels, upscale catering . . . all of which he did in lesser amounts in his first campaign. In 2012, Van Hollen spent over 21 percent of his budget raising money. To put it another way, in 2002, Chris Van Hollen's scrappy campaign spent $152,090 raising $2.9 million. In 2012, he spent $245,500 raising just $1.5 million. Does that seem efficient to you?[3]

Kent Conrad held on to his money. At least Van Hollen was more generous. He had a safe seat, so he basically raised money for others. In 2004, he transferred $70,000 from his campaign account to the DCCC. In 2006, he transferred $85,000. In 2008, the year Van Hollen coincidentally became the DCCC's chair, he transferred $705,000. In 2010, in his second cycle at the DCCC's helm, he transferred $1.7 million. Out of the $1.9 million he raised after stepping down from the DCCC in 2012, Van Hollen gave $400,000 back.[4]

In addition to raising for his campaign, Chris Van Hollen also started a leadership PAC in 2006, called VictoryNow, that raised over $2 million between 2006 and 2012. The vast majority of this money was donated to other candidates and party committees to help secure Van Hollen's party leadership position, just like the Effective Government Committee did for Dick Gephardt, but it also helped sustain the fundraising industry, sending another $155,000 to fundraisers' accounts over that same period.

I'm happy that Van Hollen is a team player and uses his excess cash to help other Democrats win elections, just like Gephardt. But both Van Hollen and Conrad raised literally millions of dollars they'd never need to be reelected.

I HAD TRIED TO CHANGE politics via a middle-class champion like Dick Gephardt. I had tried in Las Vegas, the ultimate middle-class dream. I tried to leave and be a part of the new economy with MillionEyes.com. I tried to change politics via a new underdog candidate. While of course a lot was out of my control, I couldn't help but feeling a deep sense of failure. It was a very hollow feeling knowing that the entire system of political finance was changing for the worse right in front of my face, and I couldn't do much to stop it. Doubtful I could sell ecstasy mints or resurrect my hot streak as the blackjack king of Vegas, I was again lost without a cause.

Yes, I could make money raising money, but what was the purpose? Was it to get paid? Or was there still a way to make politics work more for average voters who deserved a seat at the table? I left Van Hollen in April 2003, completely dejected. I set up a fundraising firm with some Van Hollen people in Silver Spring, Maryland.

Richard Sullivan, Dick Gephardt's new fundraiser and former DNC money man, called me and asked if I would come back to work for my old boss. I was kind to him on the phone, but as soon as I hung up, I knew the answer was no fucking way. I knew people like Steve Elmendorf and Noah Mamet were destroying the old Gephardt coalition and he had no shot at being the next Democratic nominee for president, so why would I go back for the sake of a few paychecks?

One of my firm's first clients was a single-issue, far-Left, Birkenstock-wearing group of tree huggers in Eugene, Oregon. The concept of calling wealthy individuals to give money to these nutty granolas was a much harder sell in my own mind for the next election.

On day ten of my magical mystery tour of Eugene, Stephanie Schriock called me from Burlington, Vermont, and asked if I'd be interested in fixing some New York fundraising problems for Howard Dean, the state's governor who was running for president. I was on the next plane from Eugene to the capital of maple syrup.

PART 3

MY CHANCE TO CHANGE
POLITICS FOREVER

47

I KNEW NOTHING ABOUT HOWARD DEAN BEFORE 2003.

By the time he ran for president in 2003, he had never registered on the national scene. He had been a very quiet, almost nonexistent, chair of the Democratic Governors Association during the 2000 campaign and never garnered much attention, overshadowed by the Gore-Bush race. As a fundraiser, Vermont was never on my radar, because how much money could I really expect to squeeze from ultra-liberal donors in Burlington?

I had been struggling. I knew what the problem was but wasn't sure how to fix it. I had pushed the team around Gephardt to build a donor community that represented what Gephardt stood for—pro–middle class, pro-business. Done right, it could be an unstoppable combination of working-class and new-age corporate leaders. But my idea had fallen on deaf ears.

Howard Dean represented the possibility of a new era, a new way, a clean way, a way to raise money that gave everyone a seat at the table. As I began to hear about Dean's grassroots online fundraising phenomenon—and years later, it's easy to forget what a phenomenon it was—I got excited at the thought of wealthy donors competing for candidates' attention with small-dollar donors who just believed in the cause. I thought Dean had harnessed the network I wanted to create for Dick Gephardt; he had built a reservoir of small donors like the one Chris Van Hollen owned for an instant, before he was sucked into the DC money game three weeks after winning his first campaign.

Could it work? What would it mean if it did? Could a new era of Democrats be elected without having to rely on the new power of a few wealthy elites? I was desperate to play a role. I would spend the next three years with Howard Dean and would come to understand that Dean's grassroots network wasn't about middle-class Americans who wanted a seat at the political table. Howard Dean failed the masses and the masses failed Howard Dean. In the end, Dean's grassroots donors were a tool of the small clutch of liberal billionaires, used to balance their control of the party.

The new era of small-dollar donors for Democrats on the Left and for the Tea Party on the Right has pushed the partisan rhetoric to new levels. Both sides of the partisan debate understand that to squeeze the maximum from this donor class, you must scare them. The more scared they are, the more they give.

This is how the struggle to take the party back from the rich billionaires failed.

I DIDN'T KNOW any of this at the time.

In 2000, John McCain had raised $2 million online[1] in the four days after winning the New Hampshire primary, but there was no sense he started a real political movement. Yes, he had positioned himself as a "maverick," but he hadn't really started something big. Then, burned by the George W. Bush machine in the South Carolina primary, McCain teamed up with liberal Wisconsin senator Russ Feingold to pass the Bipartisan Campaign Reform Act, commonly known as McCain-Feingold, in 2002.

McCain-Feingold was an attempt at curbing the power of big money in politics. Previous attempts at reform curtailed one form of giving but encouraged others. Look at Watergate. In its wake, Congress tried to stop shady giving by corporations, so they created political action committees, which for the first time legalized corporate and union giving from their employees and members respectively. Reformers can't dictate who will participate, or everyone loses.

Most important, McCain-Feingold capped donations of soft money to party committees, which had previously been unregulated. It didn't, however, cap elite donors' appetite to play in politics. By limiting money that could go directly to the parties, McCain-Feingold divided rich donors into two camps: the bundlers and the top 100. The bundlers were folks who would write a big check according to the new rules but who then realized that, to maintain influence within the party, they had to bundle big donations from others, too, to make an impact. Then there was the truly elite, the top 100 or so, who preferred just writing checks and didn't want to do the work of bundling. McCain-Feingold forced them to figure out ways to go around the system. Ironically, the bill brought *more* money into politics. Read on.

Where McCain didn't start a movement with small-dollar online giving, Howard Dean did. He seemed to have a movement of the masses: people who gave money, knocked on doors, made phone calls, and wrote blogs. I sensed Dean was a presidential candidate who was building a loyal following that wanted to change the direction of the country. The Democratic Party and his army of Deaniacs owned this campaign, not a few elites that wanted to control the future of the party. If Dean's small-dollar donors contributed more, then maybe they could, collectively, equal the power of large donors. It was the missing piece. Balance.

And he almost did it. By the time Dean dropped out of the race in early 2004, he had raised over $50 million, more than any other candidate by the end of 2003. An unheard-of 60 percent were contributions under $200.[2] Over 318,000 people had contributed to the campaign, more than enough to challenge any possible billionaire revolt.

The Dean for America office was on the top floor of a new building in South Burlington, aka Middle of Nowhere, Vermont. It was packed with idealistic young kids, a few older campaign hacks, and a couple of "adults" in their twenties who seemed to be in charge. I only guessed they were in charge because they wore the dress shirts.

The office felt like most national campaigns: grimy floors, grubby staff, piles of old food on card tables, stacks of stale paper. The main floor was split in two, field and finance staff on the right, communications and senior staff to the left.

I only knew one person on the finance team, Alex Pearson, who had worked for Bruce Keiloch back in my Gephardt days. The rest were newcomers, young people, nontraditional fundraiser types. It was terrifying on one level and refreshing on another. They wouldn't know what they were doing . . . but that might be a good thing. They wouldn't have relationships with the typical wealthy donors who felt entitled to something.

Those big donors would be welcome to give if they believed in the cause but not if they wanted something. And if we could figure out how to really harness this Internet thing with a steady and sustainable stream of support, a fundraiser could tell a rich donor to fuck off without consequences. It would be liberating. It was one of the more refreshing moments in my political career. I assumed that's how young people who joined Eugene McCarthy's 1968 campaign must have felt.

That first day in Burlington I sat down with Stephanie Schriock, Dean's national finance director (and now president of EMILY's List). She explained that the campaign finance team had real problems in New York. Two young people were running the show for the most important money city in the country and they needed help, fast.

By that, I think she meant she wanted my Gephardt connections to wealthy donors. I was happy to go and right the ship, if just to get out of the office in Vermont. One full day in Burlington, that was it for me. I got to New York the next morning.

THE DEAN FOR AMERICA New York fundraising team was down in the West Village in Manhattan in a small tech company's office. That made sense. Dean was changing the way campaigns used the Internet, so naturally we worked out of a tech incubator office.

It was cramped, two little offices shared by three staffers. Emily Wurgaft ran the show, Patrick Anderson raised LGBT money, and Giovanna Gray was the assistant. Not the most experienced crew, and I could tell they didn't have experience with sophisticated New York donors.

Presidential campaigns in New York are very different from anywhere else. Not only is the money important (unlimited rich people in the city who can write checks), but New York is the one state that requires months and months of work to produce a slate of delegates for the presidential nomination.

The Democratic Party had set up so many rules that you had to have women, African Americans, Asians, LGBTers, and so on, on a candidate's slate in exactly representative proportions. Whoever wrote the rule meant well, but it is an insane logistical requirement that basically means a full-time staff has to recruit a balanced slate. Emily, Patrick, and Giovanna didn't have the experience to meet the challenge. I hoped I'd not been sent to New York to do this.

Ethan Geto was running the show in the Midtown office. Emily whispered in my ear like it was some top-secret information that they had been sharing an office, but she had to leave because Ethan made a pass at her. I tried not to laugh. I didn't know Ethan personally, but I knew of him. The middle-age gay man and cofounder of the Human Rights Campaign likely had no intention of actually flirting with Emily. This was typical of the Dean for America campaign: young, well-intentioned, inexperienced Kool-Aid drinkers.

The team had set up a few fundraisers for the next couple days that I couldn't fix. Even with the excitement of small donors, I was there to provide entree into big New York money. After all, that was my specialty. I went along with what they'd planned and just tried to figure out how to get some more money down the line from the donors I knew.

The first event that weekend was out in Westchester County at elite donor George Soros's home. I thought he'd invite other big, important rich people, a circle of friends who must be able to both contribute and bundle lots of money for Howard Dean. At first, I was disappointed because of the catch: Soros was on a mission to defeat President Bush, and he really didn't care who did it. Soros wasn't endorsing Dean, and he wouldn't go out of his way to rally his network to raise money. All we got was the use of his name and his home to attract more donors.

His house had a large open floor plan with a backyard overlooking the rolling hills of upstate New York. Soros sat off to the side, way down at the edge of the yard, reading. He didn't leave that seat until it was time to introduce Howard Dean. He didn't mingle and he left immediately after

Dean spoke, avoiding the minions who'd paid a paltry $1,000 to show up at his home.

I didn't understand what he was up to. He had done the same for John Edwards, John Kerry, and Dick Gephardt. He was putting his name behind *any* Democrat. An altruistic view suggests he just liked every Democrat. The truth was hidden. He was working with a small cadre of billionaires to exploit the new McCain-Feingold rules in an attempt to take over the Democratic Party's agenda. Hosting presidential candidates was just a sideshow to him, an attempt to play nice and retain influence with the establishment now that his own donations were capped.

I HAVE NO IDEA how much money we raised that day at the Soros estate. *Nobody* knew. Money was flowing in so fast for the Dean campaign that we couldn't stay on top of missing checks, and donors who didn't make good on their commitments never got harassed for the money. This was the exact opposite of the McAuliffe way, and I loved the contrast. It gave us all the sense that everybody was in it together, a team: big donors, small donors, finance staff in NYC, and finance staff in California. It was all one glorious, equal shit show.

Governor Dean was coming back to New York City the next week for some meetings, and we had a few hours to raise money during his stop. I had some old donor friends at Goldman Sachs and Lazard Frères, folks who might just get excited about the insurgent Dean and could donate and bundle between $50,000 and $100,000 after one good meeting with the governor. Their motivation was cut and dried: to back a winner, and they wanted the winner to know they had helped.

ETHAN GETO WAS A STAR FUCKER, not a fundraiser. He wanted Dean to meet with Harvey Weinstein. Harvey cofounded Miramax Films and remains one of the most powerful people in the film industry. *Harper's Magazine* reported that in the last twenty years, seven Oscar winners have thanked God in their acceptance speeches . . . and thirty have thanked Harvey Weinstein.[3]

I was sure Harvey was a nice enough man and a decent human being, but getting him to raise money for Howard Dean would be time consuming. It's the way Hollywood types work. Not only would we have to meet with him, but Dean would have to call him afterward and kiss his ass. Our staff would have to worship him. It would be a lot of work to just get him to raise . . . what, maybe $25,000? That's a lot of money, but there are more efficient ways to get it. Harvey represented my issue with big Hollywood donors perfectly: They got all the time and the attention—after all, politicians like to hang out with famous people too—but it just wasn't worth the return.

I lost; Ethan got his meeting with Harvey. I was steaming mad but kept my mouth shut. We had a long way to go and this was just one day. Ethan and I went out to Teterboro Airport in New Jersey to meet Dean and his private plane. He was with his longtime assistant, Kate O'Connor. We jumped into a van and headed off to SoHo and the Weinstein office. Dean sat up front and barely said a word during the hour-long ride, Ethan wouldn't shut up, and I think Kate was reading *Mad Magazine.*

We got to Harvey's office and Dean and Ethan went in. Kate and I sat outside. They spent two hours in the meeting, two hours we could have used raising money elsewhere. They came out and went on and on about how well that meeting went. I was still steaming. By the end of the campaign, Harvey would write a check for $2,000 to Dean for America.[4] Never another dime, and he never hosted a fundraiser. Two thousand dollars for two hours. We raised that online in two seconds.

48

BY AUGUST OF 2003, THE CAMPAIGN WAS GETTING REAL BUZZ AND real support. Howard Dean had surged into the lead for fundraising. Amazing. The other more established candidates, like John Kerry, John Edwards, and Dick Gephardt, sat back in awe those first few months of the Deaniac revolution. That summer, the sea change was visible: For the first time ever in Democratic presidential campaigns, despite that pesky $2,000 limit, the Dean campaign had outraised the Democratic National Committee run by the king of Democratic money, Terry McAuliffe. Dean's netroots land had beaten the establishment money machine at its own game.

But it wasn't enough.

Campaign manager Joe Trippi and grassroots fundraiser Larry Biddle had the ingenious idea to stick a baseball bat icon on the website. The bat would fill up like a thermometer as people donated, until it was topped out. We'd establish different goals for each day—maybe $100,000 on a Monday, a $250,000 Tuesday—and each goal would have a different theme or justification.

Dean's supporters went crazy. Filling the bat came to represent the campaign's success. We'd hit our mark every day, and then some. I was fascinated. It took me months to organize and beg big donors to raise $100,000. This campaign was now doing that in hours and with not a second spent hand-holding rich donors.

One of the best moments of the campaign came when Vice President Dick Cheney attended a big-money lunch event in Texas, limited to a handful of people who could raise at least $250,000 for the Bush-Cheney reelect. The event's details were leaked to the press, and the folks in Burlington jumped on it.

They took a photo of Howard Dean eating a tuna fish sandwich and made a baseball bat out of it. "Why pay $50,000 to have lunch with Dick Cheney when you too can have lunch with Howard Dean at your desk for $10 or $25?" The bat exceeded the amount Cheney had raised in just a few hours. It was the ultimate way of proving that grassroots could do more for changing our political system. At least I thought that way in the moment.

IN 2004, THERE WERE about a hundred top Democratic bundlers, individuals who could raise around $100,000 from friends and colleagues. It was a small group, and they had control of the party. The next tier were those who could write a check for the maximum of $2,000. They would not raise money from their friends, but they still needed a little coddling. As I was calling the second tier in New York, I kept getting a funny response that put a smile on my face. They would donate but didn't want to go to an event; they wanted to wait for the next online baseball bat. Wealthy donors wanted to be a part of something new and exciting, they wanted to be a part of the grassroots donor community. All of us were in it together.

49

PEOPLE-POWERED MONEY HAD BEGUN TO DISTURB THE ELITE, WHO had no intention of relinquishing their grip on power. After all, these folks like it when presidential candidates beg for help. Imagine the ego boost of spending an hour or two hours every few months with a leading candidate for President of the United States of America. The conversations are very personal and very direct. They are very rarely about the general cause, doing good for the world.

Conversations are much more about what donors care about. Perhaps it's foreign policy and the need to focus on the Middle East. Take Haim Saban, an LA-based mega-donor whose claim to fame is producing the *Mighty Morphin' Power Rangers*. Saban has given close to $16 million in the last twenty years, the vast, vast majority to Democrats. He told the *New York Times* in 2004 that in a conversation he had told Howard Dean that he was, "a one-issue guy, and my issue is Israel." Don't miss Haim Saban's underlying meaning: If you want my money, you must come beg at my door, shine my shoes, echo my talking points on my one issue, and then I'll open my wallet.

Or take Ned Cloonan, head of AIG Government Affairs, who was typical of many corporate lobbyists I worked with. I would arrange a meeting during which I presumed we'd only discuss AIG's federal policy issues. Something strange happened several times, no matter who I'd bring in to see him, whether it was Dick Gephardt, Martin Frost, Ed Markey, or Howard Dean: Each time, Cloonan steered the conversation toward the flight patterns out of LaGuardia Airport. See, Ned owned a home on the New York–Connecticut border and the planes were flying too close, causing too much noise for his liking. Ned seemed to be using his position as a high-powered corporate lobbyist to get access to politicians who might try to solve a personal issue.

I wanted average Americans to have an equal say in the system. The Dean campaign was showing how that might happen with a tuna fish sandwich and a baseball bat.

The day Howard Dean raised more than Dick Cheney should have been a huge moment of celebration for everyone in the Democratic Party. It was the exact opposite. It became the day that those select few big donors panicked and started working collectively to destroy Howard Dean.

They didn't want to destroy what he was connected to, his grassroots donor army. They would have to be careful so as not to be seen as destroying Dean. They had to do it quietly. Dean helped them accomplish it.

TO BUILD ON HIS grassroots momentum and prove the campaign had national appeal, the Dean brain trust conceived a plan to hold massive rallies around the country. Fifty thousand people in Portland, Oregon, then 25,000 in New York. Impressive showings everywhere. And they cost a ton. The campaign was raising amazing amounts of money, but it was spending more than it raised. Joe Trippi and his team had no plans to manage the growing campaign; it wasn't what they cared about. Dean was just a vehicle to prove the campaign staff could change politics, and they wanted to continue spending to keep the campaign growing.

Most managers running serious campaigns would have been more reserved. They would have taken that lead in the money race and used it to
corner other candidates while saving as much as they could. The Trippiites
blew all that cash early. We had to keep finding more donors, and that
meant going back to the traditional donor network. Big donors, big events,
big amounts of time. The pressure was on to keep pace and not let the
outside world know that by early December 2003, the campaign was on
financial life support.

Time constraints on a presidential campaign are intense. Candidates
need to spend a lot of quality time in the early primary states, Iowa, New
Hampshire, and South Carolina, with a focus on voters. Fundraising is
important, but only for a few days a month. The campaign picked the first
week of December as our big money week.

Dean would do events in DC, California, Chicago, and New York. My
goal was to raise $1 million in one day, an amount never done in a presiden-
tial primary campaign. In 1991, Bill Clinton had raised $750,000 in one
day, and that was a major line in the sand. I told Mattis Goldman, a friend
and DC media consultant, that we might break $2 million for the day. So
much money was coming into the campaign in such a chaotic manner that
$2 million would be hard to confirm one way or the other. Mattis spread
the word and a reporter ran with the story.

If you know one thing in political fundraising, it's to always understate
the goal. I never intended for the amount to become public. The campaign
had to backtrack and deny that the $2 million was a real target, but once it
was out there, I continued to play it up. It was my way of letting big donors
know that Dean was going to roll to the nomination, and they better get
on board.

Things were complicated because Ethan Geto loved the big, free rallies. I was worried: Though we were taking in a good chunk of money
from grassroots supporters, would they pay online after they showed up
in Central Park for free? I had to block Ethan, deny him the opportunity
to put Dean out there, at enormous cost to the campaign, and risk not

getting anything in return. Netroots or not, we were broke and needed the cash.

So I packed December 8—my New York day—with fundraising events. They'd all be low to mid-dollar, designed to show that average Americans could afford to be a part of this campaign. Dean would arrive at 11 am for a "Woman for Dean" event in Brooklyn, then head back to Manhattan for an afternoon with LGBT supporters in Chelsea, then do a happy hour with Goldman Sachs.

At 7 pm, I arranged a "Roast of Howard Dean," then at 9 pm, the *Queer as Folk* TV show cast would host Dean for a reception, and finally we'd finish the day off at the Roseland Ballroom with a late-night "Comedians for Dean" event. This was crazy; no way could I find enough donors to pull it all off. But I needed to try so Ethan could not stick Dean in front of fifty thousand freeloaders in Central Park on one of the only fundraising days I had with Dean.

The "Roast of Howard Dean" was my idea, and it took a week to convince the campaign to do something fun. They were worried it might embarrass him, but I wanted to lighten him up. I hoped it would make Dean look more human to New Yorkers, make fun of the guy in a controlled setting, and maybe he wouldn't seem so shrill.

The campaign team in Burlington finally agreed, and we got Rob Reiner to emcee. Dean's college roommate, friends from Vermont and from his childhood would all get the chance to tell Dean stories that people didn't know. Hell, even if you didn't like Howard Dean, you might buy a ticket to just see him embarrassed.

I divided up the donor lists, first contacting those who could raise $10,000 or more to sign up to host one day's many events. Then I tried to get those who'd given $500 or $600 to give another check for that amount. We had so many targets that the process felt clean—raising money from many donors in relatively small amounts. We didn't have to rely on just a few donors who could bundle $100,000 or more; we could say no to them if we needed to without fear of getting cut off. And if we did our job right by making it seem like Dean could not lose, the big donors would be afraid of not being involved.

I set up a breakfast meeting for the top targets I wanted to hook as $10,000 hosts, including James Torrey—lifetime donations $585,000—and Diane Straus Tucker, among others. Because Dean was doing so well in the polls, some of the traditional big donors decided to come hear me give the pitch, just in case they needed to back the winner. That's what some New York wealthy donors look for, a winner to invest in; issues and policy are sometimes secondary.

The breakfast host committee meeting was on East 47th Street in a law firm conference room at 8 am. I arrived at West 47th at 7:50 am. Dammit. Trying to get across town at 8 am is nearly impossible, so I started jogging across Central Park in my suit. I ran as fast as I could, stumbling in at 8:10 am, out of breath. Some of the attendees groused about being disrespected by the late start. We sat around the conference table, just big enough for all of us.

I went into my pitch about Governor Dean and what this campaign meant for the country, for our future, for young people, and why he needed their money to win. Most important, I made it clear that Dean was going to be the nominee and now was the time to get on board. My typical speech was about seven minutes long. About halfway through the spiel, some around the table starting tearing up, rubbing their noses and eyes. "Wow," I thought for a brief second, "I'm really getting through to these people!" . . . which was odd, because my speech was about needing money to win. Not typical stuff that makes ultra-wealthy people cry.

Finally someone starting sniffing the bagels, the cream cheese, the juice. Something had clearly gone bad, but I could only smell my own B.O. from the run. Then a few people stepped outside for fresh air. I finished up and answered a few questions. Five people quickly agreed to be hosts for $10,000. Of course, before the meeting I had asked three of them to volunteer to say that, not really caring if they could raise the money. It was my way to pressure others: This guy is in, why aren't you?

On the way out of the meeting, I jumped into the elevator with a few prospects, tears still in their eyes. Surely I hadn't touched their hearts that much. Then the smell hit me. It was so bad, it had followed us into the elevator! Then in a moment of unity for Dean, we all realized that attached to the bottom of my shoe was a massive chunk of Central Park horse shit. I finally cried with them, mostly from my own laughter.

WE SPENT A FEW MORE WEEKS building momentum for the day of events. It was going to be a logistical nightmare. Moving parts everywhere, expenses through the roof, and I was struggling to handle the process. It was important to hit this day out of the park and show that New York grassroots power was real and could be harnessed into significant money. And it was important for the big-money New Yorkers to see that Dean's nomination was inevitable.

The first three events went on without a hitch. Decent crowds on a small scale that I had set up, lowballing expectations for daytime grassroots events. For the early evening events, I rented a large art studio in Chelsea for the roast and the *Queer as Folk* cast event. We split the place in two, with tables of ten for the roast on one side and a large open room for the *Queer as Folk* event on the other.

Panic set in. The 7 pm roast would be fine. We had sold tables of ten and we knew how many people had purchased tickets, about four hundred at $1,000 apiece. Even if some didn't show, the tables took up space and the room would be filled.

But lost in the fast flowing lead-up to the day was the fact that we had barely sold any tickets to the *Queer as Folk* or the "Comedians for Dean" event at Roseland after. With no tables to take up space on the other side of the art studio in Chelsea, we would need at least five or six hundred people to make it look full.

The Roseland ballroom held three thousand, and we needed two thousand to avoid embarrassment. I didn't fully understand how grassroots donors thought, what their motivations were, or how they bought tickets. I didn't know how they acted. I kept telling myself they would give at the last minute, a spontaneous massive purchase.

We had sold 150 to the *Queer as Folk* cast event and 75 for the Roseland Ballroom comic night with host Sandra Bernhard. A complete fucking disaster. After seeing the empty events, a reporter could argue that the Dean machine was over.

I had twenty-four hours to fix it.

I grabbed a few campaign staffers and we went out to Times Square and starting handing out freebies. We begged people to take them just to come see comedian Sandra Bernhard and others for a night of comedy and Howard Dean. We begged everyone we could find . . . just come, please. We even hit up the homeless on Tenth Avenue. Anything to get another two thousand people to show up. It was going to be embarrassing.

Dean's buddies didn't really have much to say about Howard at the roast, though they tried. It was a relaxed, slightly boring hour and a half as everyone anticipated a breakthrough embarrassing story, which never arrived. Even Howard Dean seemed a little bored by it all as he kept leaving the stage to make phone calls.

We had set up a little greenroom between the two events for him to relax in after the roast and before the *Queer as Folk* event. I needed him to stay in that room for a bit as I begged the people who'd attended the roast to come over to the other side for a little touch of gay humor. I needed to fill that room!

Dean was on and off the phone and unfortunately listening to the warm-up act for the *Queer as Folk* event as well. Comedian David Cross was going through some pretty funny material, with a tendency to use foul language. Nothing out of the ordinary for a comedian. Dean freaked out. "I'm going to be President of the United States and do not want to be associated with such language!" Unbelievable. He refused to go on. We had to go out and explain to the crowd of five hundred people that Howard Dean would not be speaking.

I was standing next to comedian Janeane Garofalo, who'd also done a bit that night before David Cross. "If Howard Dean doesn't go on, it's time for the comedians of New York to find a new candidate," she sighed.

I whispered back, "Right on, sister."

Dean cussed about the cuss words, using language much worse than David's on stage. The audience just didn't know what to make of the entire episode. They—well, a few—had paid real money, and they came to see Howard Dean. I told everybody that they could join us for free at the next event to make it up to them. Yeah, I was being nice. I needed the warm bodies to fill the room.

We made it to the Roseland Ballroom for the last event for the one hundred ticket buyers, some tourists we had begged, and Tenth Avenue's homeless population. The night was over. A disaster to be sure, but also a clear showing of the giving limits of small-dollar donors.

I USED EVERYTHING I had learned in over ten years of fundraising that day, December 8, 2003. It worked on one level and was a complete and utter failure on another. We raised a ton—over $800,000—beating the amount Bill Clinton had raised in 1991. Success.

But the limits of grassroots people power reared its ugly head. Going to free rallies and giving to online baseball bats had worked great for the masses earlier that year, but now that Dean was the front-runner, the fascination surrounding an insurgent campaign was fading. Some donors no longer felt Dean was the outsider who'd excited them. Netroots donors with true passion had been giving to Dean when they could afford to toss $10 or $25 at the online challenge of the day. But a snag hit around the holidays. If the choice is Howard Dean or traditional needs in December, the choice was clear for many.

I HAD ONE MORE EVENT, the next morning in Harlem. I'd scheduled it because I wanted to make a statement that everybody should have a piece of this campaign. No white politician ever raised money in Harlem, but I was determined to make it happen. David Paterson, an African American state senator and later governor, chaired the event and helped us sell out. I was most proud of this moment; the campaign was including everybody in the process.

Remember all those calls Dean had been taking the night before? He'd been speaking to Al Gore. The former VP was in New York that day and was going to endorse Dean for president. It was a very big deal for the outsider insurgent candidate to receive an endorsement from the previous Democrat nominee for president.

Unfortunately, Dean didn't trust his campaign manager, Joe Trippi, his national finance director, Stephanie Schriock, or much of anyone else for that matter. Normally for such a huge public endorsement, a presidential candidate needs a big moment like this to be tightly choreographed. Instead, Dean finally let it leak around 1 am that Gore would be in Harlem to make the endorsement official. We were all blindsided.

Every reporter in the world would want to cover the biggest moment of the campaign to date, but we had only a few hours to make it happen. You need backdrops, handouts, press passes, sound systems—and all of those things take time. We scrambled all night.

Al Gore's endorsement should have sent a message that Gore was endorsing Dean the Outsider. Instead, the mishandled moment would be the beginning of the end. It backfired, and looked like Howard Dean the Outsider had been co-opted by Gore the Establishment.

Decisions made in campaigns have an impact on how the public views you; tactical decisions can forever make or break a campaign. Dean had made a mistake with the rollout of the Al Gore endorsement, but that was not the biggest mistake the campaign made that month.

50

ON DECEMBER 13, 2003, AMERICAN TROOPS CAPTURED SADDAM Hussein, hiding in a spider hole. In response, Howard Dean made a technically correct if slightly tone-deaf statement that the world was "not safer" today.[1] Right or wrong, that day was not the day to say it.

The 2004 campaign was the first after the McCain-Feingold reforms, which capped the amount rich donors could give. The new law didn't, of course, kill rich donors' appetites to influence elections. Here, big donors and monied interests pounced, seeing their chance to hit Howard Dean as an unserious commander in chief. They set up a new 527 group—"527" refers to the part of the IRS tax code for political organizations not directly affiliated with a campaign—and within a day went up with a nasty TV ad that tied Howard Dean to Osama bin Laden. The group, called Americans for Jobs, Health Care & Progressive Values, unaccountable to anyone but its funders, bought slots for this ad all over Iowa and New Hampshire. While showing a slow-moving picture of Bin Laden, the narrator said,

> We live in a very dangerous world.
>
> And there are those who wake up every morning determined to destroy western civilization. . . .
>
> Americans want a president who can face the dangers ahead.
>
> But Howard Dean has no military or foreign policy experience.
>
> And Howard Dean just cannot compete with George Bush on foreign policy.
>
> It's time for Democrats to think about that . . . and think about it now.

Normally these attack ads would come from another candidate, a specific person to whom our campaign could respond directly. But Americans for Jobs, Health Care & Progressive Values wasn't tied to any candidate and did not have to disclose its donors. The funders were clearly scared that Dean would win the nomination, and they'd have no control over him.

Dick Gephardt had dropped out of the race one week earlier, but his ghost was still alive and well. The *Washington Post* uncovered the organization's funders, many of whom I had heard of for the first time more than ten years earlier as we sat around the Dubliner on my first day at the Effective Government Committee: Alan Patricof, Bernard Schwartz, Daniel Abraham, and even some unions scared of the Dean army, all of whom scrambled to chip in a million dollars on short notice to take down Dean.

Americans for Jobs, Health Care & Progressive Values was run by Robert Gibbs, John Kerry's former press secretary (and future White House spokesman under Barack Obama) . . . and David Jones, Jonesy.

"Our goal was to point out where Howard Dean stood on the issues and point out that he had no foreign policy experience," Jones said. "Clearly those goals were accomplished."[2]

Ten Years later, many remember Swiftboat Veterans for the Truth, the conservative 527 who attacked John Kerry's Vietnam record, as the first major unaccountable outside organization. But Americans for Jobs, Health Care & Progressive Values was really the first to play in the 2004 election, and showed conservatives how effective these groups could be.

51

THE ATTACK CAME FROM AN OUTSIDE GROUP, AN EARLY SUPER-PAC, and it's hard to respond to attacks from outside groups. Who do you fight back against? There's no candidate. The campaign couldn't attack the group's donors; that didn't really make sense. There was no script on how to respond to billionaire money that wasn't controlled by a candidate or party. The Dean campaign could have gone after generic "establishment" Democrats, but following the Gore endorsement, Dean was now more a part of the establishment, at least in the public's view. All the mistakes of the campaign were coming to a head. Led by Joe Trippi, the Dean team in Burlington then made the ultimate mistake: They tried to change the rules of campaign finance.

The Dean campaign's brain trust had a simple rationale: If outside groups could take in unlimited money, why shouldn't the Dean camp— with unlimited small-dollar potential—do the same? Up to that point, presidential campaigns followed rules that allowed for matching federal funds. For the first $250 raised from each individual, the federal government would provide a matching $250, as long as the campaign adhered to the individual spending limit in each state. If $10 million of Howard Dean's $50 million came in checks for at least $250, the campaign would have another $10 million in matching federal funds. That's real money.

It was meant to even the playing field. If everybody spent the same amount in Iowa and New Hampshire, the candidate with the best message and organization would win. John Kerry, John Edwards, and Dick Gephardt depended on matching funds, so for them, opting out had never been on the table.

But Dean was raising so much thanks to his new friends on the Internet that he and the Burlington team put it on the table. Dean announced in the middle of December that his campaign would opt out of federal limits (a common occurrence for presidential candidates today). The team thought his online prowess was an ATM, spitting out unlimited cash, and expected to use the never-ending flow of money to crush his opponents. What Trippi failed to mention to anyone was that the campaign was already broke. Fifty million dollars had come in, and $50 million had gone out. Political malpractice at its best. Had they even saved $5 million—just 10 percent—the election might have turned out differently.

Dean's decision forced every other candidate to opt out too and scramble for big money. John Kerry took out a $6 million loan against the value of his Boston home the day after the Dean campaign announcement. It's something he couldn't have done previously—to receive federal matching funds, candidates cannot lend their campaigns money. Without this immediate cash injection, Kerry would not have been able to compete in the Iowa caucus, let alone win. Dean should have cruised to victory, but he let the allure of cash—even if it was grassroots cash—do him in.

I SPENT THE NEXT FEW WEEKS collecting the checks that had not shown up on the day of the events. I was still only approaching $800,000, well short of the $2 million newspaper story amount. Alan Gifford Miller, speaker of the New York City Council, made me a deal: If I could get him $50,000, he would get me $50,000. It was a fundraiser side deal. I'd direct money to him from trusted donors who had maxed out to Dean but still wanted to help. He would he give me the same amount from his maxed-out donors. It's a way around giving limits. And it's done daily for big campaigns.

I struggled to find donors who cared about the speaker of the New York City Council. He had delivered his $50,000 already so I had to find it. At the last minute, I called Stephanie Schriock in Burlington and begged her for some checkwriters. She came through on New Year's Eve, right before the deadline.

THE IOWA CAUCUSES ARRIVED on January 19, and Dean got crushed, finishing third. That night, he screamed on national television. There's no reason to relive that moment. His campaign could have been something amazing, but it died that night.

Everybody went through the motions in New Hampshire. If Dean could pull off a victory in the New Hampshire primary, maybe he could turn things around. Nothing brings in donations like victory in hand. If he lost New Hampshire, right next door to his home state of Vermont, would the money—big and small—dry up? Dean finished second, which was respectable. But with no cash on hand, it just didn't matter. He dropped out in the following weeks, and his political future didn't look bright.

More important to me was that the new way to raise money, to do politics, had fallen short. Of course, the Dean campaign was only the first try at raising tons of money in small amounts so there was hope that with better management we could build a new grassroots donor political system. Though Barack Obama's campaigns have had success in the online donor community, it's important to remember the strategy and technology was built on the back of Howard Dean's failures. But in January 2004, we were unsure that a small dollar, online donor community could survive.

52

I DIDN'T WORK FOR HOWARD DEAN BECAUSE OF HIS PERSONALITY, his small-state charm, or his policy positions. Rather, I was attracted to Dean because of the way he could raise money. His network of lots and lots of small donors was an easy, clean way to raise money for campaigns. This was the way it *should* work. It was genius and I loved it. I wanted to see it continue to shape political campaigns even without a Dean presidential campaign.

After Howard Dean withdrew from the Democratic primary, the question quickly turned to his future. What was he going to do with his amazing network of grassroots donors? Would they just fade away?

I went back to DC with no clue what to do next. Then I got a call from Roy Neel. Roy had been Gore's chief of staff in 1993–1994 and had joined the Dean campaign to replace Joe Trippi as campaign manager toward the end. He was essentially playing the role of the adult who could help shut things down. Roy had an offer for me. Would I move to Burlington and help Dean's political action committee, Democracy for America (DFA)? DFA was an outside group itself, but one that we wanted to finance by small donors, a few bucks at a time. It would endorse candidates, not attack others. I was stoked about the chance to keep Dean's grassroots movement going.

I moved to Burlington. Tom McMahon would be the new executive director, Tom Hughes would be the field director, and Laura Gross would be the communications director. For the next ten months we would work to get Dean back from his scream and raise an astonishing $5 million for DFA. That amount may sound like a pittance compared to what Dean had raised for his presidential bid, but following the collapse of the campaign, the question was more whether Dean had any support at all. Our initial budget was for $2 million. We blew past that goal in short order.

Tom McMahon would go on to be the executive director of the Democratic National Committee the next year. Tom has a very strong focus and an understanding of the long game. It is a view that is useful and underappreciated in politics: What's the long-term goal? How do we get there? Meanwhile, both Dean and I had a very different view: Get it done today and forget about the consequences. Having Tom force Howard Dean to step back and look at the big picture changed the governor's fortunes for the better over time. It was a lesson I never learned—I wanted to change the world in one day.

HOWARD DEAN HAD BEEN laughed off stage for the Iowa scream, but we had one great thing going for DFA: Of over 750,000 people on his email lists, 318,000 had donated, a powerful army that if used correctly, could change politics forever. If we could harness these supporters and convince them to give to other candidates—candidates they'd never heard of but who stood for the right things—we'd dilute the influence of wealthy donors who had taken control of the conversation in the party.

We set out to promote candidates across the board, not just for Congress. If we could change the way a candidate for city council, state representative, or local school board raised money, we might be on to something new. Candidates for Congress generally have access to a national donor base of only very wealthy individuals, and those folks take too much time to bring around, especially if you're new to politics and they have never heard of you. Locally, a candidate might have a direct mail list to write for money, but it cost a lot to solicit money via snail mail. And then local politicians in down-ballot races might not have a list at all, especially if they were just starting out.

With DFA's seal of approval and official endorsement for candidates everywhere, we wanted to send a signal to small donors that it was time to chip in. We wanted to see this work. What we didn't know at the time was that to raise this kind of money, we would end up playing a role in increasing partisan political rhetoric.

ALTHOUGH DEAN HAD BEEN the champion of small-dollar online money, he did have his share of large donors too. Now, these folks could never be considered the top-tier big donors, they were the B team of big money. The governor wanted to keep them involved somehow too, though the time and effort put into these folks would not get us too far.

However, we needed an infusion of cash before we could get the small dollar machine running, so we invited these people up to Burlington to preview DFA and discuss how they could participate: Beth Broderick, former actress on *Sabrina, the Teenage Witch;* Rick Jacobs, a Los Angeles gay activist; Judith McHale, head of the Discovery Channel; Walter Ludwig, a political hack; and some guy whose name I forget but who was the Vermont king of maple syrup. Dean for America's top dogs. It showed why we never got traction when the heat started—we didn't have anybody in the establishment to back us up. It was refreshing to have a new breed of rich outsiders like this, but presidential campaigns are brutal, and when the attacks come, you need adults with experience around. Dean never had that.

Judith McHale would complain a few months later that I had never asked her for money for DFA. She had $25,000 to give, but she didn't write the check because I didn't specifically ask her for it during that meeting. This was the world that big donors live in: They needed to be asked. Through Dean, I was trying to reverse this relationship: If you had big money, give it because you believe in the cause, not because you want something in return . . . or worse, because you want to be begged.

I had struggled with this for ten years. I was a Democrat, I supported Democratic causes and candidates. I supported the party, the movement. If a donor had so much money that writing a $25,000 check was common, why need to be begged? Shouldn't it be the other way around, where a donor gives because the donor believes in something or someone?

It works this way for philanthropic causes: breast cancer, heart research, March of Dimes, and so on. Sure, some of those donors like being wined and dined, but a majority give because they believe in the cause. Politics is not that way, in part because they've never been pitched that way. Politicians, especially Democrats, sell themselves (see: Obama, Barack), hatred of the other side—painting the other side as evil is a politician's best closing argument—or the fear of losing . . . but never the cause.

FOR MONTHS AFTER THE CAMPAIGN, most billionaire buzzards hovered over what they presumed to be Howard Dean's political corpse. They thought that Dean was dead as a doorknob and wanted to capture his grassroots army. They came to Burlington, played nice, and pretended to be supportive of his future. What they wanted was free and total access to his list of 750,000 email addresses. They needed that army to take over the Democratic Party. Had we failed to rehabilitate Dean's standing with the activists and establishment, they could have gotten away with it.

The two big donors of 2004, George Soros and Peter Lewis, the liberal head of Progressive Insurance, did almost all of their funding in conjunction with Andy Stern, president of the Service Employees International Union (SEIU), and his deputy, Anna Burger. They pushed for radical change across all Democratic institutions, including the labor movement. They would eventually split off from the AFL-CIO and form a new alliance with the Teamsters, Laborers' International Union of North America, and a few other smaller unions. It would only last a few years before they all went back to the AFL-CIO.

If labor is anything, it is grassroots involvement. Unions work their members to get involved in politics, causes, and labor drives around the country. Dean's grassroots movement scared them; it was outside union control with very few actual union members. If anything, a new political power base of 750,000 people could be a threat to Andy Stern.

Elite billionaires don't have much in common with labor. They shared a vision of a Democratic renaissance, but they didn't completely agree with what that vision was. Soros was as focused on creating a global liberal utopia as he was on building one in the United States. Andy Stern was focused on getting more members for his union, more *dues-paying* members.

What was clear right away was that wealthy billionaire donors wanted control and access to Dean's new army of political donor activists. They wanted to use their money to take control of the Deaniac machine, with or without him.

But since we had a people-powered movement, I thought I could play them off one another and kick-start Democracy for America with some cash.

Jonathan Soros, George's son, flew up to Burlington and spent the day with Dean and our staff to talk about DFA. What he really wanted was to find a way to use our list of 750,000 names for his project he was working on, America Coming Together. ACT spent over $20 million in 2004 trying to elect John Kerry. It was a super-PAC before super-PACs, and having the Deaniacs get involved would make a big difference—ACT could say they weren't just the rich guy's club. In the end, ACT ended up being a waste of a lot of money, and it proved to the wealthy liberal elites that they had to change the way they invested.

Jonathan left without committing to support us, and I held on to our email list, but I called the staff at the SEIU and told them that ACT and I had a very good meeting and that we hoped that they would contribute a large sum. The back-and-forth went on for a few days. SEIU could not decide on how much to give because they didn't know whether they'd get our email list in return.

So I decided to make the decision for them. I called Peter Lewis's office and told his staff that Jonathan Soros had committed $500,000. Would Peter match it? Then I called Jonathan Soros and told him that the SEIU said he would be giving $500,000, and I wanted to thank him right away.

If I got away with it, that would be a cool $1.5 million to kick-start the new Democracy for America. I knew there was a short window before I'd be found out, so I demanded the money right away, saying we needed it to pay for our servers or would lose our list of 750,000 names.

It took twenty-four hours before the phone starting ringing off the hook: "Lindsay, who told you that Soros was giving $500,000?" And "Lindsay, who told you that Peter Lewis would give $500,000?" I had no good answer, of course. I tried to be as generic as I could and said I couldn't remember. They tried to call me out and get me in trouble, but I was a fundraiser, I was just doing my job: squeezing money out of the system.

Each had budgeted $100,000 for DFA, but since they couldn't figure out if they had or had not actually committed, Soros and Peter Lewis decided to each give $250,000 for a total of $500,000. I won this little battle with the rich liberal elites, and I didn't have to give up a thing.

53

DEAN HAD STOKED SOMETHING AROUND THE COUNTRY, AND NOT just the grassroots. The private sector wanted to understand his movement and figure out how they too could harness the power of the masses. It was the dawn of the crowdsourcing era, in a way. The governor was getting $50,000 or so a speech as he traveled around the country for the next six months. I would tag along and set up meetings with the grassroots donors on these trips. It was an ideal way to make him money and keep our project going.

Howard Dean was a tough man to travel with. He was a stickler for money, which I actually admired, but this meant lots of red-eyes and weird flight times. It makes some sense, but flying from Burlington to San Francisco in the morning, having meetings all day, and flying back to Burlington on the red-eye was tough. He wanted to remain anonymous on his flights, fine with me. But he was ridiculous. The deal was that I would sit on the aisle, he would sit at the window, and he would wrap his head in a towel so nobody would see him.

We split up the trips: Tom McMahon would go, then I would go. It was the only way to stay sane, as Dean was on the road six days a week. We came to the conclusion that Dean's wife probably wanted him away as often as possible.

OF COURSE, WE RAN INTO a few hiccups along the way. Puerto Rico might have been the scene of the crime for my pot smuggling "network," but it was also a drug island for big pharma. Many of the top pharmaceutical companies had set up shop down there for tax reasons and cheap labor. Evan Morris worked for one of them as their DC lobbyist. The majority of lobbyists played the game well, giving money because they have to, not involving themselves excessively or demanding too much time, like wealthy national donors. Evan was different. He demanded time just like your average political billionaire.

Donors who spend so much time schmoozing with politicians develop avenues to communicate with them, cutting staff out of the process. What that means is that the fundraiser can't control the relationship, can't block it when it becomes inappropriate, and can't remind donors that they owe money. Dean continued to think that he should have direct contact with these folks. He was the boss, and why should his donors have to go through the staff?

Evan called Dean and told him that he had something set up in Puerto Rico. He could arrange for his buddy, a trial lawyer named Jimmy, to pick us up at Dulles and fly us down to San Juan on his private jet. If this request had gone through me, I would have had a lot of questions: Who was the attorney? Where was the money coming from in Puerto Rico? Is this the best use of our time? Dean didn't ask any of these questions, but he did tell Evan it sounded like a great idea.

We flew down to DC early that morning. With an hour to kill, I had set up a meeting with the Kerry campaign just to touch base and continue to build some love between the establishment Democrats and Dean. We wanted to make sure Dean didn't get screwed at the national convention with a 3 pm speaking slot (the best slots are in prime time). Joe Lockhart and Ann Lewis, two of the more senior veterans of Democratic politics, sat down with us. Dean led with an over-the-top suggestion to save the campaign for Kerry: John Kerry should fly to Baghdad the next day and hold a press conference about how stupid the war was. I had to look away so it didn't appear as though I was agreeing with him.

WE LEFT THE KERRY OFFICE and set off for the private plane terminal at Dulles Airport. We arrived before Evan and Jimmy. A bunch of folks in cowboy hats sat in the lounge with us and snickered at Dean. They were all waiting for Republican House Majority Leader Tom DeLay to fly off for a golfing trip to Europe, the one that would eventually land DeLay in legal trouble for inappropriate campaign contributions and force him to resign from the House. He'd be acquitted later, but the joke's still on them.

Finally Evan and Jimmy showed up and we jumped onto the cramped old plane, with just enough seats for all of us . . . not what we thought we would be flying to Puerto Rico in. I looked at Dean and didn't say a word. But I wanted him to know that I had a job to do: to protect him from agreeing to stupid shit like this.

On a private plane, the flight to San Juan from Dulles should be about three hours. This plane was so old that after five we'd only made it to Samson City, Florida, and had to stop for fuel. All that time with Evan and Trial Attorney Jimmy was painful, as I had to sit there and listen to them spout off, and we still had another three hours to go. We arrived in San Juan as the sun disappeared. Exhausted and miserable, Dean went straight to a little fundraiser with the governor of Puerto Rico. We raised about $10,000, which was at least worth some of pain.

The next morning we flew over to Vieques island. Turns out Jimmy had dragged us to Puerto Rico because he was suing the U.S. Government over the Navy's use of Vieques as a bombing range for the last forty years. I was sympathetic toward his clients, but he was essentially using Howard

Dean as a type of advertisement to attract other potential clients to meet him. He didn't give us a dime.

Why Evan Morris, a pharmaceutical lobbyist, had set this trip up made no sense. I guess he was trying to use the allure of Jimmy's potential donation to become closer to Dean. It was the credit game in a new form. Evan was typical of everything I felt was wrong with money in politics; he hung around rich people, trying to use money to exert influence on politicians. This is why I wanted to see Dean's money army succeed.

54

DURING THE PRESIDENTIAL PRIMARY, THE FACES OF THE GRASS-roots had seemed distant to me. I didn't really know these people that well. After all, that was the point of the movement—as they gave money through Dean's website, the fundraiser was cut out of the deal. It was what I wanted. I was mostly in New York City, hanging out with any rich person who was open to supporting Dean.

As we went around the country—Portland, Seattle, Philadelphia, Chicago, Texas . . . anyplace we could generate a gathering of ex-Deaniacs—I was shocked to learn who these people really were. They weren't average Americans who wanted a stake in the political process. After a few trips to engage with them, to energize them, I had developed a sad opinion. You know the bar scene in *Star Wars?* Don't think of these people as the misfits who are in the bar; these people are the ones the bouncer wouldn't let in to begin with! They weren't the "normal" folks who showed up for other candidates: the retirees, the party faithful, the idealistic kids. Some truly loved Howard Dean, as in were *in love* with him. Others clearly had never had the social skills to participate in other more normal campaigns. But the online world Dean created had brought them out of their shells.

They weren't an easy bunch to manage. Just as the wealthy elites felt entitled to something for the money they gave, this new mass army felt entitled to something for the emails they sent, the blogs they wrote, the money they gave, and the orange hats they would wear (the orange hats caused major issues for Dean in Iowa, as his chaotic "army" showed up and invaded the state).

Keeping some of these folks at bay from both physically attacking Dean (those in love with him) and those who wanted to drive his agenda into some radical new antiwar movement did make me feel like a bouncer at that bar in *Star Wars* some days.

Months and months after he'd dropped out, these people still loved Howard Dean, and only Howard Dean. Their purpose was to keep his revolution going. Their second common thread was that they truly hated George W. Bush. The hatred was not the normal, "I am a Democrat, he is a Republican," which we could have done something with because that would have been a disagreement over values. To these people, it was much more personal.

Even though 2004 was John Kerry's summer, the leftover Deaniacs never spoke about him. Bush was the devil, Dean was the savior, and they couldn't care less about John Kerry. They didn't give a shit about the Democratic Party, its values, or who was going to win the election if it wasn't Howard Dean. It was a real eye-opener that Kerry was in trouble—how was he going to win if he couldn't even muster the enthusiasm of the party's base? Kerry was clearly the candidate for the establishment elite Democrats, who had gone out of their way to destroy Howard Dean.

One of my main assumptions—that Dean's grassroots campaign was composed of average folks—had been shattered. The die had been cast. My new quest was figuring out how to engage middle-class Americans to participate in the political process. Money was a part of politics, we weren't going to change that, but I wanted to give average Americans a voice. It had been my goal since working with Dick Gephardt's network in the mid-1990s.

55

DEAN'S CAMPAIGN DIDN'T HAVE MUCH CONNECTION TO THE DC INsiders, which was kind of the point. But Tom McMahon and I still wanted to at least make peace with them. Dean's grassroots dollars were as green as anyone's, so if the insiders could accept Howard Dean's grassroots help, a few could validate his efforts through Democracy for America.

First we met with Nancy Pelosi and Harry Reid. We offered what we could: Dean's ability to raise money in small dollars. We would set up joint fundraising accounts in accordance with the law, one each for the party's campaign committees, which we called DFA-DCCC and DFA-DSCC. Dean went batshit crazy: He didn't want to help them. He didn't understand why Tom and I would ever agree to help these insiders. We ignored him. He had no choice if he wanted any chance of rehabilitating his image after the scream. He needed to help some mainstream Democrats, not attack them. We went on to raise a significant amount of money for the DCCC and DSCC in the summer of 2004, and most important, we brought some grassroots money for Pelosi. It was a hard sell, but it worked.

We did events in Seattle, Los Angeles, Chicago, and New York. All were packed with grassroots supporters, singing praises of Howard Dean and even Nancy Pelosi. It was the beginning of the Democrats taking the House and Senate back in 2006, and Dean had led the way.

OVER THE NEXT FEW WEEKS we had two more meetings with the Kerry campaign. Dean harbored a notion that Kerry would pick him for vice president. I doubted it. Tom McMahon had set up a meeting with the

Kerry folks in DC. I went along for kicks. As we walked in, Kerry's new deputy campaign manager, Steve Elmendorf, greeted me. The same Steve Elmendorf who had derailed any chance Dick Gephardt had to be president, first in the late 1990s by insisting that we only focus on big donors, then in 2004 as Gephardt's presidential campaign's chief of staff for the same reason. Steve chatted with us about how much John Kerry appreciated what Dean had done but clearly didn't understand what Dean for America, or how we were trying to fund campaigns differently, was really about. I smiled.

Steve requested that Dean go to Hawaii for the Kerry campaign. The message was clear: *We want Dean out of the way, don't want him talking to the press.* He should go knock on doors far away from Main Street, USA. Tom and I walked out of this meeting and I told him I was sure that Kerry would lose the election. What would that mean for Howard Dean?

56

ON THE SAME TRIP TO DC, WE WENT UP TO THE HILL TO SEE MY OLD friend Steve Jost. He had managed the Van Hollen campaign, but he also knew what he was doing with party politics. He had a game plan: how Howard Dean could take over the Democratic National Committee after the election.

Wow. Tom and I put it together on paper: how to get the fifty state party chairs and crucial DNC members to support Dean, the beginning of the "50 State Strategy," where we wanted Democrats elected in every state across the country, not just the blue ones. We'd have to work quietly, openly supporting John Kerry, though we were sure he was toast. We presented the plan to Dean in July 2004 in Burlington. He rejected it outright. He was, however, open to supporting another candidate for the DNC chair.

I wasn't sure if he had strong enough coattails to sweep someone else into the job. His choice was Tina Flournoy, a powerful, behind-the-scenes Clinton operator who'd kept communication lines open between the Dean and Clinton worlds. She's now Bill Clinton's chief of staff. Dean presented how she could win; she spent about two seconds thinking about it. She didn't want to be out front, didn't like public speaking, and just didn't want the job. Dean seemed shocked.

We went back to work for the Democracy for America candidates and other efforts for Dean. We made the best of the situation, not knowing what to do after an election we were convinced John Kerry was going to lose. What would the grassroots movement do? What would happen to Dean?

Dean changed his mind that September. He would run to be the new DNC chair. Finally, if he won, it would be our chance to build a Democratic Party that everyone could have a piece of, a table where everyone got a seat.

We designed the process, whipped votes, and evaluated potential opponents, the most serious of whom was my old pal Martin Frost, the one politician in America who loved dialing for dollars, the one who drove me to smoke years prior because of his intense focus on money. Winning would redeem Dean, a chance to come full circle from his scream, a great comeback. In just a matter of months, disgraced Dean would be back on top.

I was excited at the possibility of working for an outsider who could come in and shake the party establishment. The DNC was a country club for the party elite, currently under Terry McAuliffe's waning tenure. I thought Howard Dean was the perfect candidate to burn the country club down.

What really happened over the next few years was not the story of an outsider trying to burn down the country club but rather one of Dean the outsider desperately trying to join it. Dean did not use his position as DNC chair to fundamentally change political fundraising, as he might have. Rather, he became part of the ruling hierarchy. Look where he is now—an advisor in the government affairs practice at the massive law and public policy firm McKenna Long & Aldridge.

57

THE 2004 ELECTION WAS HARD ON THE DEMOCRATIC PARTY AND even harder on its donor network. The party had raised more money than ever. The DNC, the Kerry campaign, and outsiders like billionaires George Soros and Peter Lewis, had banded together to throw in millions of dollars to candidates and an evolving network of liberal organizations to defeat George Bush.[1]

Elite donors—the top one hundred—feared the prospect of Howard Dean as party chair. He was unknown except for his scream and was thought to be uncontrollable. They began to whisper that he might not be the best face to put forward. The underlying sentiment was against the rise of Dean's grassroots donor network. Rich donors sensed they might start losing influence.

After the McCain-Feingold legal changes, mega-donors could give only $25,000 to the DNC and other party committees. Before it, they could give a few hundred thousand dollars in soft money to the DNC and secure the privileges of a top-dog donor and all that came with it—lavish attention from elected officials, a say in policy and campaign strategy, a friend to call when they got in trouble, and maybe even an ambassadorship when Democrats won the White House. If they wanted to remain big players, they now had to write a check for $25,000, then ask friends, colleagues, and family to give that kind of money, too. The ability to be a checkwriter had just been devalued thanks to McCain-Feingold, while the value of raising from others had skyrocketed. The checkwriters of yesteryear now had to bundle too.

It turned the world upside down. Bundling meant work: calling friends, hosting events, and hounding people. Billionaires don't like doing that. So instead, the top mega-donors formed super-PACs before super-PACs were blessed by the 2010 *Citizens United* Supreme Court decision. They could give unlimited money with, at the time, no disclosure rules. They claimed that they were responding to conservative organizations like the Swift Boat Veterans for Truth—the GOP-linked outside group that had attacked Democratic nominee John Kerry's credibility as a Vietnam veteran during the general campaign. If they couldn't beat the system, they would build a new one.

Driven more by a liberal ideological agenda, a group of elite donors basically broke off from the Democratic Party around and after the 2004 election. Soros, Lewis, Colorado software mogul Tim Gill, San Francisco environmentalists Susie Tompkins and her husband, Mark Buell, Texas trial lawyer Fred Baron, SEIU (a union that was always close to Soros), and several others set out to go around the institutions they blamed for the 2004 loss—the DNC, DC establishment Democrats, and the consultant class—and build a progressive architecture that reflected their own liberal utopia, with very different old middle-class priorities from the Democratic Party. Though these donors would still give to Democrats, the party's candidates would now have to kowtow to an agenda built from outside. Their agenda was focused on environmentalism, LGBT rights, and getting out of Iraq . . . all reasonable issues, but make no mistake that they are different priorities than the party's traditional focus of helping the middle class get ahead. And the party can only do so many things at once.

For many of these donors, the new vehicle was the Democracy Alliance, a new front in the battle against big money. Conceived by Clinton operative Rob Stein after watching the 2004 election results with George Soros, Democracy Alliance required a $25,000 entry fee and $30,000 in annual dues. "Partners" were required to donate $200,000 a year to a network of think tanks, watchdog organizations, and single-issue groups that fit the alliance's agenda. Instead of fighting for the middle class, Democracy Alliance money was rooted in a mishmash of single issues tied to the vague liberal priorities designated by its donors. What's more, the group was shrouded in secrecy, with no disclosure rules tied to its giving. No one knew its membership list. Democrats now are making the case against the "evil" Koch brothers; Democracy Alliance gave the Kochs the playbook in 2005. The *Washington Post* wrote it up like this:

> Trial lawyer Fred Baron, a member of the alliance and longtime Democratic donor, agreed: "The piece that has always been lacking in our giving is long-term infrastructure investments."[2]

The small, self-selected group of very wealthy elites decided to create a demand for their money by providing political infrastructure for Democrats: voter databases, left-wing radio to compete with right-wing talk shows (Air America), think tanks, advocacy organizations, and many other projects that they would select to fund. Organizations that made the approved list of recipients included the Center for American Progress, Media Matters, EMILY's List, ACORN, and Campaign for America's Future, as well as other organizations, the vast majority of whom have a strong liberal agenda. Compromise is not in their DNA.

The strategy was the driving force behind the direction of the party, one not coming from elected officials. Elected representatives would become a sideshow in the battle to build a political infrastructure to drive the message and get voters to the polls. The mega-rich wanted to wrest control of the party away from its elected officials and leaders. These donors did something that no other group could do: They used money to insure politicians needed them without giving money directly to politicians. A rough calculation suggests that Democracy Alliance partners gave $500 million by 2012.

The mega-rich hadn't formed full-fledged super-PACs quite yet, but elite donors were figuring out the ways to control politics. And by the 2012 election, candidates could go ask elite donors to give to super-PACs that supported them. How crazy is that? *Please support this outside organization that supports me, though it can say anything you want it to, even if I disagree. But it will support me. I think.* Democracy Alliance was the first step down this road, not just for regular rich folks who could write big checks but for something more ominous: handing over complete and unaccountable influence on the party agenda to donors with no official connection to it.

OF COURSE, TRADITIONAL WEALTHY DONORS still had sway within the party, but they were in shock after the 2004 loss and couldn't get their act together to oppose Dean's candidacy for party chair. It was clearly time for a real shakeup at the DNC, and the desire for something new allowed the anti-Dean elites little room to offer an alternative.

The election for the party chair is conducted by the official members of the DNC, 447 votes from state party chairs, state-elected DNC members, and superdelegates, including every Democratic member of Congress. Former White House confidant Harold Ickes; DCCC chair and my nemesis Martin Frost; Simon Rosenberg, head of the New Democrat Network; and a young operative named Donnie Fowler ran, but none could unite support to counter Dean.

We outworked all of them. Dean went around the country and met with state chairs and promised a new "50 State Strategy," which meant the DNC would invest its cash in all fifty state parties, not just the swing states. That meant cash for the long-suffering state parties and votes for Dean in return.

To ease some of the party establishment's fear, Dean went to the Capitol and met with Democratic leader Nancy Pelosi, Whip Steny Hoyer, and Senate Majority Leader Harry Reid. We walked in to meet with Reid, and being a great politician, he thanked me for the work I had done in Nevada in 1998. Nancy Pelosi was the most striking: She seemed ambivalent to Dean, as long as the DNC invested in House campaigns. She clearly didn't like him, but her demand for money in House races was an amazing example of the effect of big money in politics. Back in 1995 when she was a back-bench member from San Francisco, I had worked an event with her in California, and she had been more of a champion of the average middle-class voter. Now, sitting with her for five minutes, her focus was on the richest of the rich and what they could raise for her. After all, a lot of that money lived in her backyard.

58

EVER THE SHOWMAN, TERRY MCAULIFFE HOSTED A BIG GOING-away party for himself as he stepped down as DNC chair. He had the DNC spend about $100,000 to deck out a massive hotel ballroom in downtown DC. All the political leaders showed up, including John Kerry—who had just lost the election—and Bill Clinton. They all got up on stage to publicly thank Terry. Terry extolled all the great things he had done as party chair. He'd raised more money, implemented new technology, and built a new building.

Taking a parting shot at Dean, he ended the speech by reminding the crowd that he had raised over $300 million in 2004 and that the next chair—the vote hadn't taken place yet, so Dean's victory, while expected, wasn't official—should raise at least $100 million in 2005. Total bullshit. A presidential year is when you raise the most, and the year you raise the least is always after losing a presidential. In fact, in 2001 after Bush beat Gore, Chairman McAuliffe had led the worst year the DNC had had in over ten years. But that didn't stop him from putting a bull's-eye on Dean's head, and mine: If you don't raise $100 million, you will be a failure.

THE VOTE FOR DNC CHAIR was a runaway win for us. The winter meeting—in which the actual voting takes place—was set for early February, but by mid-January, we had the votes and only Martin Frost was still in the race.

The deal was sealed. It was a Saturday afternoon when the vote count was announced, and victory was ours.

Howard Dean had asked me the previous night to be the new national finance director, the head fundraiser for the entire Democratic Party. It should have been a moment of great joy—I was officially at the top of my profession, a dream job for political fundraisers everywhere. But I wasn't dying to do the job, I'd been trying to get out of fundraising for years. I knew the hell I was about to walk into: Big donors and bundlers who wanted to run the show, dealing with outside groups, a constant fight for dollars, managing a staff of over fifty people. Nobody in their right mind would ever want this job, but I had spent thirteen years raising money and wanted to change the relationship between donors and politicians. If I was ever going to change the role of money in my party, this was my only chance. I couldn't control the Democracy Alliance crowd, but I wanted to take power away from the wealthy mega-donors who remained in the party's orbit. I didn't have much choice but to say yes. I thought Howard Dean wanted the change too, but he proved not to be up to the challenge.

We celebrated a bit and agreed to meet early the next morning at the DNC.

THE DNC STILL HAD THE STAFF left over from the Kerry campaign and Terry McAuliffe's tenure. Dean's inner circle sat down and decided that we would ask for everybody's resignation and start fresh. We set up the transition team, seven of us, that would hire all the senior staff. Despite Terry McAuliffe's insistence on raising $100 million, we budgeted $50 million for 2005. We didn't have much time to waste. I had to get moving and start raising money.

On Monday we gathered all the staff, over a hundred still working, and told them they had to put in resignation letters that day. A stun to some, but they should have realized this was coming. The transition team would hire new staff over the next six weeks until all the senior staff was in place. I was given a little leeway in hiring a few folks right away. I needed them. We brought in Julie Tagen as deputy finance director; she had worked for Dean for President too. We hired Jay Patterson as my assistant.

That was the end of the early hiring. Internal politics would stop me from going forward with others for a while. Determined to make the changes, I had to wade through the bullshit first. See, Julie is white, Jay is white, and I am about as pale as they come, so I wasn't allowed to hire another Caucasian before the first minority. Andrew Wright was one of the few really talented fundraisers I knew, and I wanted him on board early. I am a lifelong Democrat and support diversity, of course, but most of the fundraisers I knew were white, and I was chomping at the bit to get going. But Andrew is also white.

The transition team met nightly to go over top prospects. We all knew Tom McMahon would be executive director, but he is white so we could not announce him yet. We still needed a communications director, political director, field director, and so on. I wanted to move fast; the sooner we got a minority hired, I could move on and start hiring staff.

We sat one evening and talked about communication director possibilities: Karen Finney had worked for Hillary Clinton and was the leading choice. I didn't care much; when you don't control the White House, messaging is run by folks on Capitol Hill, not us party hacks at the DNC. But Karen was a minority, which was all that mattered. As soon as she was hired, I could open the floodgates.

It was our second week in charge. I almost gave up that night; I should have. The conversation about Karen was not at all about her ability to do the job. We did spend over two hours, however, wondering whether Karen was "minority enough." More precisely, did Karen have two black parents or just one? Really. Leah Dougherty, Chairman McAuliffe's chief of staff who was sticking around to work for Dean, made a few phone calls to find out Karen's lineage. It was a sickening night, but Karen made the color cut and was offered the job the next day. Then I was able to hire Andrew Wright.

With so many young Democrats looking for work in DC, I had to interview hundreds of people for fundraising jobs. Three hours a day interviewing potential hires. I had to keep internal politics in mind, so on each resume I wrote down a number from one to ten, "10" representing a big fight with the diversity team, a "1" meant I was home free. It had nothing to do with talent, contacts, networks of donors; it all had to do with how hard I would have to fight to hire them.

I made one statement to every person I interviewed: "The DNC finance department is now under my watch, and I have one rule: Everybody has a seat at the table. A donor who gives $10 is a Democrat, a donor who gives $25,000 is a Democrat. Period." This was not about diversity, which I thought was a given; rather, elite donors would take up no more space at the table than grassroots supporters. I was making a point not only to new staff but also to the big donors they talked to: "You are not going to control the system. We welcome your participation, but this is about everybody and this is about winning."

59

EVEN THOUGH THE ELITE OF THE ELITE—THE DEMOCRACY ALLIANCE crowd—were setting up an outside operation, some stayed in the DNC's orbit too. That way, they could exert influence from as many angles as possible. Of the two hundred top party bundlers—folks who max out to every party committee and then bundle hundreds of thousands of dollars more from their rich friends—we set up meetings with as many as possible early on, not to ask them for money but to explain the plan we had for the new DNC under Chair Dean.

We had just lost the election and we were trying to get the party to rebound. The high-dollar donors and bundlers were so important to our ability to raise early money that Dean and I spent about 60 percent of our time in the first months going around the country and letting the rich donors vent. These meetings allowed donors an opportunity to unload on us, to yell, to formulate their own plans of action to fix everything. It was painful.

If you piss off even a few major bundlers, they can cause major revenue problems. They have that much sway. That's why my focus was on building a grassroots network. If we had a million small-dollar donors in a given year, we could afford to piss off a thousand and still have 999,000 who'd donate. Of course, these mega-donors didn't deserve the level of attention and the time we gave them, but we had no choice. We needed money, and fast, with salaries and bills to pay. That's why we didn't spend any time building the grassroots network at first; I hadn't changed anything in my first weeks on the job.

Howard Dean and I went out to Los Angeles to take our beatings. One of the first was breakfast at the Beverly Hills Hotel with Sherry Lansing, the CEO of Paramount Pictures, who had given $23,000 to the DNC in 2004 and thousands to individual Democratic candidates.[1] She brought David, her sidekick. Sherry was pleasant enough and gave her opinion on the state of the party. She wanted to fix our communications problems, and she was willing to move to DC to do it.

Sherry was a boilerplate elite donor who believed she could run things better. We listened for over two hours. She came up with a simple budget of $25 million for her program. She could help raise some of that, but only a few million. Dean thanked her and told her that we would be in touch. We got into the car and he told me to try to get a check out of her before we (me) called her back and told her we would not be bringing her on board as the new communications guru. Now, Sherry is a smart and powerful executive, but there's no way we could deal with someone accustomed to that sort of power at the DNC.

That afternoon, the *New York Times* called me and wanted to know more details about the new DNC communications program being run by Sherry Lansing. Fucking big donors. David, her sidekick, had leaked the story to the *Times* that Sherry was coming on board. The *New York Times* ran a story about the "possible" coming of Hollywood to the DNC.

When we didn't let her execute her communications plan at the DNC, guess what? She didn't write another check for four years, when she gave $26,200 just before the 2008 election of Barack Obama.

I WENT TO TEXAS with one of our young finance staffers, Kate. A few days in Houston, Austin, and Dallas to try to get these rich individuals to get over a lost election and look forward. It was a sad few days as we couldn't secure meetings with the top bundlers and spent a lot of time just getting old Dean for President donors to meet with us. Some big folks, like Arthur Schechter, former ambassador to the Bahamas thanks to his bundling for Clinton, sat down with us, but he complained just the same: "The party was out of touch with America and it was time to change." I doubted we were talking about the same types of change.

After the second day in Texas, Michael Vachon called to say he needed me to come to New York and meet with the team that had "changed" Colorado. Michael was George Soros's right-hand political man and in control of access to the Soros billions. I had to go.

We sat around a conference table overlooking Central Park as five elite donors from Colorado talked about how they had changed the party in their state essentially by ignoring it. They had gone around the institution and created a winning formula of outside groups. Jared Polis—who is now in Congress from Colorado, a seat he ran for after selling his online greeting card company for $780 million—was thrilled about killing off the state party. He talked about the inability for the Democratic Party to function, and if we wanted to change the country, we had to create new tools to raise money, to contact voters, to get voters to the polls. The Colorado groups were funded by Democracy Alliance partners.

How was I supposed to take that conversation? I believed in reforming the party, especially how it raised money. But I was more interested in propping up state parties, not in destroying them. The parties were accountable to their memberships, while shadowy outside groups were unaccountable to anyone but their financiers. What if an elite outside group didn't like one of our candidates? Maybe thought someone was too moderate for a district? What's to stop those outside groups from supporting another candidate who otherwise wouldn't have had a shot? It would divide the party. My job was to get Democrats of all kinds elected, and that meant working within the party structure.

The meeting was a clear indication that Democracy Alliance would continue to build new institutions outside of the party, a subtle way for Soros to point to a future ignoring it. And while he did eventually give $41,750 to the DNC under Dean's tenure, he also lavished $2 million on MoveOn.org's voter fund . . . and spread countless millions more to other groups whose donors weren't disclosed.

Conversations like this only reinforced in my mind the need to double down on sustainable small-dollar donations, to make the party strong and competitive with these outside groups. Today, nearly every state has a parallel organization of big donors that's outside the party but runs ads nominally in support of Democrats.

60

FROM DAY ONE, I STARTED SENDING SIGNALS THAT CHANGES WERE coming.

The DNC's funding streams were big donors, direct mail, and some new online money. Each stream had a different net profit, and direct mail—that is, mailing solicitations to people's homes—had the smallest return, between 2 and 5 percent. The cost makes a difference. If it cost only about $20,000 to raise $100,000 from rich donors, it made financial sense to spend more time raising from them. Of course, there were too many other costs associated with raising from them.

Direct mail was a mess for the DNC. Consultants who had been around for years had stale formulas and prewritten text for each solicitation. I asked them to be more efficient, but they fought hard to protect their turf.

I knew how to get them to reform. When we brought direct mail in house for Democracy for America, we reached an 11 percent return, much better than 2 to 5 percent. Increasing the margin on direct mail would mean decreasing reliance on rich donors. If the Democratic grassroots ever could compete with the big donors, it would be because we did become more efficient, like bringing down that cost.

The previous year, McAuliffe had ended an old practice of splitting the proceeds from direct mail with state parties. Each state party received 8 to 10 percent of the net funds raised from direct mail within its state. Think of Florida. Say the DNC raised $1 million from Florida by direct mail and netted $100,000, the Florida Democrat Party would have gotten $10,000. That mattered, but state parties hadn't been receiving it under the McAuliffe regime.

If I couldn't get the consultants to bring down their costs, I'd kneecap them. I went to Dean. I told him I wanted to reinstate the state split for all direct mail. He agreed because the practice fit in with his 50 State Strategy of building up state parties.

I WAS STARTING to put my team together over the next few weeks and months, but I also didn't have the patience for the internal politics. I wanted to break down internal walls as fast as possible. At the time (and still today), the DNC finance department is broken into desks: Gay and Lesbian, African American, Asian American, Women, Small Business Leaders, Young Donors, Veterans, and more. Each desk has a full-time staff. In addition, there are regional directors: Midatlantic, New York, California, Midwest, South, and Northeast, all of whom have two to three staffers.

The entire concept made no sense. I was a Democrat and I wanted donors around the country to give because they were Democrats too, and only because of that. I made a push to get rid of the demographic desks. Why couldn't we just have a team of fundraisers that raised money for Democrats? A novel idea, right? Donors should give money so the Democratic Party and its values would win, not because of some fundraising program that matched up with a donor's identity or personal beliefs. Word got out. The desk staffers, fearing their jobs were under threat from my plan, talked to the donors they dealt with.

Rich bundlers reacted quickly. One decision was particularly costly. When I refused to let Evan Morris, the big pharma lobbyist who'd arranged the shady trip to Puerto Rico with Dean the previous year, serve as the small business chair, he showed up at my office and literally ripped up $75,000 in checks he had bundled.

Andy Tobias had been the elected treasurer of the DNC since 1999 and was the head of the Gay and Lesbian fundraising desk. He is also an author who writes about personal finance because—guess what?—he has, and came from, a lot of money. Tobias panicked. If I took away his program, he would lose his official connection to gay political finance networks. The day I made my suggestion to get rid of the desks, he went to Howard Dean and asked that I be fired.

Under threat, Tobias wanted to fire the change agent. Great. I knew I was in for more trouble, but I was not going to let the old guard stand in my way. Getting rid of the desks was a minor change that was still on my mind, but I had bigger plans. I would make life tough for the desks, especially Andy Tobias. He might have been the elected treasurer, but as finance director, I got to hire the people who'd work for him. As I interviewed hundreds of potential new staff, I was on the lookout for two things: diverse staff and the worst possible candidates. Now, I hired some great people too, but if I couldn't automatically get rid of the desks, I'd sabotage them. I hired Tom Petrillo to be a gay and lesbian fundraiser under Tobias. Tom had been working as a barback in a gay bar. I figured I would kill off Andy by bringing in inexperienced staff. Not only was Tom not qualified for the job, but every time I walked by his desk, I could see him chatting on dating sites like Manhunt and Gay.com.

61

IN 2004, THE DNC UNDER JOHN KERRY'S CANDIDACY AND CHAIR
Terry McAuliffe had been able to attract 3,700 contributors to give the
McCain-Feingold restricted maximum of $25,000. Even though my ul-
timate goal was to end these donors' influence, I needed a few months to
implement my changes. These folks would give some money to bridge the
gap, I hoped.

Early in Dean's tenure, we invited all of them to DC for a private meeting, an all-day affair with presentations from Dean and senior staff at the
Mandarin Oriental hotel. It was time consuming but worth the effort. In
the end we could convince only about 150 to fly to DC. Most donors were
still pissed about losing in 2004, were tapped out, didn't trust Dean, and
blamed the DNC for failing. But 150 was a good start.

One of the few big donors to come was Fred Baron, a smiling, gray-
haired famous Texas trial attorney, who was also part of the Democracy
Alliance crowd of liberal billionaires. I had been raising money from him
for years, and we had a good professional relationship. That morning I
pulled him aside to get him to listen to my plan. But before I could get
my pitch out, he asked for a favor.

"Senator Leahy is moving a new bill through the Senate, and it's going
to really hurt us trial attorneys," he said over his rounded glasses.

"Blah blah blah," I thought. "This is the DNC, and we don't do policy." Well, we do service donors.

"Now, since Chairman Dean is also from Vermont like Pat Leahy,
would Howard mind calling his home-state senator to ask for some
help?"

I pulled Dean aside and told him Fred's request. Dean had a plan: I
told Fred we would call, then we walked down the hall and Dean pulled

his cell phone out of his pocket. Fred could see Dean calling, but couldn't hear him.

"Well, good morning," Dean said to the staffer who'd answered in Leahy's office, "What a great day it is in DC." Then they chatted for a minute. "Does anyone else around want to say hello?"

In all, he talked with three or four staffers in Senator Leahy's office for about ten minutes. He turned and walked back toward Fred and gave a big thumbs-up. Dean didn't say a word, but Fred sure thought Dean had talked to Leahy. Job done.

I SMELLED AN OPPORTUNITY. We had just done a "favor" for Fred, and now I wanted one from him. Rather than just pitch him, I asked Fred to gather a few of his big-dollar friends in the room, folks he trusted and could persuade to give money if he asked. We all met outside in the smoking area of the Mandarin Oriental—eleven big donors and bundlers with no idea why they had been summoned outside.

I made my pitch. "If the DNC does what I want it to do, we will never need any of you again. Yes, we need you now to bridge the cash-flow gap today, but you've done so much for us that I don't like asking for so much money. The future of the Democratic National Committee is grassroots donors and grassroots only. I want to start a program called 'Democracy Bonds,' an effort to capitalize on Chairman Dean's grassroots fundraising success and get one million donors to pledge $20 a month to the DNC. I want to give you all a break and eliminate big donors altogether."

I thought I would have a few more months to develop the Democracy Bonds program, but when Fred Baron essentially asked for a quid pro quo, he opened the door. I went for it. I had not presented this to anybody else, but I wanted to shove it down his throat. The idea did not go over well with my mega-donor focus group. About thirty minutes after our little chat outside, Fred walked up to me in the main meeting room and whispered in my ear: "Lindsay, I've always liked you, but we have no choice now. We have to destroy you. We can't allow small donors to dilute our influence. You can raise some money from them, but it is not okay to give them any power."

I smiled all the way home that night. I had drawn my line in the sand. It would work. All I needed was for Dean and the senior staff to back me up.

62

I TALKED WITH JOE ROSPARS, THE WHIZ OF ONLINE EFFORTS FOR the Dean presidential campaign who had joined us at the DNC. He loved the idea and went right to work designing a physical "Democracy Bond" that we would send to everyone who signed up. The deal was simple: Agree to give $10, $15, $20, or $50 a month to the DNC and invest—buy a bond—in the future of the Democratic Party. With a plan and some backing, I thought we could get to a million bondholders in three years.

We announced the new plan to the entire staff and asked everybody to spread the word and sign up their friends. We sent out an internal email at 9 am. By 10 o'clock, I'd been summoned to Howard Dean's office. The freak-out had begun. Andy Tobias knew it was coming, so he had arranged for the DNC's attorneys to be present and argue that using the word "bond" might bring a lawsuit from the Treasury Department. Really. It was the best he could come up with on short notice to derail my new program. His stalling tactic worked for a while, but then the lawyers approved the use of the word "bond." Amazing.

Over the next few days, Andy Tobias, Fred Baron, and their crew went to work destroying me. Reporters starting calling about our alleged DNC fundraising problems. A series of stories ended up being printed that week about the failures of the Dean fundraising operation. It was clear to anybody in the know what was going on, but nobody on the outside was in the know.

HOWARD DEAN'S RAISED VOICE ISN'T RAISING CASH

One hundred days into his tenure as the high-energy, higher-decibel chairman of the Democratic Party, Howard Dean is in trouble with party moneybags. . . .

Dean wowed the faithful in '04 with his Web-based fund-raising magic. But major business donors still count, and in his new role as party honcho, the feisty doctor seems to be struggling to connect. . . .

"It appears that the chairman has come to the conclusion that he doesn't need major donors," sniffs one fat cat. "He hasn't made any effort to reach out."

Personality factors aside, Dean's business-bashing '04 campaign makes him a hard sell in corporate circles. "There's a wait-and-see attitude from business and major contributors," says Nathan Landow, a Maryland developer and big-time donor. "This guy has some work to do to get the comfort level up." William W. Batoff, a Philadelphia real estate developer and longtime Democratic fund-raiser who backed President Bush in 2000 and 2004, is less diplomatic. "Howard Dean is the wrong person to be chair," says Batoff, who claims he will help fund the Dems' congressional efforts but will boycott the national committee while Dean reigns.[1]

After a week of hit pieces—mostly attacking Dean and his allegedly unpredictable style—Andy invited me to breakfast to chat about the future of DNC finance. With rounds of negative press, he hoped he'd have leverage on me. I had to say yes to breakfast. We met at the Hamilton Crowne Plaza on 14th Street in Washington. Andy played nice for a few minutes and then announced his idea.

"If you're excited about the Democracy Bonds program," he said with a smirk, "why don't you just do that and let me hire a new finance director to handle the big donors?"

I laughed in his face. "This isn't just about the Democracy Bond program succeeding," I shot back. "It's just as much about using my position to put you and the money you represent into a box. I can't change the party if I let you continue to occupy politicians' time and wield influence." Andy was clearly shocked by my full-throated response: "Under absolutely no circumstances am I leaving."

He cried. I am not kidding. The elected treasurer of the DNC was sitting at breakfast at a nice hotel and he started crying because I wouldn't do what he wanted me to.

AFTER A FEW WEEKS of looking for legal reasons to kill Democracy Bonds, the attorneys could not come up with another reason to delay the program. We launched the Democracy Bond program the next day. Here's what Howard Dean wrote to Democrats in an email:

> I've set a personal goal to secure the ongoing resources the Party needs each month, and I'm trying to get there with Democracy Bonds. By getting your Democracy Bond, you're making a commitment to make a monthly contribution the Democratic Party in order to:
>
> - Reform the political process by building a political party beholden only to the people, not the special interests
> - Build the Democratic Party from the ground up in every precinct so that we can compete everywhere
> - Win elections in every state and territory of the United States, at every level of office
>
> "Democracy Bonds" are about building a community of Americans with a stake in our common future—locally, nationally, and globally. They will bond together a person in Alaska and a person in Missouri in common cause for a political process where parties are accountable to ordinary people and their concerns.
>
> You can only buy one bond. You can decide to commit more money per month, depending on what you can afford, but the principle is democratic with a small-D—one person, one bond. Every person can be a stakeholder in our party.

Eighteen thousand people signed up in the first month. They gave an average of $12 a month, which may not sound like much, but over $200,000 had become automatic revenue every month. If I could have signed up 1 million donors at $12 a month, I'd have changed politics forever. A few weeks after the launch, I sent this message to Democrats everywhere:

Dear Fellow Democrat,

Six weeks after the launch of Democracy Bonds, the response has surpassed all expectations. More than 20,000 Democrats—from bankers to waitresses—have made a monthly commitment to fund our party for the long-term.

The Democracy Bonds community can tell you a lot better than I can why this commitment is so important. I've included some comments from a recent online discussion about Democracy Bonds below this note.

Building a community of small donors giving monthly is the key to funding the 50-state strategy that you mandated—a sound, sustainable financial base is the only way we can build a truly national party and fight every race at every level.

Tonight, Governor Dean and Democracy Bond holders in Boston will be building that community even more at the first-ever Democracy Bonds rally.

The buzz is real, the potential for this program is real, and the impact of your small monthly donation will be real. Join the community now or, if you're already a Bond holder, pass this link to a friend: www.democrats.org/democracybonds
Thank you for everything.

Lindsay Lewis
Finance Director
Democratic National Committee

63

AT THE TIME, RAHM EMANUEL CHAIRED THE DCCC AND CHUCK Schumer headed the DSCC. Two solid political thinkers who had one thing on their mind: winning back the House and winning back the Senate in 2006. Dean's 50 State Strategy was not on the radar. Why waste money on states that didn't have Senate races or competitive House races?

Dean was committed to the 50 State Strategy. Rahm and Schumer knew the future was in bigger money, in winning back Congress in 2006 and the White House in 2008. They wanted Dean to get his head out of his ass and put the DNC's money into the races that mattered the most.

By July 2005, they were fuming so badly that we had to set up a meeting. Schumer couldn't make it over to the DNC building, so he called in while Dean, Rahm, and I sat in the room. The call was cordial for a few minutes. Dean sat behind his big desk, and Rahm pounced back and forth across the room. If not for Schumer on the phone, he might have taken a swing at Dean. The call lasted about ten minutes, and Rahm stormed out. Dean smiled and said, "Fuck him." A few years later Rahm would fuck Dean back when he became President Obama's chief of staff. Dean got no post in Obama's cabinet.

I remained loyal to Dean and smiled to myself about this sideshow. I wanted my Democracy Bonds to work. If they did, these stupid battles would disappear. The money flowing in from small donors would ease all ills.

THE PRESS HITS KEPT COMING, and the big Democratic donors were using conservatives to attack us. Conservative commentator Robert Novak wrote:

> Democratic National Committee (DNC) fund raising under the chairmanship of Howard Dean shows a disappointing $16.7 million raised

in the first quarter of 2005, compared with $34 million reported by the Republicans.

That tends to confirm dire predictions by old-line Democratic fundraisers of a fall-off in money if Dean became chairman. He had promised to bring in heavy individual contributions, as he did in his 2004 campaign for president. But the DNC in the first quarter received only $13 million from individuals, compared to $31 million for the Republican National Committee.[1]

It was getting thick and rough, almost to the point that the seventy people working for me thought they all would lose their jobs. I did what I could to protect them and take the heat directly; I didn't want to tell them that they didn't matter. If we could pull off the bonds, they wouldn't matter to the DNC finance department. The reporters who wrote the stories had been fed by big donors, who requested anonymity in exchange for juicy insider gossip.

Howard Dean didn't care about any of the negative press. He had figured out what he was now doing as party chair, and that included a lot of hobnobbing, attending ritzy parties, and becoming popular with the establishment. He had come to DC to burn down the country club, but he was having so much fun now that he wanted to join.

Dean was the first real outsider to serve as the DNC chair since the 1970s. That was something the Democratic "nonestablishment"—the congressional back benchers, the state party chairs, the small party caucuses— really appreciated. This "nonestablishment" love shown Dean made him feel secure in his new job. Attack all you want; Dean had friends to back him up. He was going to bring the regular guys into the establishment's country club. Bringing in new voices was novel and commendable, but it made those folks who were trying to change things, like me, bigger targets to the establishment, who felt threatened. And Dean left me on a cliff.

Howard Dean didn't care about the source of money like I did; what he did care about was the total amount—just raise it, from somewhere.

Democracy Bonds were just another revenue stream, not, as I saw them, a new tool that could fundamentally alter politics. Had Dean embraced Democracy Bonds with passion, they would have had bigger success.

STEVE GROSSMAN HAD BEEN the Dean for President national finance chair—an honorary but important title—and when these hit pieces started appearing, he called Dean and said he could fix the problem. He told Dean that he would like for me to come up to Boston and spend the weekend with him so he could teach me how to fund-raise.

This was one of the more painful conversations I ever had with Dean.

"This is embarrassing," I told him. "I don't want to waste a weekend with a donor who thinks he knows best."

"I know," replied Dean. "But can you just go up there and humor him?"

"I don't want to. These folks are out to get us. I'm trying to change things around here, and you need to back me up."

He said he would back me, but he didn't do as much as he should have. The bigger prize for Howard Dean was joining the elitist club. He needed big donors to validate his new role as chairman. Against my wishes, I went off to Boston on Memorial Day weekend. I took a cab to Steve's office and we chatted for a bit. I pretended to be interested and eager to learn. I was neither. That night I had the pleasure of sleeping in one of his sons' bedrooms. As I've mentioned, I am six-five; the bed was a child's single. I did my best to get an hour or two of shut-eye.

The family had breakfast together, then Steve and I went off to the living room. He had a pad of paper out and asked questions about how was I feeling, what was wrong, what kind of tree would I be if I could be one. He jotted down every word I uttered and looked over what he had written down. Was I supposed to pay him for the hour of therapy?

He had a new idea. We spent the next three hours role-playing fund-raising calls. Really. I have spent thousands of hours successfully calling people for money, but Steve—like most big-money donors—thought he knew better.

Steve went into the kitchen and I called him. He first played an angry trial attorney in Mississippi, including the Southern accent. Holy shit. I played along and tried to sell this "trial attorney" on supporting the DNC. He said he was all tapped out. I said thanks for the time and hung up. Then I called again, and this time he was a woman from San Francisco who cared about the environment. I made my pitch about the Dean 50 State Strategy. "She" also said no. I hung up.

This went on for the next few hours. What he didn't know was that I had explicitly taken this job to stop these little kinds of games. I didn't want the trial attorney in Mississippi or the single-issue donor in San Francisco to have that much say over the future of the party.

I have never spoken to Steve Grossman since so I have no idea if I passed his fundraising class.

64

WHEN ANDY TOBIAS WAS NOT CRYING, HE WAS TRYING TO RAISE money. His big event every June was the LGBT fundraiser in NYC. He was always able to raise $1 million or close to it. We needed the money.

Andy had set up the event in the lobby of a new building in Chelsea. It was under construction, and that was his theme: The DNC is being rebuilt by Howard Dean. All the waiters and staff had to wear yellow construction hats. The event would include a little speech by gay activist and screenwriter Tony Kushner, followed by Howard Dean. I sat in my seat and went virtually berserk.

I couldn't be upset about the million bucks. Rather, I was upset because the room had one woman. One. In the entire world of LGBT donors, Andy had managed to find one woman: Fredrike Merck, of the Merck family fortune, an eccentric donor who had been helpful to the Howard

Dean campaign. Two hundred donors and one woman, exactly what I was against. Andy had made it clear he was out to get me, and now he was shoving it down my throat. I went up to him and asked if we should change the name of his fundraising operation from the LGBT desk to the MWLA desk: Men Who Like Andy.

I saw him go over to Dean later on that night and whisper in his ear. I knew I'd be called to the chairman's office when back in DC. I didn't care.

I DIDN'T STOP TRYING to control Andy Tobias. I wanted somebody who would help bring other LGBT groups into the fold. The program at the DNC was focused on the richest of the rich in the gay donor network, but hundreds of groups worked for the LBGT community, and they had little say. The DNC needed the LGBT community, not just for the money, as Andy thought, but for more outreach in what we did across the country.

Julie Tagen suggested her friend Donald Hitchcock, who was Paul Yandura's partner (an advisor to billionaire donor Peter Lewis and former head of the LGBT desk at the DNC). Donald was not a fundraiser, but that did not bother me; I was looking for something bigger. He was perfect, someone who'd anger Andy and bring some fresh air into the DNC.

The backstabbing started on day one. Andy was livid. He scolded me for hiring somebody he didn't approve of. Tom Petrillo was upset because he thought he was actually in charge of the LGBT outreach for the DNC. In one move I had accomplished so much.

Donald immediately set up meetings with the leaders of all the top LGBT groups—Human Rights Campaign, the Victory Fund, and others—with Howard Dean. This is exactly what I wanted, buy-in for everything we were doing, not just from Andy's elite checkwriters.

I was soon gone from the DNC but later dragged into a court case. Hitchcock had sued the DNC for discrimination for being fired and had dragged Dean and the rest of the staff into court proceedings. (The case was later settled out of court.) I had no idea what led to Donald's termination, but I did know that Donald was forcing the likes of Andy to change; now they had to pay attention to people outside of elite checkwriters. I scored this as a victory.

65

AFTER THE SUCCESSFUL LAUNCH OF DEMOCRACY BONDS, WE HIT A wall. Over the next few weeks, the program grew at a snail's pace. I wanted to know why. The Dean presidential campaign had over 318,000 small-dollar online donors, but we were struggling to get past 20,000 Democracy Bond holders. If the grassroots could be made to understand that this was the moment to take control, I thought they'd step up.

I hired the pollster Cornell Belcher to discover why Democracy Bonds were selling slowly. We set up focus group meetings in New York, Chicago, Denver, and Los Angeles. Each focus group had twenty people and would be run by one of Cornell's staffers. Nobody knew they had shown up for a DNC focus group. I sat behind the two-way mirror and listened in.

The results were distressing, and exactly the same no matter what city we were in: Grassroots donors had given so much in 2004 and we had still lost. They would give again only if money was tied to a specific action, not a general belief in the party's values.

To this day, it is the most important, and depressing, conclusion I have ever heard. It didn't click with Cornell or anyone else watching that we had to do something, something active, something radical, something crazy to get them to give money. The grassroots would never contribute for the sake of giving to a general cause; their donation had to mean something. In other words, the grassroots were telling me that they were just like the elites, the billionaires, the ultra-rich. They wanted something tangible in exchange for a contribution. When we finished the week in Los Angeles, I went back to my hotel and broke down. In order to get a large amount of support from the grassroots, we would have to be radical. We would have to be over the top.

I had lost the war before the first battle was over. But I was so tied to the success of Democracy Bonds that I still tried to win that first battle. I returned to DC and begged Dean to go radical on the war in Iraq—be the Howard Dean of 2003, come out and scream about the war. Go crazy, dammit! This would energize grassroots donors to sign up. We could still grow the Democracy Bond program.

Now that he was more focused on being validated by the establishment, Dean resisted. Screaming about the war in Iraq wasn't the right thing to do, but I wanted to get grassroots donors on board no matter what. He wanted to play nice with the people he had railed against just two years before. This was what Washington does to outsiders; I just thought Howard Dean would be stronger.

Dean's refusal to go crazy on one level was right: Going crazy to please the hard-core lefties over Iraq would have been superficial and felt like he was using the issue just to raise money. Dean had come to "power" by giving voice to those angry at the party establishment. But he was part of the establishment now and couldn't speak in exactly the same way. He could hardly attack himself. This is always a problem with anti-establishment victories, something the Tea Party on the Right is still adjusting to today.

But he was wrong on another level. We needed money from the grassroots, and we needed lots of it. I had done a good job pissing off major donors; Dean had done the same. If we created some controversy, perhaps the grassroots would respond to defend Dean (and donate to him)? It was a gamble I wanted to take, but Dean did not.

My desire to raise money through hysterics was a bit hypocritical. I had tried to eliminate the single-issue desks and make donors give only because they cared about the Democratic Party. By going crazy, I would essentially be creating a new "desk," one that would raise money from the single issue we chose to exploit: in this case Iraq. That's not a sustainable model over the long term.

This was my moment of clarity. I, thus the average American, could not win at raising political money. No matter how you played the game, the game would be tilted to one set of donors or another. Big donors would give if politicians gave them the time and the attention they craved. Grassroots donors would give if you did something "crazy" to motivate them. The rest of America, those who don't live politics 24/7, who don't care about elections except in the weeks leading up to them, and those who'd never consider contributing to a politician, had no seat at the table.

I had misjudged what the grassroots could do and what they are, I had burned my bridge to the big donors, I had burned my bridge to the establishment. As a fundraiser on a mission to make a difference, just a few months into my tenure at the DNC, I was really a very lonely person with very few options.

66

THERE WAS MORE BAD PRESS, EVEN THOUGH IN 2005 WE WERE IN the middle of raising $51 million, more money than any party committee ever had the year after losing a presidential campaign.[1] Plus, when Dean went around the country to raise money, he was doing much of it on behalf of the state parties, the first serious DC help they'd gotten in years.

But the stories took a toll on me. Dean was focused mostly on the 50 State Strategy, and outside of a few stars like Andrew Wright, we were struggling to raise money. We maxed out with 31,000 Democracy Bond buyers.

Elite donors had freaked out; they didn't like Dean and they didn't have a friend in Dean's finance director. And I had just found out that grassroots donors were motivated by the same things as big donors: actions, not beliefs. I was gradually realizing I was fighting a war I could never win by myself. I was outnumbered and outgunned.

I had grown up in a liberal family that had fought the good fight for those not represented by their leaders. I had now spent fifteen years raising money from rich individuals, corporations, and grassroots donors. It hit me on a dark night in late July: The corporate donors were the best for the system, the lobbyists who just dropped off their checks and smiled at the member of Congress. Both the grassroots and elite billionaires were motivated by the same thing, and that was a major problem.

If our system of political finance system requires our politicians to raise so much money and spend so much time doing it, it's a broken system. The art of legislating has become a secondary concern for those elected to Congress who must spend at least fifteen hours a week raising money from rich donors. When the chair of the DNC has to spend ten times more of his schedule with donors than he does with precinct workers, party stalwarts, and those who put time into doing real political work (registering voters, getting voters out to the polls, crafting messages, etc.), the system simply doesn't work. When it takes radical, crazy, heated pitches to gain real money from the grassroots, the system doesn't work.

I had to get out. It was just a matter of when and how.

Late that August, Hurricane Katrina hit New Orleans. The DNC had planned three big events in California that week. How could we possibly go raise money from disconnected, rich elites when thousands of poor and middle-class Louisianans—the folks I wanted us to represent—were dying? It was exactly what was wrong with the Democratic Party money machine: hanging with the rich while the poor and middle class suffer.

I had to fight with Dean and others to cancel our California events. It shouldn't have been that tough, but it was a sign of the times—the pressure to raise money couldn't stop even for a hurricane that had destroyed a major American city.

Eventually, Dean gave up his fight to go to California, and I sensed my opportunity. I decided to write him a letter about the failures of the Democratic leadership. It was my resignation and an attack on his leadership. He called me in, and I sat with him in his office and explained that he could have really changed the party if he had fought to keep his outsider credentials, but now he was nothing more than a servicer for elite establishment donors. He had let them win. He could put a good face on it, show that he was changing the party with his 50 State Strategy, but he wasn't.

I resigned that September 2005. He gave me three months to find a replacement, but I left the DNC then and never went back.

George Soros and Peter Lewis were working both outside and inside the system, forming the party's ideology through outside groups, while they and others continued to demand the time of the officials who ran the party. Democrats were in full control of the elites, the rich individuals with singular personal beliefs that they put into action via the time and money they give.

The relatively small amount that the party needed to raise in 1990 had allowed everybody to have a seat at the table. The new need for massive amounts of money reserves seats only for those who can afford to buy them.

By using money to build around the party, the rich elites have essentially killed it. Today, it is more important to be supported by one of the groups funded by Democracy Alliance's original donors than it is to be supported by the Democratic National Committee.

The grassroots from both parties have driven the conversation to the fringes: In order to raise enough for the Tea Party or the Democratic National Committee, you must scream louder and attack with more passion. The system doesn't work for the Average Joe.

Less than a year after taking the job as finance director for the Democratic National Committee, I was gone. I didn't care. Howard Dean went right back to trying to join the country club, as reported by the *Washington Post:*

> In November, influential Florida lawyer Mitchell Berger hosted a breakfast for Dean in Fort Lauderdale. The following month DNC finance chairwoman Maureen White held a dinner at the New York home she shares with her husband—financier Steve Rattner—that raked in

$250,000 for the DNC and, more importantly, gave Dean face time with a handful of fundraising heavy hitters within the party.

Dean has also huddled individually with prominent Democratic donors on both coasts of late, a group that includes actor-director Rob Reiner, New York venture capitalist Alan Patricof and investor Bernard Bergreen. [Former DNC finance chair Alan] Solomont recounted that Dean has tracked him down by phone in France, Israel and the Caribbean over the past year.[2]

AFTER I QUIT, I did some consulting work for some godawful candidates who never had a chance. Walter Ludwig was one of those outsiders who had joined the Dean presidential campaign, and he was doing consulting work for some long-shot candidates. I joined him. He is one of those fast talkers who never really produces anything. I don't think he has won a single campaign to this day, but he still goes out and hustles for candidates. This is what happens when more and more money comes into the campaign world: Consultants charge money to "advise" campaigns on how to raise that money.

We were the ultimate used car salesmen, just like too many political consultants. We landed a few candidates: Ford running for the Senate in Minnesota, Mfume for the Senate in Maryland, and so on. We would sit our candidates down and tell them to raise money all day, every day. It's the only way we will get paid. And that's what we did. The more the candidates raised, the better chance we got at getting paid. It wasn't about winning at all.

A few months later, I quit the consulting work; I was taking money from candidates who could not win; why?

I sat at home and watched TV, drank, smoked, and tried to figure out what was next. I doubted I could ever make a difference again. I had had my shot and I had been defeated. If I can take any comfort in my career, in 2006, Democrats won back the House and Senate, a goal I'd been working for my whole career. By May 2007 I was dead broke.

EPILOGUE

I WALKED INTO DICK GEPHARDT'S FUNDRAISING MACHINE IN JUNE of 1992. I walked out of the Democratic National Committee as a departing national finance director in late 2005. In all those years, I watched the part-time fundraising required to run for Congress move to a full-time occupation. I watched campaigns for Congress go from costing well under $500,000 to $1.5 million, and often much more. I've raised—or helped raise—over $200 million myself. I watched the grassroots donors on both sides of the partisan aisle create a new need for partisan warfare. Most important, I helped a few wealthy individuals with narrow concerns hijack the Democratic Party, demanding the attention of its politicians and altering its agenda.

After all those years and dollars, I've constantly asked myself how to limit the role of money in politics. Good government reformers have offered a slew of answers.

Should Congress write a law banning lobbyists from contributing? The John Roberts Supreme Court—as it did again with *McCutcheon v. FEC*, just days before I wrote this—will kindly remind you about defending free speech and that contributing political money does not equal bribery.

Should we limit contributions to, say, $100? That sounds all nice and clean, except you will put all the power in the hands of the big employers and big membership groups, like large companies and unions. Employ

100,000 people, and you can ask them in their "free time" to contribute $100 to a political action committee because a certain member of Congress is just so damn good for America. Get just five hundred to pony up and you have produced a hefty $50,000, enough to give the maximum to five members. Do that a few more times, and your company could run a House committee that controls legislation that pertains to your business. But if you employ just fifty people? Good luck.

And good luck getting Congress to write either law.

Maybe we need a constitutional amendment limiting political money? Good luck there too. The process is so daunting—two-thirds majorities in both the House and Senate or two-thirds of state legislatures—that it's just a pipe dream.

Rather than worrying about limiting money, focus on the other aspect: time. Time is money, right? If you can't control the money, then control the time.

CONSIDER THE OPTIONS a member of Congress has to raise money: from lobbyists, corporate and union political action committees, national rich donor networks, grassroots online donations, and super-PACs supporting them. Raising money from each is time consuming in its own way.

Raising money from the lobbyist and PAC community might be more transactional—politicians take a check and might be lobbied—but it's time consuming, as members must attend fundraising events every night. It's certainly out of control, but not for the reasons most people think. Lobbyists aren't buying votes; the relationship is the exact opposite most of the time. Members of Congress have become adept at figuring out the campaign value of proposed legislation. They don't talk about it, and they certainly don't mention it back home.

Proposing damaging legislation puts fear into industry leaders. It's the most sure-fire way to raise money. These bills don't get very far in the legislative process. That's because lobbyists rush to cut checks to every member on the relevant committee. The press, President Obama, the general public all reverse blame by holding out lobbyists as the evil actors in this process.

They are wrong. Raising money off damaging legislation has become basic economics. Congressional committees with fundraising potential have grown in size over the past twenty years. Congress is the same size, of course, but the number of members who sit on the Ways and Means Committee, Financial Services Committee, and Appropriations Committee has increased dramatically. Why? Because they can raise money by serving on committees. A member of Congress can vote on a bill, then walk down the street to a fundraiser and collect a check related to the vote. Members couldn't do that if there was a time-based restriction on raising money when Congress was in session.

What about those wealthy donor networks around the country? The problem is time spent coddling them. Raising money from a rich billionaire is not as simple as picking up the phone and asking for a contribution. That just doesn't work. Members of Congress call these people, travel around the country to see them, and take weekend trips with them. They do a lot with a very few select individuals who can write big checks and bundle checks from others.

The time members spend with these people gives them leverage. It is no longer about one wealthy person helping a candidate because the donor believes in the candidate. This relationship has been reversed as well. Now members of Congress believe they need these wealthy donors. Members believe they need to know donors, they need to care about what they care about, they need to be a champion of the donors' priorities.

Super-PACs play mostly at the presidential level, just as I saw starting with the Howard Dean campaign in 2004 and as the country has seen since in the 2012 election. They play the outsider game and change the party's agenda to fit the needs of their patrons. There are fewer super-PACs focused on congressional races, and most of the super-PAC money for congressional campaigns is raised by a few members of each party's leadership, which, of course, takes time, and plays into the hands of elite billionaires controlling the party's agenda in an unaccountable fashion.

Why not try to raise exclusively from the grassroots? That shouldn't take much time, right?

The idea had so much potential. The basic concept of millions of people giving to the cause because they believe in something was what kept me going in my dark days. It was the holy grail of clean elections. Except that it wasn't. In order to raise grassroots money on the large scale, you have only one choice: scare people, be obnoxious, throw bombs. And that takes time too.

The most successful members of Congress raising grassroots money for the past few cycles have been the Alan twins, Allen West (R-FL) for the Republicans and Alan Grayson (D-FL) for the Democrats. These men get up every day and spend time finding ways to scream about the other party. After spewing out partisan hatred to fire up the base, the Alans (and others, of course) sit down at a computer and type up the next crazy fundraising email.

It works. Others do the same, as do party committees. But being violently partisan steals time too, the time (and credibility) a member has to actually legislate. And it prevents members from crossing over to the other side to try to do something bipartisan. Base supporters online will destroy a member who compromises these days. Then the online money will dry up. This kind of overly partisan hyperbole has left us with fewer pragmatic centrists to actually govern.

MOST STATES, a majority of American cities, the UK, Canada, Australia, and most democracies around the world restrict the length of a campaign. Very simply, they might not restrict the amount of money a candidate or a party can raise but they do restrict the amount of time a candidate has to ask for campaign cash.

That's why I'd propose the following: Candidates, parties, committees, super-PACs, or any group that participates in federal elections can raise money for only one hundred days before a primary election and one hundred days before the general election. And Congress cannot be in session during that time. This is not restricting anybody's free speech—donors can continue to give as much as they want, but only one hundred days before the vote. (Of course, this brings up a separate discussion of scheduling primaries.)

When campaigns lasted only a few months and needed fewer dollars, the big donors didn't get the servicing they get today. A member of Congress would be elected in November and would have at least another fourteen or fifteen months before needing to worry about money again. Members wouldn't have to keep a scorecard on how much money new legislation might raise, they wouldn't have to run around the country and beg billionaires to help them, they wouldn't have to scream at online donors and sacrifice any hope of working on bipartisan legislation.

What about those grassroots donors? Won't they just go away if they can give only in the last hundred days? The exact opposite would occur. First, members couldn't profit from partisan bickering. Second and much more important: A short campaign means that the grassroots donations count much more. That $25 actually goes to helping elect somebody, not to pay the fundraiser, the travel bills, the weekend trips with lobbyists. It goes directly into the election. Grassroots groups of all ideological varieties will understand that.

OVER THE COURSE of my career, I met a lot of people, I raised a lot of money, I had a donor end up dead, and I tried to change a system that favors one class of donor over another.

And after nearly fifteen years and $200 million, I understand that the only way to address the ills of money in politics is to limit the time politicians can spend raising money.

NOTES

PROLOGUE

1. Cited in Stephen Labaton, "The 1992 Campaign: Campaign Finances; Despite Economy, Clinton Sets Record for Funds," *New York Times,* October 24, 1992. Available at: http://www.nytimes.com/1992/10/24/us/1992-campaign-campaign-finances-despite-economy-clinton-sets-record-for-funds.html

CHAPTER 1

1. Federal Election Commission, Congressional Candidate Table 1: House and Senate Financial Activity from January 1, 1989 through December 31, 1990. Available at: http://www.fec.gov/press/summaries/1990/tables/congressional/ConCand 1_1990_24m.pdf
2. Russ Choma, Center for Responsive Politics, "Election 2012: The Big Picture Shows Record Cost of Winning a Seat in Congress," OpenSecrets.org, June 19, 2013. Available at: https://www.opensecrets.org/news/2013/06/2012-overview.html

CHAPTER 3

1. Federal Election Commission, Congressional Candidate Table 5a, Top 50 House Campaigns by Receipts, January 1, 1991–December 31, 1992." Available at: http://www.fec.gov/press/summaries/1992/tables/congressional/ConCand5a_1992_24m .pdf

CHAPTER 10

1. Federal Election Commission, Congressional Table 1, House and Senate Financial Activity, 1996. Available at: http://www.fec.gov/press/summaries/1996/tables /congressional/ConCand1_1996_24m.pdf

CHAPTER 13

1. Steve Elmendorf's campaign contribution records are available through the Federal Election Commission, by searching for him in their disclosure portal at http://www .fec.gov/finance/disclosure/norindsea.shtml

CHAPTER 14

1. David Johnson and Jeff Zeleny, "Congressman Sought Bribes, Indictment Says," *New York Times,* June 5, 2007. Available at: http://www.nytimes.com/2007/06/05 /washington/05jefferson.html?ex=1338782400&en=f8ac6372594c21f5&ei=5124 &partner=permalink&exprod=permalink

CHAPTER 16

1. Discussed in CNN AllPolitics, "Clinton Ok'd Using Lincoln Bedroom for Contributors," February 25, 1997. Available at: http://www.cnn.com/ALLPOLITICS /1997/02/25/clinton.money/

CHAPTER 17

1. See 1997 FEC filings for "Gephardt in Congress" and the "Effective Government Committee" to see where money was returned to John Huang. Only available on microfiche at the FEC's office in Washington, DC.

CHAPTER 24

1. Federal Election Commission, Congressional Candidate Table 1, 1998. Available at: http://www.fec.gov/press/summaries/1998/tables/congressional/ConCand 1_1998_24m.pdf

CHAPTER 26

1. Center for Responsible Politics, opensecrets.org, "Election Stats: 1994," Available at: http://www.opensecrets.org/bigpicture/elec_stats.php?cycle=1994
2. Cathy Booth, "Can't Buy Me Love? Airline Tycoon Wants to Be California's Governor, and He's Getting Ready to Spend His Way There," CNN, December 1, 1997. Available at: http://www.cnn.com/ALLPOLITICS/1997/11/24/time/cal.gov.html

CHAPTER 28

1. Many of the finer details in the proceeding several paragraphs are from Jon Ralston, *The Anointed One: An Inside Look at Nevada Politics* (Las Vegas: Huntington Press, 2000), pp. 67, 122–200.

CHAPTER 30

1. Jane Ann Morrison, "Former Jones Fundraiser's Tactics Come into Question," *Las Vegas Review-Journal,* October 21, 1998.

CHAPTER 31

1. John L. Smith, "Details of Russo's Meddling with Midler Make for Stormy Story," *Las Vegas Review-Journal,* August 25, 1998.
2. Aaron Russo's campaign contribution reports are available via the Nevada Secretary of State's web portal: https://nvsos.gov/SOSCandidateServices/Anonymous

Access/CEFDSearch/BrowseReports.aspx?nd=0001998_Election_Reports%5c
0001998_Candidate_Contributions_And_Expenses%5c000Russo%2c_Aaron
Sol(REP)

3. All the money (amounts, dates, donors) I raised for Jan that we discuss in the sub-sequent section can be verified through a link to her campaign disclosure filings through the Nevada Secretary of State's web portal: https://nvsos.gov/SOSCandidate Services/AnonymousAccess/CEFDSearch/BrowseReports.aspx?nd=0001998 _Election_Reports%5c0001998_Candidate_Contributions_And_Expenses%5c 000Jones%2c_Jan_Laverty_(DEM)

4. Jon Ralston, *The Anointed One: An Inside Look at Nevada Politics* (Las Vegas: Huntington Press, 2000), p. 200.

CHAPTER 32

1. See Jan Jones's disclosure forms for the donations from Wynn's casinos. Available through the Nevada Secretary of State's web portal at https://nvsos.gov/SOS CandidateServices/AnonymousAccess/CEFDSearch/BrowseReports.aspx?nd=000 1998_Election_Reports%5c0001998_Candidate_Contributions_And_Expenses %5c000Jones%2c_Jan_Laverty_(DEM)

CHAPTER 34

1. I know a lot about the Binion family from having spent plenty of time in Vegas, but I don't know everything. We pulled background information from a variety of sources, like John L. Smith's *Of Rats and Men: Oscar Goodman's Life from Mob Mouthpiece to Mayor of Las Vegas* (Las Vegas: Huntington Press, 2010), and Cathy Scott's *Death in the Desert: The Ted Binion Homicide Case* (n.p.: AuthorHouse, 2011).

2. Cy Ryan and Jeff German, "Binion May Have Violated Campaign-Finance Law," *Las Vegas Sun*, August 4, 1999. Available at: http://www.lasvegassun.com/news/1999 /aug/04/binion-may-have-violated-campaign-finance-law

3. See Jan Jones's disclosure forms for the donations from Wynn's casinos. Available through the Nevada Secretary of State's web portal at https://nvsos.gov/SOS CandidateServices/AnonymousAccess/CEFDSearch/BrowseReports.aspx?nd=000 1998_Election_Reports%5c0001998_Candidate_Contributions_And_Expenses %5c000Jones%2c_Jan_Laverty_(DEM)

CHAPTER 35

1. Cindy Cesare, "Binion Retrial: Murphy Breaks Down," *8 News Now*, October 22, 2004. Available at: http://www.8newsnow.com/story/2464145/binion-retrial -murphy-breaks-down

CHAPTER 38

1. Numbers on self-funding for the Fine and Goodman campaigns are taken from Jane Ann Morrison, "Developers Help Mayoral Candidates," *Las Vegas Review-Journal*, April 29, 1999, and an Associated Press article, "Mob Lawyer Wins Vegas Mayor Race," June 10, 1999. The articles differ about how much Goodman gave himself, $140,000 or $160,000. I say "$140,000" in the text to stick with the more conservative estimate. It was years and years ago, I hardly remember the

exact amount. I do remember very well, however, that Arnie gave exactly zero of his own dollars.

2. Mike Zapler, "Health Problems Force Bingham from Mayor's Race," *Las Vegas Review Journal,* March 9, 1999.

CHAPTER 39

1. Todd S. Turdam, "A Colorful Lawyer Is Running for Mayor," *New York Times,* May 2, 1999.
2. "Winning Las Vegas," *Campaigns & Elections* 20, no. 7, August 1, 1999.
3. Mike Zapler, "Polls Show Goodman in Lead," *Las Vegas Review Journal,* April 29, 1999.
4. "Adamsen's Ads Attack Goodman," *Las Vegas Sun,* April 30, 1999. Available at http://www.lasvegassun.com/news/1999/apr/30/adamsens-ads-attack-goodman
5. Mike Zapler, "Mailer Attacks Goodman on Megan's Law," *Las Vegas Review Journal,* April 30, 1999.
6. Number on donations and expenses from Jane Ann Morrison, "Developers Help Mayoral Candidates," *Las Vegas Review Journal,* April 29, 1999.

CHAPTER 41

1. Justin Mayo, "State's Top Donors," *Seattle Times,* July 25, 2004. Available at: http://seattletimes.nwsource.com/news/local/politics/top50donors.pdf

CHAPTER 43

1. Juliet Eilperin, "And the Winner Is . . . House Democrats," *Washington Post,* March 25, 2000. Available at: http://www.washingtonpost.com/wp-srv/WPcap/2000-03/25/063r-032500-idx.html

CHAPTER 45

1. Mark Shriver's disclosure is available at http://www.opensecrets.org/politicians/alsorun.php?cid=N00013806&cycle=2002
2. Ibid.
3. See Chris Van Hollen's July 2002 quarterly FEC filing, available at: http://docquery.fec.gov/cgi-bin/dcdev/forms/C00366096/54053/#SUMMARY
4. Jo Becker, "Van Hollen's Rush for Dollars; Party Leadership Gets Involved After Coffer-Draining Primary," *Washington Post,* October 6, 2002.
5. See Ira Shapiro's FEC filings from 2002, available at fec.gov

CHAPTER 46

1. All Van Hollen's numbers are derived from his Federal Election Commission filings publicly available at www.fec.gov and the data produced by OpenSecrets .org, available at: http://www.opensecrets.org/politicians/summary.php?cid=N00013820&cycle=2014
2. We crunched these numbers ourselves. We went through a lot of microfilm at the FEC, pouring over hundreds of itemized disbursements from Conrad's 1986

campaign and his 2000 campaign, identifying various itemized costs from both. Since this data is older, unfortunately it is not online.

3. All data are from Van Hollen's page at OpenSecrets.org and derived from his FEC filings.
4. Ibid.

CHAPTER 47

1. Richard Rapaport, "Net vs. Norm," *Forbes Magazine,* May 29, 2000. Available at: http://www.forbes.com/asap/2000/0529/053_print.html
2. Institute for Politics, Democracy, & the Internet, in collaboration with the Campaign Finance Institute, "Small Dollars and Online Giving: A Study of the 2004 Presidential Campaigns," March 2006. Available at: http://www.cfinst.org/pdf/federal/president/IPDI_SmallDonors.pdf
3. *Harper's Magazine,* "Harper's Index," March 14, 2014. Available at: http://harpers.org/archive/2014/03/harpers-index-359/
4. Harvey Weinstein's donation to Howard Dean was given on December 31, 2003, and can be viewed at the Federal Election Commission's Individual Contributor disclosure portal, available at: http://www.fec.gov/finance/disclosure/norindsea.shtml

CHAPTER 50

1. Associated Press, "Dean: America Not Safer After Saddam's Capture," December 13, 2003. Available at: http://www.foxnews.com/story/2003/12/16/dean-america-not-safer-after-saddam-capture/
2. Jim VandeHei, "Kerry Fundraiser Helped Finance Anti-Dean Ads," *Washington Post,* February 11, 2004.

CHAPTER 57

1. Grim, Ryan, "Peter Lewis Leaves Democracy Alliance, The Liberal Donor Network," March 21, 2012. Available at: http://www.huffingtonpost.com/2012/03/21/peter-lewis-democracy-alliance_n_1368551.html
2. Jim VandeHei and Chris Cillizza, "A New Alliance of Democrats Spreads Funding, But Some in Party Bristle at Secrecy and Liberal Tilt," *Washington Post,* July 17, 2006. Available at: http://www.washingtonpost.com/wp-dyn/content/article/2006/07/16/AR2006071600882_pf.html

CHAPTER 59

1. Federal Election Commission, donor record lookup for Sherry Lansing. Available at: http://docquery.fec.gov/cgi-bin/qindcont/CT/160896.00/2/(lname%7CMATCHES%7C:LANSING*:)%7CAND%7C(fname%7CMATCHES%7C:SHERRY*:)

CHAPTER 62

1. *Bloomberg Businessweek Magazine,* "Howard Dean's Raised Voice Isn't Raising Cash," June 5, 2005. Available at: http://www.businessweek.com/stories/2005-06-05/howard-deans-raised-voice-isnt-raising-cash

CHAPTER 63

1. Robert Novack, May 7, 2005 at Real Clear Politics. Available at: http://www.real clearpolitics.com/Commentary/com-5_7_05_RN.html

CHAPTER 66

1. Greg Sargent, "DNC's ATM Withdrawals: Watch for the Clinton-Dean Show!" Available at: http://nymag.com/news/intelligencer/16052/
2. Chris Cillizza, "Dean Answers with New Money Man," *Washington Post*, January 15, 2006. Available at: http://www.washingtonpost.com/wp-dyn/content/article /2006/01/14/AR2006011400965.html

INDEX